Elizabeth Montgomery

Reminiscences of Wilmington, in Familiar Village Tales, Ancient and

New

Second Edition

Elizabeth Montgomery

Reminiscences of Wilmington, in Familiar Village Tales, Ancient and New
Second Edition

ISBN/EAN: 9783337081867

Printed in Europe, USA, Canada, Australia, Japan

Cover: Foto ©Thomas Meinert / pixelio.de

More available books at **www.hansebooks.com**

REMINISCENCES

OF

WILMINGTON,

IN

FAMILIAR VILLAGE TALES,

ANCIENT AND NEW.

BY

ELIZABETH MONTGOMERY.

SECOND EDITION.

WILMINGTON, DEL.
JOHNSTON & BOGIA, 420 SHIPLEY STREET.
1872.

FROM THE "COMMERCIAL PRESS" OF JENKINS & ATKINSON,
WILMINGTON, DEL.

PUBLISHERS' PREFACE.

The inquiring mind naturally seeks to know the *beginnings of things*.

Therefore, the Author of the mind, who knows perfectly its requirements, in becoming also the Author of a history of the universe, for the use of man, commences it with:—"In the beginning."

Do not these facts distinctly convey to us a divine intimation that *we ought to treasure up the past?*

While we should mark well the current "signs of the times," we should also keep in present view the historic past. Because it is out of that past that the present has sprung, and from thence also are derived the lessons of history and experience.

It was from considerations like these, doubtless, that "The Reminiscences of Wilmington" were originally written.

The authoress, a lady of piety and intelligence, in this volume sought to open a vista in perpetuity, reaching into the past far enough and wide enough to enable the successive inhabitants of Wilmington, henceforward, to look back upon the early scenes in the eventful history of their beautiful city,—those first beginnings of its noble present, and of its more promising future.

But the motives that originally incited to the *production* of this book, are now equally urgent for its *reproduction*.

It is a book of permanent value, for reasons already explained.

It is, also, as a glance at its Contents will show, a work that must prove highly entertaining to young and old, of every class and walk in life. Those who are already acquainted with it, will want to possess it. And those who have not read it hitherto, will find in it charms as fresh and fascinating as if it had just now come from the gifted pen of its authoress.

That the book is of marked interest and value is clearly proven by the fact, that since it has become rare—being out of print—fabulous prices have been offered for it and refused.

Our aim is now to bring this rare volume within the reach of all; and no one should permit the opportunity to pass without putting it into his own library, for safe keeping and convenient reference.

PREFACE.

Having delayed so long to write you the promised story of other times, what shall I tell you of the months which have insensibly fleeted away? Will it suffice to say, three sheets of paper were soon filled and read to an elderly lady, my valued friend, who advised the story onward, and in a few brief weeks "dust to dust concludes her noblest song?" That one spared a little longer has amplified the narrative from the tablet of memory gleaned a little here and there, by sea and by land, of war and of peace, mingling mirth and woe, to portray village life in the lights and shades of olden days, and to recount what we have heard and known, and such as our fathers have told us. Much care has been taken to come as near the truth as memory, unaided by notes, can recall.

My lot in the morn of life was to while away hours listening to traditionary lore, that sprinkled my pathway, and passed off as the early dew. Ere noon the verdure faded, and gave place to other views, and naught was left but a train of yellow withered leaves. As the sun grew dim to me beyond the western hills, to you it was rising in eastern grandeur, gilding your joyous morn of childhood; and in turn you evinced a fondness for such legends; oft would you cling to my chair and entreat me to tell you a story of old time, thus awakening my energies to gather the fragments, though the shades of evening were falling. Now and then a starry light would shoot across my way, and brighten up some old relic that would fill the mind with reminiscences on the very brink of oblivion, and turn the thoughts back even to the early fathers and their adventurous journeyings o'er the trackless ocean, from the icy regions of the north to these western shores.

On the spot where they trod, pitched their tents, and planted a colony, we meditate on their doings, and glory in our Swedish ancestors, not as mighty men of renown, but as the salt of the earth that preserved its savor, pioneers of the choice spirits who to the red men proclaimed peace, and said "we have come to do you good."

Yon old edifice, to this day is a monument of their good faith, reared in a wilderness where they worshiped the God of their fathers; and whence the glad tidings of Gospel light first shone on the benighted sons of the forest by whom they were encompassed.

In the infancy of their colony, a peculiar people, called Quakers, mingled with them—distinct in their tenets, each adhering to their own, and if agreeing to differ in matters of religion, to live like brethren, somewhat resembling the Apostolic age. Though their possessions were not held in common, they shared their comforts without money and without price. To this Christian example and influence, no doubt, the community owes a debt of gratitude for the morality and good order which was so long proverbial.

More recent events oft intervene with respective claims to attention; and blending those as they present themselves may not be the least of our errors to the nicely fastidious, for we "take no note of time" as the knell of departing hours hastens us on, but ask of you that most excellent gift of charity, and to have in remembrance that "the days of our age are three score and ten years," then we all do fade as a leaf, and that these sketches are from the memory of one past the full time alloted; besides, never, no never, in her brighest hour had she the least pretension to be a writer of stories. Strange, that on the verge of her pilgrimage, though solicited by friends to offer the public a little volume, she should comply, being fully conscious of its defects, and of the propensity to criticise. But even such must own, "with me it is a small matter to be judged of you," "when the Lord is at hand, and will make manifest the counsels of the heart." Reader, though thy endowments be of the highest order, the frosts of seventy winters will silver o'er thy locks and blight thy noble powers; may the benign Giver of every good then grant thee, yea, even thee, so small a portion that thou canst do likewise.

CONTENTS.

CHAPTER I.

Wilmington and its Environs—Arrival—New Zealander—A Legend of Other Days—Prospect Hill—Joshua North, Esq.—Confiscated Estates—Dr. Wharton—Brandywine Mills—A Voyage to New York—General Washington—Joseph Tatnall, Esq., ... 17

CHAPTER II.

Race Banks—Waterfalls—Isaac Kendall—Amusements—Cottage of A. H. Rowan, Esq.—Winter Sports—A Sad Calamity—Crossing the Dam—Moonlight Party—Bold Scenery—Tablet Rock—Old Snuff Mill—Isaac Jones, Esq.—Old Barley Mill—The Brandywine—Floodgate—Rattlesnake Run—Wild Scenery—Freshets, ... 26

CHAPTER III.

Old Paper Mill—The Original Paper Machine—Description of the Mills, Cottages, &c.—Picturesque Scenery—Kentmere, the residence of Joshua Gilpin, Esq.—Giant's Footrock—Pic-Nic—Rokeby—Hagely—Jacob Broom, Esq.—Cotton Mill—Ruins, &c.—Lost in the Wood—Messrs. DuPont's Improvements—Eleutherian Mills—Explosion—Alarm—Change of Scenery—Fine Mansions—Gen. Lafayette—Rockland—William Young, Esq.—Relics of Gen. Washington—J. Brindley, Esq.—Swedes, . . . 38

CHAPTER IV.

King's Road—Bancroft Woodcock—Dr. James Tilton, Sen.—Old Letter—Cæsar A. Rodney, Esq.—Dutch Dolly—Fine Scenery—Col. Townsend—Carl Christopher Springer—Old Cottage—J. Springer—Introduction to the Sixth Generation of his Pastor, ... 54

CHAPTER V.

Almshouse Inmates—Of High Order—Mr. B.—M. Martel—Mrs. B.—Burnt March 25th, 1804—Tamar Way—Frederick Craig—Mantua—Delamore Place—Col. Davis—Tusculum—J. M. Broom, Esq.—Dr. Read—Dr. Martin—Richardsons-Latimers-Swedish Families-July 4th, 1794-Celebration, 67

CONTENTS.

CHAPTER VI.

Long Hook—Major Jaquett—His Father—Whitefield—Major P. J. enters the Army—Description—Visit of an Old Soldier—The Avenue—Night Walk—Blackbeard—The Alarm—Surrender to Bull Frogs—Solomon, - 78

CHAPTER VII.

Major Jaquett—Battles—Brandywine—General LaFayette—Bell McClosky—Colonel Hazlett—General Smallwood—Guilford C. H.—General Green—Camden—Baron deKalb—Delaware Regiment—Singular Incident—Virginia—Patriotic Lady—Return—Joseph Tatnall, Esq.—Mrs. Jaquett—Bennet—Lord Cornwallis—Monckton Park—George Haines, Esq.—Robert Morris, Esq.—A thrilling story—Judge Bedford and lady—Mysterious events—Hays's family—An eventful day—General Washington, President of the United States—Eden Park—P. Bauduy, Esq., - - - 86

CHAPTER VIII.

English Fleet—Panic—Hessians—Deserter—Battle of Brandywine—Tranhook—Fairfield—Old Ferry—Swedish Colonists—Rocks—Cave—Indian Mounds—1812 War—Mud Bulwark—Hon J. A. Bayard—Peace—Note—Major Cass, - - - - - - - - 103

CHAPTER IX.

Cemetery—Swede's Church—Ancient Customs—Rev. Erick Biorck—Rev. Petrus Tranberg—Rev. Israel Acrelius, Historian—Mr. Benzell—Rev. Lawrence Girelius—His Successors—Chapel—Old Church Dilapidated—Renovated, 110

CHAPTER X.

A Ghost Story—Esquimaux—Cemetery—Solemn Funeral—A Sad Accident—Dr. Capelle—Adventures of a French Soldier—Dr. Bayard, - - 122

CHAPTER XI.

Sketch of Miss Vining—Ex-President Jefferson—Gen. Lafayette—Duke de Liancourt—Duke d'Orleans—Gov. Dickinson—John Vining, Esq.—Mrs. V.—Miss V.—Visits Philadelphia—Wm. Henry Vining—Decease of three brothers—Miss V.—Closing Scene—Jane Mauthrell—Mrs. Curtz—Alice Hough, - - - - - - - 133

CHAPTER XII.

Banks of the Christiana—Melancholy Catastrophe—Irish Trade—King's Ships—Primitive Customs—Packets—Capt. J. Foudray—Capt. Samuel Bush—Mode of Traveling—Steamboat—Wharves—Jonathan Rumford, Esq.—Eleazar McComb, Esq.—James Brian—Ship Building—Thomas Willing—Barney Harris—William Woodcock,   -   -   -   -   142

CHAPTER XIII.

A Singular Incident—Brig Friday—Capt. J. M.—Prizes—Robert Morris, Esq.—Brig Nancy—Capt H. Montgomery—Sails under British Colors—News of Independence—Arms the Brig—Invited Guests—St. Thomas's hauls down the Flag—Hoists the first American Flag in a Foreign Port—Lands Ammunition and Arms—Explosion—Lieut. Weeks Killed—Scuttling a Brig—Raising Her—Cargo arrives Safe—Capt. H. M. fell in 1780,   -   -   151

CHAPTER XIV.

A Swedish Minister—Catastrophe—Capt. H. Geddes—Shipwreck—A Singular Incident—Solemn Reflections—Capt. S. Lovering—Mr. A , a British Agent—Adventures of a Lady—Anecdote of a Sailor—Algerines—Captures—Cruelties—Bondage—Prisoners Ransomed—Arrival—Capt. Penrose—His Story—Remarks on their Character,   -   -   -   -   161

CHAPTER XV.

Journal—An Ancient Race—Dey of Algiers—Officers—Ceremony of Introduction—Fast—Story of a Turk—Tunis—Bey's Palace—Swedish Consul—Ornaments—Slaves—Coffee handed—Ancient Carthage—Canal—Pieces of Antiquity—Bey's prediction of America—Costume—Adventures of a Female—Coasting Trade—Captain Cuffee,   -   -   -   -   172

CHAPTER XVI.

Visitations of the Yellow Fever—Every House Crowded—Ship on Fire—Its first appearance here as an Epidemic—In 1798—Intense Alarm—Death of Citizens—Touching Scenes—A few Philanthropists—J. Miller—James Lea—John Ferris—Dr. Vaughan,   -   -   -   -   181

CHAPTER XVII.

Walnut Street—Old Trees—Amusements—Fairs Folly Lane—Anecdote—Dr. David Bush R. M., Esq., —D. E. N. B—Gov. M'Kean—Separation—Adventures of a Young Lady,   -   -   -   -   188

CHAPTER XVIII.

Methodist Meeting-house—John Thelwell—Stone Meeting-house—A Noted Lawyer—White Hall—Vandever's Island—Old Swedes' Cemetery--Remembrances of the dead, - - - - - - - - 194

CHAPTER XIX.

French Street—Mrs. Way—I. H.—Capt. E Brown—Allen McLane, Esq —J. Stapler, Esq.—School—Gov. McKinley—Town Taken—Anecdotes—Escape of Capt. M. and Capt. K—Fleet—A Young Lady—De Sonrei—Monsieur Garesche—Betty Jackson—Change in Scenery—Old Mansions, - 205

CHAPTER XX.

King Street—Capt. Giles—A thrilling story—Gilpins—Anecdote—Mrs. Wallace—Eli Mendenhall—Capt. Jeffries—William Cook—Trinity Chapel—Dr. E. A. Smith's family—Capt J. Nicholson, - - - - 217

CHAPTER XXI.

Other days—Mr. Crip's Pottery—Sad Incident—J. Keating, Esq.—Peter Provenchere, Esq.—Affecting Incidents—Messrs. Hilles—J. Maule—Boarding School—Baptist Cemetery—Potter's Field—Story of the Water Works, 225

CHAPTER XXII.

Market Street Bridge—Dr. Monroe—Mrs. D.—An Adventure—Bank—Dr. Pascal—J. Springer—J. Brobson—Hotel—Sailor's Exploit—Smoke House—J. Webster—Post Office—J. Niles—David Bush, Esq.—Major Lewis Bush—Indian Queen, - - - - - - - 232

CHAPTER XXIII.

Peter Brynberg—Book Store—Old Bank—Printing Office—Robert Hamilton, Esq.—Adventure of Mons. Bergerac—The Dawes Family—Gen. Stockton—Job Harvey—Town Hall—Michael Wolfe, - - - 238

CHAPTER XXIV.

Abijah Dawes—French Army—Gunning Bedford, Esq.—Dr. Franklin—Dr. McKinley—Governor Dickinson—John Rumsey, Esq.—Old Academy—Its changes—Professor Patterson—Funeral Procession—Old Presbyterian Church and Cemetery, - - - - - - 245

CHAPTER XXV.

Front street west of Market—Eleazar McComb, Esq.—Francis Way—Major Patten, - - - - - - - - - 255

CHAPTER XXVI.

Shipley Street—Wm. Jones—Up Second Street—Sheward's Brewery—Tan Yard—Z. Ferris—Cold Bath—In Shipley Street—Dr. Nicholas Way—Post Office—Ziba Ferris, Sen.—The Maid of Erin—A Tale of Other Days - 257

CHAPTER XXVII.

School—Henry Pepper—Wm. Cobbett—St. Andrew's Church—Billy McDougall—Dr. Gibbons—College—M. Bradford—Woman in a Well—John Bull—Boarding School—Caleb Seal—St. Peter's Church—Sisters of Charity—Friends' Meeting House—Cemetery—School, - - - 266

CHAPTER XXVIII.

A Legend of the Revolution—D. D. B.—Gen. Robertdeau—Miss V.'s visit—Marriage—Seclusion—D. D. B. enters His Majesty's Service—Mysterious news—A Perilous Journey, - - - - - 275

CHAPTER XXIX.

The Hermit—Recruiting Party—Evening Mists—Village—Tavern—Gen. Green—Secures Her Passage—Recognition—Dr. B.—Retreat—Susy—The Meeting—Reconciliation—Dr. S —The Parting—A Ride—Baggage Wagon—New York—Crosses to New Jersey, - - - - - 282

CHAPTER XXX.

Safely Landed—Meeting her Infant—Captain L. hastens her on—Contempt of the Officers—Unsightly Dress—Apologies—Prosperous Voyage—Joyful Meeting—Charleston—Noble Lords—Royalty Triumphs—Anecdotes—Rebels Revive—Gen. Green—Sails to Nova Scotia—Their Arrival—Gloomy Scenes—Usefulness—Visit to the Barracks, - - - - 289

CHAPTER XXXI.

A fortnight passed—Resolution—Mrs. B. studies medicine—Coarse fare—Discontent—Stores arrive—Energy—Popularity—Amusing incidents—Improvements—News from London—Sails for Boston—Explores the States—Wilmington selected—Black oak bark exported—Death of Dr. B.—Mrs. B.'s residence in Virginia—Devoted to Slaves, - - - 300

REMINISCENCES OF WILMINGTON.

REMINISCENCES

OF

WILMINGTON.

CHAPTER I.

Wilmington and its Environs—Arrival—New Zealander—A Legend of Other Days—Prospect Hill—Joshua North, Esq.—Confiscated Estates—Dr. Wharton—Brandywine Mills—A Voyage to New York—General Washington—Joseph Tatnall, Esq.

Of all the towns that I have seen, none appears to me more pleasantly located than Wilmington; nor to possess greater advantages for an agreeable residence. If this be prejudice of opinion, it arises from habits of early affection; for there is an attraction in the name of birthplace, home of our childhood and youthful associations, when the rays of life's morning sun brightened all our prospects, and even the spot is hallowed that has been bedewed by the tears of sorrow, as the last earthly resting-place of a beloved parent. This feeling must be the gift of our great Creator, or how could the Laplander relish his coarse fare, and with gratitude thank his Maker for his icy region and long dreary nights as the favored spot of Heaven?

In giving you a description of this pretty town, as I have chosen to call it, I may indulge a little, yet will strive to keep to the truth; hoping that ere long you may come here and see whether these things are really so. There will be added some reminiscences of olden times, connected with the early settlement of this place, and of the revolutionary war, &c., as these were related to me by my venerated grandfather and other worthies, now silent in the grave, with more recent events of my own day. Such a variety of subjects cannot easily be arranged in order; and no doubt some incidents will be disposed in bad taste. I shall write them down as they occur to my memory.

Wilmington is surrounded, one half by a rolling country, the other half by water; it stands on rising ground, gradually sloping to its watery bounds; thence for miles it is skirted by beautiful meadows, with an extensive view of the noble river Delaware, on the east, and its tributary streams, fancifully winding through those meadows, stretching their courses past the town, where a drawbridge is thrown across the Christiana to let small vessels through, as it is navigable four miles beyond.

On the other hand, the Brandywine takes its course to the mills, where vessels stop. There is a bridge connecting the flourishing village of Brandywine with Wilmington; also a drawbridge a little below, for vessels to pass through, and for the railroad.

This is a romantic stream, long celebrated in story, and takes its name from the loss of a vessel at its entrance, laden with brandy and wine. It winds its way for a great distance, and gives water power to many factories, as it descends from its source. The distance from one bridge to the other is a little more than a mile, in a direction nearly north and south.

You can see all the shipping passing; some floating down, heavy laden with our country's produce going to distant lands to reward the farmer for his toil; and though you must rejoice in the success of your neighbor, and the prosperity of your country, your heart will sadden at the thought of how many loved ones there have never, no, never returned.

This town bears a sad remembrance of disasters at sea. Many of our youth, the hope of their parents, ah! and some reckless ones too, sailed from here, with a fair breeze and light heart, and found a watery grave in the ocean; and the fate of some was never known. Yes, and many in the prime of life left widows and orphans to mourn their sorrowful bereavement. The hoary-headed sire, too, who had braved the perilous ocean, and had his hair breadth escapes, and almost attained his three score and ten years, resolved to go but once more, went that once, and so ended his voyage of life; the places that knew him once know him no more.

"They that go down to the sea in ships, that do business in great waters, see the works of the Lord and his wonders in the deep."

Here, the view on the other hand changes the scene; every thing here looks cheerful. See the fleet of vessels, large and small, under full sail, returning from foreign lands, laden with the luxuries of life to enrich the merchant, and gladden many an anxious heart! With a good spy-glass, you can read the name of that ship, and see the men on board. How briskly they move about, and how joyously, so near their destined haven! In an hour or two, they will have the inexpressible happiness of embracing their long absent friends.

The three vessels you see close to the shore enter the Christiana; they sail down, then turn gracefully round, and sail up. Two of them are side by side, taking the same course. The small one slips into the Brandywine, and now they part, one to the right, and the other to the left.

Does not this remind you of the interesting story of the good old patriarch Abraham, whose exemplary conduct with his kinsman, Lot, was so striking? When their herdsmen differed about the pasture, he affectionately said, "Let there be no strife, I pray thee, between me and thee, and between thy herdsman and my herdsman; for we be brethren. Is not the whole land before us? You take either the right or the left." Lot chose the well-watered plains of Jordan, which now seem before you; for here are flocks and herds in rich pasture, well-watered; their fields of waving grain, promising the husbandman a golden harvest; meandering streams; vessels under full sail; steamboats plying; railroad cars whizzing past; and all this you can see at one glance.

Before we leave this view, I will describe to you an exciting scene which occurred here a few years ago. A cannon was fired opposite the town from a ship under full sail. She "rounded to" into the creek; then the spy-glasses were drawn out. They saw she was a dark, dirty-looking ship; but soon discovered that she had many a light heart on board, and plenty of oil, to give light to our dwellings. The sails were lowering (for, unless the tide is high and the wind low, heavy laden vessels cannot pass the bar at the entrance), the steamboat was going down to tow her up. It was a whale ship that had been absent three years. Now the boys halloo "A whale ship." This cry was echoed through the town, and the people ran from every direction. You would have thought they came from the Rocky Mountains, where a vessel had never been seen.

On her arrival at the wharf, they crowded on board, and such a cheering! It was indeed a merry day; for many prodigal sons had returned who had been to a far country, and fed upon husks, and had often sighed for their father's house, where there was bread enough and to spare. This was a temperance ship, and they had been sent by their friends, on the long hazardous voyage, in hopes to correct their evil habits, and had arrived safe and well, with good resolutions to amend their lives, were met by their affectionate relatives, rejoicing that their sons who had been lost were found, and the dead were alive again; and now the fatted calf was to be killed to make merry with their companions.

A quantity of beautiful shells, and whalebone, was brought in this ship; one piece I saw from the bone of a whale that reached from the floor to the ceiling, of the breadth of two hands, turned at the ends and fringed like a feather, and highly polished.

One man on board attracted much notice; he was stout, thick set, with straight black hair, and Indian feathers, his complexion of darker hue; he was from New Zealand, and a sprig of royalty, too, the son of a prince. But, O, shocking! he was a cannibal, and owned he had eaten human flesh: now he abhorred the thought that it should be known; his family opposed his coming here, and said the Americans made slaves of every one that came to their country. But this did not deter him; he behaved well on board, made a good sailor, and was kindly treated by the officers and crew of the ship.

Many little presents were given him in town, such as tools, knives, beads, &c. Mr. L. gave him a silver dart, the length of your finger, with his name inscribed thereon. This he called his little harpoon, and was much pleased. Silver was more precious with him than gold. When the locomotive appeared, he danced and clapped his hands in ecstasy; but the steamboat was his delight; whenever it arrived, he left everything, ran and threw himself flat on the wharf to examine the wheels, laughed and jumped, and said the people of his country would never believe him when he should tell them what he had seen.

Two years after he left here, he returned; Mrs. and Miss Lovering were sitting in the parlor, in the same position where he had taken leave of them; he entered with a handkerchief full of beautiful shells, and threw them down at the old lady's feet, saying, "For mother—give son some," (the gentleman who gave him the dart). Their language has but few words to express their ideas, but he was grateful; they gave him a box of little articles to take home. He was now dressed like a gentleman, with his gold watch and gold chain around his neck, and he said he intended to build himself a house when he returned home, and live no longer in a bark coop.

Now turn a little to the north. There is a fine view of the "Shellpot hills," partly topped with handsome trees; at the foot is the little gently flowing stream that bears the same name, paying its tribute to the Delaware.

In days gone by, near this spot lived a respectable farmer, who had a very pretty daughter, one of the belles of her day; she had many admirers, but rejected their offers, although some of them were unexceptionable. A son of a neighboring farmer now paid his visits to the mansion; and though there were no cliques at this day, respectable people all visiting each other, yet in the case of marriage connection there was often opposition from pride of family. Such was the feeling here. The father expressed his disapprobation to his daughter, who was amazed at the father to suppose he was admitted as a lover.

However, his visits were continued, and the old gentleman remonstrated again, and again was re-assured that all was imagination; yet he felt uneasy, and pressed the subject further, when the young lady became angry, and in a passion, wished, if ever such an event should happen, the devil would take her off; hoped that her father would now feel at ease, and never renew the subject.

Time passed on, and perseverance in the farmer's son overcame the young lady's scruples; the high-minded father had to submit; arrangements were made for the wedding; the guests had assembled; the minister, Mr. Girelius, with the bridal party, were standing on the floor to perform the ceremony, when, O, sad to relate, the lady, pale and trembling, with distorted features, exclaimed aloud, "There he comes!" clapped her hands, turned around, and fell on the floor a lifeless corpse. What an awful change of scene; one moment dressed in her bridal robes, the next shrouded for the grave!

An old lady who was present justly observed to a friend of mine in speaking of it years since, it could only be felt by the persons who witnessed it, and never be described. It was supposed that her feelings became so excited at the recollection of her rash speech as to bring on a spasm, which caused her sudden death.

This is one of many warnings that might be given to young persons, to guard against rash wishes or promises. But we have one recorded in Scripture that ought to be all sufficient. Jeptha's rash vow, "that if the Lord would deliver his enemies into his hands, and let him return in peace, whatsoever came forth from the doors of his house to meet him should be offered up a burnt offering to the Lord," behold his daughter came to meet him with timbrels and dances; she was his only child; when he saw her, he rent his clothes, and said, "Alas, my daughter, thou hast brought me very low."

The house you see opposite is called Prospect Hill; it formerly belonged to Joshua North, Esq., a wealthy and respectable man, but a very active Tory in the Revolution, who was obliged leave the country. His property was confiscated, as were many valuable estates on the river shore, owned by simple-hearted men, who really did no harm; but being exposed to the enemy, who took their cattle by force, yet paid for them, receiving the pay was their only crime, when he so guilty persuaded those their lives were in danger to escape with him; they went, leaving their families to be deprived of their estates.

This was the case of Jacob Derrickson, a wealthy farmer, whose ancestor was one of the Swedish colonists, and proverbial for his active benevolence. He never gave the poor man the crumbs from his table, but shared with a bounteous hand the choicest product of his farm, while his house was the stranger's home; his good deeds were still in remembrance, and the sympathy of the people expressed for his son. Gen. Washington kindly sent for him to return, but it then was too late. His descendants are yet here.

Doctor Wharton lived there for many years. He was a gentleman of great literary attainments, educated for a Roman Catholic priest; officiated in his profession for years; he then recanted, entered the Episcopal Church, and succeeded Mr. Girelius, the last Swedish clergyman. After some time he removed to Burlington, N. J., where he was an acceptable minister until called away by death, lamented as a scholar of the highest order, and an estimable man.

The next high point of land is Mrs. Elliott's; from her portico you can see "Fort Delaware," twenty miles below, and with a good spy-glass see the men at work, and how they are occupied. This family are of olden days, respectable farmers.

We will now take a view of the Brandywine Mills, and say something of their past and present history, and of their original proprietors. These mills, like the stream that sets them in motion, are of great notoriety, and have run unrivaled in the full tide of their glory for the greater part of a century. Recently, they have been shaded by those of greater magnitude and more modern structure; yet it is doubtful whether they have been rivaled in business; certainly not in their exports of corn meal. The situation is so accessible by water that vessels can unload and re-load at their doors.

The first mill was built above the bridge, near the northwest corner of the city bounds, by Oliver Canby, whose descendants continued this business until very lately with great success and respectability. Samuel Canby was one of our most respectable and wealthy citizens; we often admired his erect and stately figure even to old age, when he died leaving to his heirs a reputation of more real value than his wealth.

William Canby was an example for honesty and benevolence, a truly religious man. His character cannot, we think, be better portrayed than in the words of the prophet: "I am old and grey-headed; have walked before you from my childhood unto this day; behold here I am; witness against me before the Lord." "Whose ox have I taken? or whom have I defrauded? Whom have I oppressed? and I will restore it you." And they said, "Thou hast not defrauded us, nor oppressed us." And he said, "The Lord is witness this day that ye have not found aught in my hand." They answered, "He is witness."

Thomas Shipley built the first mill below the bridge, then two others. The first one is now owned by the city, and used for pumping up water to supply the inhabitants. He was the ancestor of a very respectable family here; one of whom lately declined the business. His grandson, Samuel Shipley, sold one of the mills within a few years, the building of which and digging the race, exclusive of much labor done by persons in his employ, cost just two thousand pounds. One of the grandsons is now a partner in the extensive commercial house in Liverpool of Brown, Shipley & Co.

There are at present thirteen mills in operation. These, with the mechanics employed, make Brandywine a busy place. Formerly the wheat was conveyed in buckets to the upper stories. Then Oliver Evans' machinery was introduced.

This reminds me of an anecdote. On the day the cars commenced running from Wilmington, there was some excitement, and I met an old gentleman in the street in high glee, who stopped me, and said he remembered when a boy listening to Oliver Evans telling his father the time was not far off when it would be only a day's journey from Philadelphia to Baltimore, and that carriages would be invented to go without horses. This his father thought so preposterous, he clapped him on the shoulder and said, "Why, Oliver, I always thought thy brain was a little cracked, now I know it; farewell."

The lots where the mills stand, on this side the creek, were purchased of my grandfather Peterson, who owned the first vessels that carried flour to New York and Philadelphia. A contract to that effect was made with the miller at the time of the purchase; and although it may be traveling a little out of the way, I will give you a sketch of the habits of those early days, as it comes in place here.

The journey to New York was so great an undertaking that few persons attempted it, and those were thought travelers. My grandfather's business often required his attention there. On his return, crowds of villagers would come to hear the news, and of the wonders he had seen in that astonishing city. On one of his visits to Mr. Rutger's, a wealthy brewer of that day, and whose descendants now have large possessions there, after settling their accounts, grandfather dined with him, and was an invited guest to a bridal supper, given to his daughter on her return from a journey that evening.

As the vessel was to sail at daylight the next morning, he wished to be excused; however, his invitation was so pressing it was accepted; and he did not leave until after eleven o'clock at night, when a servant was offered to conduct him through a huckleberry swamp on the way. As it was bright moonlight, and he familiar with the path, this civility was declined. When about half way through, the moon disappeared, and grandfather, losing the path, wandered amidst thorns and briers till day dawned, his clothes completely torn off. This swamp long ago was the very centre of New York. Col. Rutgers, the son of that gentleman, occupied the same house a few years since.

Joseph Tatnall was the most distinguished of those worthy men whose memories deserve notice in this community; and the rising generation ought to be informed that Mr. Tatnall was a true patriot. He alone dared to grind flour for the famishing army of the Revolution, at the risk of the destruction of his mill. His house was the home of Gen. Lafayette during his sojourn here, and that patriot remembered his kindness. On his return to New York in 1825, he required for Mr. Tatnall, then deceased. As he passed through Brandywine, he requested that the procession might be detained a few minutes at his son's door, while he paid his respects to the representatives of his worthy friend.

Gen. Washington, and other officers, received his hospitality during their residence here; you will hear more of his patriotism in the sequel. When President, and passing south, once he alighted at Mr. Tatnall's gate, entered the yard and knocked. Mrs. T. came to the door, and wished to send for Mr. T., but the General preferred to go to the mill, and leave his chariot at the gate. These gentlemen walked back to the house, followed by crowds of boys, rejoicing at the fine chance offered them to see the man whom the people delighted to honor. One of the joyous boys, lately deceased, an old gentleman, related the incident with much zest as a remembrance of General Washington.

The business of Mr. Tatnall was very extensive, as you may conclude from one circumstance. Mr. Lloyd, a great grain grower in Maryland, came to sell his wheat; went to Mr. T., who agreed to take all he had. Mr. Lloyd smiled, and said, "Why, sir, my grain will amount to forty thousand dollars." The reply was, "I will take it," to the great astonishment of that gentleman, and perhaps not less so to the gentry of the present day to hear that he paid the cash for it. It is creditable to his descendants to say that the mills are now owned by his sons and grandsons, the latter being the principal millers.

Thomas Lea, son-in-law to Mr. Tatnall, was among the useful, enterprising, and wealthy men of his day; was often heard to say how much he had been blessed; everything seemed to prosper in his hands; his family were just as he wished they should be; he had secured for them a competency of this world's goods, and he could now take his ease. He built the largest mill on the Brandywine. When it had been a short time in operation, and was filled with the finest grain, lo! trouble came upon him like a mighty rushing wind. The destroying element, in a few hours, consumed and laid in ruins this queen of the mills.

The loss was great, though to him trifling; the fire was tremendous, and the fragments continued burning for a week. Next, the afflictive hand of the Almighty was laid heavily upon him; death entered his domestic circle, and removed a beloved daughter, by that direful disease, consumption, that slays its thousands and tens of thousands; and a daughter young and lovely.

Son after son went to that "bourne from whence no traveler returns," until seven out of nine of his children, men and women, were the inmates of the grave. One son died in a strange land, whither he went in pursuit of health. His riches took wings and flew away. Lastly, disease seized his mortal frame, and brought down his gray hairs in sorrow to the grave.

"If a man live many years and rejoice in them all, let him remember the days of darkness." "The dust shall return to the earth as it was, and the spirit to God, who gave it."

James Price, another son-in-law to Mr. Tatnall, was suddenly removed from prosperity and usefulness, apparently in the prime of life. He was lamented as an excellent and worthy man.

These persons were all of the society of Friends; plain, straightforward men, calculating the cost before entering into any contract, expecting to pay the uttermost farthing, and from their own purses too. When you reflect on the present way of conducting business with the facilities to accomplish every project, those persons of olden times must be placed among the highest order of enterprising men, and to whom this community is much indebted for its present prosperity.

CHAPTER II.

Race Banks—Waterfalls—Isaac Kendall—Amusements—Cottage of A. H. Rowan, Esq.—Winter Sports—A Sad Calamity—Crossing the Dam—Moonlight Party—Bold Scenery—Tablet Rock—Old Snuff Mill—Isaac Jones, Esq.—Old Barley Mill—The Brandywine—Floodgate—Rattlesnake Run—Wild Scenery—Freshets.

Now we will stroll up the race bank, and view the beauties of this charming place. A mammoth willow graces the entrance, and more than fifty years have passed since the French residents built bathhouses over the stream on this side for their own use, though they generously left the keys near, where any one could accept their proffered kindness, and it was fully appreciated. They also had benches placed in this race, where the servant women stood in the water to wash clothes, drying them on the grass, and we well remember the snowy whiteness of their linen by this cold water process.

That house on the left hand, so prettily situated, was long the residence of James Canby, one of our most respectable and active citizens, now owned and occupied by our worthy Bishop Lee.

Here are four races, two on each side the creek, one far above the other. That stream flowing so gently beneath, at times rises to a great height, and in all its majestic grandeur, like a furious torrent, sweeps everything before it. At others, the water is so low you can step the rocks across.

Early in June it displays all its loveliness; then the forest trees that mostly shade these walks are dressed in their full verdure; the declivities are crowned with a variety of wild flowers of every color and hue; the vines in their different shades of green are twined around the trees; the birds are singing melodiously; the water falling over the dams, and sprinkling its sprays around, dashing and foaming through the flood-gates, like mineral waters sparkling with fixed air: fishes sporting in the stream; whole schools of young people of every age are skipping along the banks, climbing the rocks, and fancifully decorating their heads with wild flowers. Here and there pic-nic parties, amusing themselves in the neighboring wood. Animated nature gives an expression to the scenery, while inanimate adorns it with its richest garb, all mingling their offerings to ornament the spot.

Here let us pause. Shall we not present our offering to the Lord? and meditate on his works, "and talk of His wondrous doings; when our lives are fallen unto us in pleasant places, and we have so goodly an heritage." Let us pray for his counsel to guide us in all our ways, that at the last he may receive us into glory.

Swimming and bathing were amusements here, and for more than half a century hundreds of boys were taught to swim by a kind-hearted old man, lately deceased, Isaac Kendall, whose efficiency in this art will be long held in grateful remembrance by fathers and sons, and even grandsons who have been entrusted to his care and taught this useful exercise.

His instruction was gratuitous, yet he seemed amply rewarded by reciprocal enjoyment. Children were regular visitors at his little cabin, collecting pictures and pasting them on the wall. His innocent and lonely life was cheered by these youthful guests.

We are just below that building long known as the Old Barley Mill, near the creek. On this spot, in 1797, stood the cottage of Archibald Hamilton Rowan, Esq., a distinguished Irish gentleman who opposed the government at home, and joined the "United men," although he said he never favored rebellion, but only a reform.

He was imprisoned, and made a wonderful escape through the interposition of his wife, a true royalist, who had access to the prison at all times, and arranged her plans judiciously. Her equipage attracted notice, and drew more persons together than usual on this occasion.

Mrs. Rowan entered the prison, with her female attendant only, and an over-garment for him to slip on. A person resembling Mrs. Rowan, dressed in his clothes, was in waiting. At the moment the keeper was turning the key to let them out, the alarm of fire was given, so suddenly that all was confusion. The woman remained in the prison, and he stepped into the carriage, attired in the garments of this female, and the gentleman sprang out at the other side, mounted a fleet horse that was ready, and went off at full gallop. In the meantime, Mr. Rowan rode to the vicinity of Dublin, and escaped on foot.

As soon as he was missed, the person on horseback was pursued. Some time was spent in following up this delusion. Handbills were instantly out, headed "Rowan in the smoke, and Ten Thousand pounds reward." A man ploughing lent him his horse. This he soon rode down, and in crossing a stream, he entreated the boatman to hurry. "I am trying to get you away, sir; for I know you," was the reply; "and I am a poor man, and could now make my fortune, yet would never betray such a friend to my country as you." This he spoke with strong feelings, as a proof of Irish generosity and noble-mindedness.

When he came to the fishing-boat provided for his reception, the fishermen covered him with their seine; and some difficulty occurring, they were compelled to put back to the shore. Just then the police officer appeared. There were many boats, and all were diligently searched. As this one was the last, he began to despair, and was almost ready to surrender, when one of the police, using harsh expressions, said "the devil had a hand in his eluding all their efforts to capture him, and they might as well give over the pursuit."

The boat was then pushed off, and he safely landed on the coast of France. When on board, another of the handbills was presented him. He encountered some difficulties in that country, whence he came to this, and wandered about until he made Wilmington his resting-place.

For years he was an exile here. He boarded with Mr. Armor, near Wilmington, for months, and worked in his garden like a day-laborer, and left everything flourishing, when he took a room in the suburbs of the town, over a back building attached to the house of a very peculiar old bachelor, who, being himself eccentric, many droll things occurred. He had a kind of stairs or ladder, on the outside, to descend without interrupting his host, whose repose was often disturbed, lest the stranger should commit suicide.

He had many things sent him from home as curiosities. One night, the snow being deep, and crusted on the top, he put on an enormous pair of wooden shoes, such as are worn in the bogs of Ireland, and went down the stairs clattering and making a most awful noise. The host was in bed, and too much terrified to rise and see what it was; but lay covered up almost suffocated, till morning, when lo! to his great surprise and horror, he saw evidently the track of a giant's foot in the snow, who he had no doubt came to his house that night in pursuit of the stranger.

He soon after left him, and built this cottage of rough boards, with several small rooms, each having a fine name. On the inside he pasted paper to make it look neat.

The young people frequently visited him to borrow his books, as he had a valuable library. His only companions were two dogs, named Sally and Charles, after his wife and youngest son. They followed him everywhere, and seemed to understand all he said. I have heard him order them to shut the door, and reprove them for not cleaning their feet before they entered a lady's house, when they went back to the door and rubbed their feet on the mat.

Mrs. Rowan sent him a lock of her hair, that turned gray the night he made his escape from prison. She was a lady of great beauty and accomplishments, and was prohibited from having any communication with him on the forfeiture of her estate; yet she always found a way to supply him with ample funds.

He lived in this humble manner, and at one time made spruce beer, and wheeled it in a barrow through the streets to sell. All this was done for effect, as his doings were known in England.

At another time he set up a calico-printing establishment, and sent his address to a friend.

> "It was once Hamilton Rowan, Esq.,
> Now it is calico-printer and dyer."

He had many friends here, and was greatly respected. One day he came to town and left fire in his stove; when he returned his house was in ashes. Some men saw the flames in time to save a few articles; but nearly all his valuables were consumed. He then went to live in the old house opposite the barley-mill, where he remained to reside during his stay in this country.

Many offers were made him to return; stating that he need only to ask pardon of the king, and it would be granted; but he declared he would never bend his knee to majesty.

His wife and family were permitted to meet him in Hamburg, to take a final leave. They met, and through the intervention of friends, he was permitted to return, on giving his promise never to meddle with the affairs of government. Thus, after passing years in humble life, he was reinstated in the bosom of his family, with an income of thirty thousand pounds sterling per year.

His friends here were never forgotten. They often received remembrances of him in the shape of presents, and several men far beneath his rank were entertained at his house, merely because they were from Wilmington. He had a room in his house called Wilmington, where he retired to soothe his feelings when he became excited on any subject.

A ship sailed from here to Hamburg, while he was there; and he invited the captain, with two lads, to a most sumptuous dinner, given to the nobility, and introduced them as the sons of his friends, and spoke with much feeling of the hospitality he received in this place.

Among Mr. Rowan's curiosities was an instrument he carried in a side pocket, placed so as to touch his hip bone, by which he could tell how many miles he walked an hour, and whether he went too fast or too slow. This was made by his wife's direction, to enable him to take proper exercise while in prison. He likewise had a sword cane with a compass on the top, less than a dollar in size, to direct his steps when he was wandering through the woods.

He was a warm-hearted friend, and gave many proofs of it under trying circumstances. In the memorable year of '98, when the yellow fever first appeared at Wilmington, William Poole, a very worthy miller at Brandywine, a friend of Mr. Rowan, was seized with that alarming disease, which every one seemed to fly from. As soon as he heard his friend was ill, he proffered his services, which were thankfully received, and he nursed him with unremitted attention until he recovered.

Many little notices of friendship passed between them after his return to Ireland.

"Return to thy place and abide with the king, for thou art a stranger and also an exile."

Fishing among the rocks and streams was an amusement enjoyed by numbers; being so well shaded it afforded pleasure to all who were fond of that sport. Young people, in skipping the slippery rocks heedlessly, have unexpectedly taken a plunging bath, to their great annoyance and the merriment of their companions; sometimes it has been attended with danger.

Amidst the dreariness of wintry winds and chilling frosts,—that have stripped the rugged oak of its foliage; disrobed all inanimate nature; forced the feathered tribes to wing their way to more congenial climes, and the fishes from their wonted channel; driven the insect world into their cells; stilled this resistless torrent and fitted it up for a sporting-place for youth,—even at this cheerless season they are to be found in the full tide of enjoyment.

Many can recall hours pleasantly spent at the old barley mill, sliding and skating; groups of young persons and schools assemble here to enjoy the healthy exercise. Those of riper years, too, have had their hours of recreation. In days gone by, A. H. Rowan and two Scotchmen, John Fleming, long a worthy townsman and propietor of the mill, with his friend William Key, have played a Scotch game called golfing. They drew a circle on the ice, and had a stone round but rather flat on one side, in size and shape much like an old-fashioned roll of tobacco; in this a handle was placed, by which it was pushed over the ice, something like pitching quoits. This game has long been forgotten, like those who took delight in it. "There is no remembrance of thee in the grave."

A dangerous sport practiced here in those days by the younger class was riding on a whirligig. A post was secured in the ice, with a hole in the top, through which a long pole was passed; a sled was attached to each end by a rope; on these the riders were seated; four or six men holding the middle of the pole, forced it round with such rapidity that a dense mist enveloped the whole circle. This play has also passed away like a tale told, while the first named is kept up, amusing to spectators who come here to witness the feats displayed in skating. Some with great dexterity cut ciphers and write letters, others have little girls holding on to their coats as they skate, or in sleds fastened to their waists, flying over the ice in full glee; many are skilled in the art of sliding to a great distance, others are popping down at every attempt, yet not discouraged, so absorbed in pleasure they are regardless of the intense cold.

Joyous as these sports may be, on some occasions they are mingled with sorrow. Thirty winters have gone since, on a fine morning, a few school girls came here at noon to slide; and, as there was water over the edge of the dam, they prudently declined to venture. A fearless one sprang on, the ice broke, and in a moment she was gone, and through great exertion taken from the water a stiffened corpse.

Adverse providences had cast a gloom over the dwelling of her widowed mother. The angel of death had hovered around and borne away, in the bloom of youth, one and another of her loved ones. They were especial objects of anxiety; she wept over them as they sickened and died. For this blooming daughter of thirteen she had no such tears to struggle with, having left home but a few hours in gayety and health.

Crowds were running towards Brandywine, and one of the family inquired the cause; being informed a child was drowned, this afflicted widow could feel for other's woes, and when a sympathizing friend entered to prepare her for this sad event she met her in tears, but with fervent gratitude thanked her Maker for the safety of her little ones; her manner unnerved the affectionate friend for the painful duty.

The name of Mary was scarcely uttered, when the earthly tenement of this beloved daughter was borne in; but the buoyant spirit that so lately animated the lovely form had fled. This was an agonizing scene to see the bereaved mother lay her hand on the breast of her darling child, in hopes some warmth still remained; but all was in vain. She came forth like a flower, was cut down and fled away like a shadow. "Remember now thy Creator in the days of thy youth." "The living know that they shall die, but of the day and hour no man knoweth."

Mrs. Jane Dauphin often compared herself to the wreck of a ship floating upon the ocean, stripped of every means to guard against the tempestuous sea, expecting the next wave to dash her into the fathomless abyss. "Be merciful unto me, O, God, for my soul trusteth in thee. Yea, in the shadow of thy wings will I make my refuge until these calamities be past."

In reviewing gone-by events, many individuals will be associated of olden days almost forgotten, others of more recent date, though slumbering in the dust, live in memory. To some of those we know, a brief tribute of respect may not be improper.

The friend alluded to was a widow, and acquainted with sorrow, but not so overwhelming, and was always a friend in need. Whenever Mrs. Mary Black approached the "house of mourning," it was to weep with those who wept, and her gentle spirit was fitted for errands of mercy. If to visit the sick, her presence was soothing and her offering acceptable. God had blessed her with abundance, and as a practical Christian, she bounteously gave to the poor of the land. "I will shew thee my faith by my works."

We will now resume our stroll and cross the dam where two races terminate, and ascend the narrow rugged path to the bank on the right, and leisurely walk up to the flood-gate, thence through the wood to the old snuff-mill, and narrate whatever claims a lingering look. Yon clump of rocks, so steep and sloping to the margin of the race brim-full, turn the thoughts back half a century and revive an incident in early life.

On an evening excursion to this romantic place, a youthful party full of glee seemed to vie with each other to pass their hours in social joy. The night was beautiful; a brilliant moonlight rested on the trees and grass, glittering on the limpid stream in pearly rays. The girls frisked over the grassy way, through green bushes, with their white dresses flowing, leaping rocks, singing and chattering merrily. A village beau playfully called them a heartless clan, while he was displaying his eloquence to awaken their sympathies for his pitiable fate, just parting from his lady-love and in despair. They were as gay as larks.

The knell of time warning them to wend their way home, all rushed to this spot, and scrambling up the rocks to reach the top, a shout from the sentimental orator proclaimed "we have won the race," for a smart lassie had kept by his side, who reminded him of the fitness of this rock for a lover's leap; now he could perform an exploit to sustain his pretensions. At this moment a mis-step of hers called forth his gallantry. He, too, slipped, and in they plunged, he being over ordinary size, made a tremendous splash. The whole party screamed at the top of their voices; and an echo above resounded through the wood, and the loud rumbling noise seemed as if the flood-gates had given away, and the mighty rushing waters were about to overwhelm them.

But their fears were soon succeeded by peals of laughter, to see the hero and heroine gathering themselves up, and slowly creeping up from their aquatic freak, thoroughly drenched and looking aghast. In a doleful tone, the lassie exclaimed, "Am not I in a rueful plight? How shall I go through town, or enter my home in such a dripping dress?" Years rolled on ere the story was forgotten, yet it was no rare adventure to plunge in here.

In advancing, the shore grows bolder, and the scenery wilder. A precipitous ledge of rocks arrests our attention, rising nearly twenty feet perpendicularly, and you gaze in wonder how this can be; names cut in the stone from top to bottom, where no resting-place is found for the sole of the foot. The ascent adjoining is rugged and abrupt, covered with bushes, and some noble forest-trees. That ridge of rocks overgrown with pendant moss, and goodly-sized saplings, growing out of the clefts, amaze us, for we see no soil to nourish the roots.

At the old snuff-mill, associations of childhood cling to memory, when in simplicity a child would receive, and be pleased with a trifle, and carefully preserve it. The first time I was here, the wrapper on a roll of tobacco took my fancy, as I had never seen the like. It was an engraving of four men seated at a table smoking pipes. The first was represented as saying, "Good tobacco;" the second, "Yes, excellent;" the third, "Who made it?" and the fourth, "Isaac Jones." A workman kindly gave me one of these labels, and being fond of pictures it was long valued.

Isaac Jones was proprietor of this property. Yon old stone house was his summer residence; his family attended the Swedes Church. One or more are interred in its cemetery. As the second bell rang on Sunday morning, his old-fashioned carriage was seen regularly driving down the lane, and it may not be improper here to say that Mr. Jones was ever ready to contribute liberally for church purposes. Though a very plain man, he was the first to propose the purchase of an organ for Trinity chapel, and promised to be the largest contributor. Ere it was completed, he was consigned to dust.

We have heard that his heirs received but a small portion of his possessions. The property has fallen into other hands, and large paper mills are erected there. "Surely every man walketh in vain show; he heapeth up riches, and knoweth not who shall gather them."

We now return to the old barley-mill, and must tell you more of it. Fifty years ago, a calico-printing establishment was set up here by A. H. Rowan, the Irish gentleman previously mentioned. This place had long been used by John Fleming for cleaning barley. A large bleach green, over the race, was managed by an Englishman. In later years the mill was enlarged, filled with spinning jennies, and called Rockburn; these were superseded by carding machinery, then owned by one of our worthy townsmen, Joseph Bringhurst.

Spindle-making is now carried on, and the machine shop conducted with good order and decorum, by a woman regularly taught the art of making spindles by her father. Since his decease, she has managed this business, and is said to excel in workmanship; when her daily labors are over, she passes the twilight in improving her musical powers on the violin, and she plays with skill and taste.

Near yon silvery sheet of water is a spot of spongy oozy soil where flags and lilies of rare beauty grow.

The Brandywine is an extremely crooked creek, flowing over and through rocks and through hills and dales in fanciful curves, varying its depth. Within a few miles of town you can cross over five bridges, four covered, and one wire footway, where you ascend a ladder, and step on slender boards, that rock with your weight, and the only support is a wire not as thick as your finger. It is a considerable height above the water, and to look down it seems a fearful pass. In some places flats are pushed over by holding on to a rope. In others boats are used.

It may be termed likewise a whimsical stream, for at one time the dams are a dry path, and you can step across the rocks, and the whole looks like a rocky ridge in a thirsty land. At another time the roar of the water-falls are deafening, tumbling over furiously; and then again, on your next visit it may be a gentle, limpid stream, so inviting that a seat on a rock is involuntarily taken to be refreshed by its cool shade, in the view of reflected mills, vessels, trees, and people; ay, even our own shadow.

The pathway here is completely overshadowed, and in part secured by a stone wall, then a strong abrupt descent filled with briery bushes. Here and there a few gradual slopes covered with shrubs and vines, so interwoven that they form arbors, and jutting rocks hang over, that shield the view from persons walking the banks. Thus secluded, they are resorted to for bathing.

Near the head of this race, Caleb Seal and Joseph Shallcross, a century ago, were partners in a mill, where the neighbors sent their grists and waited till they obtained their flour. It may have been the first mill on the creek, for the Indians still held their possessions in places, and lived in wigwams, the ruins of which I remember.

At this flood-gate the water is deep, and it is dangerous to fall in. You cross a flat log, perfectly safe, if you are careful. Now and then a benevolent hand has rescued a young person from a watery grave.

The whole border, hill and glen, is covered with wild flowers of every color and hue. The sweet-brier and crab-apple blossoms are fragrant, and beautifully contrast with the dog-wood and honeysuckle. Laurels and roses are plenty. The admired Brandywine cowslip has been so long sought that it is nearly rooted out, and the rare curious plant, Noah's ark, almost extinct. But the neat pretty little Quaker girl keeps its footing, blooms long, and is very abundant.

In summer and in autumn, fruits and nuts may be gathered; and as reward always sweetens labor, one is sure to be amply repaid for a toilsome walk of ups and downs, crossing logs or leaping rocks. However the attractions may vary with the seasons, they never fail.

We must next descend a ravine of solid rocks, through which a rivulet runs, that has worn the stones smooth; and it is nearly dry. Many ramblers on these banks remember Rattlesnake Run. It commemorates reptiles that flourished here in the days of "auld lang syne." In later years, they and "copperheads" were scarce; yet, when the dead leaves moved beneath the feet, the apprehension made one tremble.

Black-snakes were numerous here. My lot was only now and then to see a garter or water-snake glide into the race. Many a group of school girls have scampered over this grassy way to clear the track from such intruders.

The general aspect of this place is extremely picturesque, exhibiting pleasant windings of the stream, thickly wooded hills, lofty cliffs, and valleys filled with odoriferous shrubs and patches of wild flowers, diffusing their sweetness in the air, as they put forth blossoms in the spring. The thick foliage of summer offers a shady retreat near the cooling waters; but the autumnal scenery excels in splendor, when on a bright day, as the sun's rays are softened by evening shade, and the foliage beautifully variegated, just changing its colors; the groundwork still green, but diversified and dotted with clusters of crimson leaves of every tint, and hues of yellow and brown, here and there speckled and streaked glossy leaves. The distant view resembles a terraced flower-garden, or green-house plants, tastefully arranged tier over tier, so that imagination can readily form gorgeous bouquets, wreaths and pyramids.

Hence the pathway winds through a glen, and the stream in view points the way, or a stranger might become entangled in briers and thorns. The woody heights stretch across like a screen, and the approach to the buildings curves into a little dingle, through which a gentle streamlet murmurs, and bushes entwined with vines darken the way and remind us of an entrance into a cavern. Quickly a glimpse of curling smoke, rising among the trees from cottages interspersed on the brow of the hill, and the old paper-mill bursts upon your sight.

Here everything is full of life; clangor of mills, humming of machinery, din of busy men hurrying to and fro, waters roaring, rending of rocks resounding through the lofty heights; for it is on the border of a kingly stream, that gives the power of motion to a vast amount of machinery above and below, where thousands of men, women, and children are employed, besides scores of animals and numberless vehicles freighted with manufactured commodities, destined to a distant market. We may safely say the vehicles contain an abundance of the staff of life, and much of life's destroyer. They return laden with the raw material, produce and merchandise. Here the farmer has a market at his door, and the laborer can earn bread enough and to spare. Here the poor man may become rich—rich in the comforts of life, but mayhap here, too, the rich man may become poor.

There are times when this kingly stream rises in majestic grandeur, and stone walls must bow. Ah! the very stones must be rooted from the earth that for ages they have clung to as their birthplace. And costly machinery that has drained his coffers of thousands is rent into atoms, or unfitted for service. And the poor man's garner, too, and the couch whereon he rested his weary limbs, must go; and perhaps his cabin is not spared. Amid all this devastation, he, homeless and penniless, may yet gratefully thank his Maker for the blessing of life.

From one familiarly acquainted with this region half a century, you may expect to hear how things were in gone-by days. The storehouse of memory could furnish incidents of deep interest for a long narrative, were it in skilful hands; as it is not, a brief and simple story must suffice of this old mill, in operation before the present century.

CHAPTER III.

Old Paper Mill—The Original Paper Machine—Description of the Mills, Cottages, &c.—Picturesque Scenery—Kentmere, the residence of Joshua Gilpin, Esq.—Giant's Footrock—Pic-Nic—Rokeby—Hagely—Jacob Broom, Esq.—Cotton Mill—Ruins, &c.—Lost in the Wood—Messrs. DuPont's Improvements—Eleutherian Mills—Explosion—Alarm—Change of Scenery—Fine Mansions—Gen. Lafayette—Rockland—William Young, Esq.—Relics of Gen. Washington—J. Brindley, Esq.—Swedes.

ALONG a curve of the Brandywine Creek, about two miles above the City of Wilmington, where the stream forms a semicircle for nearly a mile, was situated the estate of Joshua and Thomas Gilpin, at which the water power had been formerly appropriated to the manufacture of flour, and various other objects. But on the revival of trade and some of the manufactures immediately after the American Revolutionary war, it was converted to the making of paper, which was established there in the year 1787, and continued by the usual process into the commencement of the present century.

In the progress of invention and improvement, however, which has been so remarkably developed in our day, the Messrs. Gilpin extended their concern here very much, and established a new process; it was the art of manufacturing paper by machinery, so as to make a sheet of paper continuous and endless in length, and originating there, was the first establishment of this kind in America.

The paper was made on a revolving cylinder, all the machinery for which was made on the spot, and it was entirely successful. It was a novel accomplishment of skill and talent, and was very much admired as forming so very important an improvement; the previous and old method having been to make paper by single sheets, by a tedious and laborious process of the workmen by hand labor.

The machinery requiring great accuracy in its construction, was in progress for some time, but was put into use in August, 1817, and about the end of the year began to furnish paper for market; first for the *American Daily Advertiser* at Philadelphia, and for other newspapers, and soon after for elegant editions of extensive works, and for writing. In May, 1821, Lavoisne's great Atlas in letter-press and colored copper-plate engravings was published upon this machine paper, by Mathew Carey & Son, of Philadelphia, and this is noted by them in their edition of the work.

The establishment of this machinery necessarily created great jealousy and envy, for it was calculated to alter, as it soon did alter, the whole system of paper manufacture through the country; and it eventually furnished to the American public the means of a greater and cheaper supply of this prime material, for the extension of knowledge and literature, and which could not otherwise have been obtained for the extensive demands of our wonderfully extended country.

But the establishment underwent difficulties and disappointments commensurate with its importance.

A patent for the invention had been taken out in the year 1816, by Thomas Gilpin, but this was done before it was perfected and in use—and after it was completed, its importance was so obvious that every method was taken to procure a knowledge of it; so that eventually, by obtaining information from time to time of some of the work people, and close inspection of the patent, sufficient ideas were obtained of the machine to evade the patent, and similar machinery in rivalship was got up and experimented upon in New England; and this was first introduced at the paper mills at Springfield, Massachusetts, where paper by machinery was produced about the year 1825, and from thence the process was quickly spread through the country.

Besides this, the estate sustained calamities of various character. On the 22d February, 1822, an overwhelming flood extended over all this part of the country, and by it the creek rose to the height of more than twenty feet, which caused the destruction or ruin of most of the establishments, and on this estate to carry away to a great extent the dam, the races, machinery, and some of the buildings. In addition to this, in the month of April, 1825, one of the principal mills, with the machinery in it, was destroyed by fire.

These extensive calamities were followed by a further freshet, which took place over all the country, in the spring of 1838, by which these works were more extensively injured than by the former one; for being the lowest down on the creek they were more exposed to the flood. The large bridge below them, on the Philadelphia road, was carried away on both occasions. The proprietors of these mills having thus continued the Brandywine manufacture of paper, on the estate, for exactly fifty years, it was discontinued and the estate sold, and the buildings were then appropriated to the manufacture of cotton, which became a more extensive object through the country.

The statement of the machine, and freshets, was handed to the author by Thomas Gilpin, Esq.

It has been already stated that the old mill was in operation before the close of the last century, but it was not so extensively known beyond this vicinity before the improvements, which were made soon after the commencement of the present one; from thence it progressed to great notoriety. Citizens and strangers often resorted to this estate for a pleasant walk, and to enjoy its beauteous scenery, as well as to see the novelty and skill of mechanism, visit the wonder-working machine that could turn out an endless sheet of paper. Paper-making is too well known to need a description. Yet as things here were on the most approved plan, and order and neatness presided, we will venture to sketch one apartment in the old mill—a large salle on the lower floor, where more than thirty women were seated on high stools, at a long table placed before the windows, each one having a knife to pick the motes from every sheet; and they were dressed becoming their occupation, with a clean apron as smooth as if an iron had just been rubbed over it. Not a cobweb marred these white walls, nor was dust allowed to soil the floors.

Just above this, a large and modern stone building was occupied in the same way. Many departments of the business were carried on in each of these houses. The stone house below was used for assorting and cutting rags, and another stone structure for extracting colors. In this, immense kettles were fixed in furnaces built of stone that seemed immovable; yet the memorable freshet of 1822 swept the whole of the lower works away, and part of the building also. One of these heavy coppers landed on the Pea Patch; and the chain bridge connecting Wilmington and Brandywine was carried down the stream for some distance, and landed on the marsh, doing but little injury to the wood work. Flat-boats often conveyed paper on the water from one mill to another; but it was generally taken in wagons to the Wilmington wharves. Large quantities of bank note paper were made here. We have seen whole pieces of new silk handkerchiefs cut to mix with the rags, to designate its manufacture.

It is nearly thirty years since the old mill was burnt. The fire took place at noonday, and could not be accounted for; but it was on a day when public business was to be transacted, and strangers had assembled. The lighted sheets of paper flew through the air to a great distance, presenting a grand spectacle. The ruins stood for years. Close to the mills was a carriage road. Except this, the foreground was of steep hills, covered with grass and mostly shaded by noble trees. The hills were ascended by steps cut in the earth, or boarded and walled up. On the left was a fine clump of trees, and a swing with an armed chair, nicely arranged, where hundreds of youth have whiled away pleasant hours.

> "And memories of the loved,
>   The loved and far away,
> Live in those dark and heavy boughs,
>   And hang upon each spray.
>
> How can ye, thoughtless winds,
>   Sing there with so much glee?
> My eyes are dimmed with sadness now,
>   How can I sketch the tree?"

The axe has been laid at the root, and the woodman has not spared those trees.

Tier upon tier of stone cottages, yellow-dashed and well ventilated, rise up before you on these hills, shaded by forest trees, each having a yard nicely paled and ornamented with shrubs and vines, climbing to the roofs, mingling taste with comfort.

As a manufacturing district, it was long proverbial for the neatness and orderly conduct of its population. One trait in the character so remarkable we must not omit to note. The Messrs. Gilpin were the proprietors—the younger one of whom, Thomas Gilpin, resided partly in Philadelphia; but when here, occupied a very pleasant cottage, at which he generally received his friends. His garden was filled with fruit and flowers, with some choice lemon-trees in full bearing. There was a green-house adjoining, and an ice-house, in which the work people were allowed to keep their provisions, and to have daily access to it.

He having no family, and having to attend to the business in Philadelphia, he passed only a part of his time on this estate; but when absent, the house was left to be opened for the use of his friends, and such strangers as were brought by them to see the works. Here they stayed, and had the plain refreshments of water, cheese and crackers, "for the string of the latch was never pulled in;" yet nothing was ever disturbed, for a corresponding respect was paid by the guests to the attention they were accustomed to receive.

One anecdote, to show somewhat of the character of some of the parties, may be worthy a place in the reader's attention.

In the rosy month of June, notice was sent of a party of the young and sportive for the privilege of a day's recreation, and one of the cottages was prepared for them. The owner passing by a trio of young ladies, when seated in the wood, observed to them that they had a beautiful party, to which one of the young ladies replied, "Yes, and there are three brides among us." The observation he then made was, "Then I hope you are the three." But one of them, with what emotion must not here be betrayed, said, "No, there's no such good luck."

In an elevated and picturesque situation, on the upper part of the lawn, near the top of the hill, but surrounded by a forest grove, stands the very neat cottage of the higher order, built by Joshua Gilpin, Esq., and called Kentmere. It is beautifully situated, with an extensive view over the valley of the Brandywine and the Delaware; with gardens and walks around it tastefully arranged. This mansion is too well known to be further described, where many visitors from the neighborhood and cities have been so hospitably entertained. Mr. Gilpin resided here with his family the latter part of his life; and died there in the year 1841.

In the day of prosperity, the large stone house opposite the mill was occupied by Lawrence Greatrake, who managed the concern of paper-making. Death summoned him suddenly, in the vigor of life, to leave this extensive business and his large family. A youthful son succeeded him in the management of the establishment for years. It was a beautiful spot, and all around it was kept in the neatest order, shaded by trees, shrubbery, and vines. Yet no withered leaves or broken branches marred the rich verdure on this hill. The mistress of the mansion, Mrs. G., arranged all within her bounds in good taste.

The court in front was adorned in beauteous order, with many flowering shrubs. The balcony in the rear overlooked the creek and mills, and far beyond; and the steep hill descending was covered with rich grass, and handsome trees well trimmed, so that the view was not obscured. On one side was the garden, with a serpentine walk the whole length of the high ground, and planted with different species of trees and shrubbery, consisting of some hundred varieties, completely shaded. Here and there was an arbor, decorated with vines and furnished with stools painted white. This presented the most picturesque view. At the entrance of the estate was a neat cottage, called a lodge, at which the road divided into three ways, with a large gate to each; a private one led to Kentmere, a lower one to the mill below, and the centre one to this house and the mills above.

There are many who gratefully remember the civilities tendered to them by this family, especially those caught in rains or thunder storms in their rambles up these banks, and sought shelter under their roof. Some far away, who have been educated at Hilles's boarding school, may not forget the memorable evening when the entire school fled to this mansion to seek an asylum from a pelting rain, and the perplexity, as night approached, with no appearance of a change in the weather, and how George Greatrake exhibited his kindness in ordering the large covered mill wagon, geared with four horses, in which fifty or more girls were closely packed like reams of paper, standing erect, secure from the rain. They had a merry ride; though slow, it was sure and novel; a carriage conveyed the teachers home, and this was deemed an event in their life.

The daily crowds of visitors here one would think must be wearisome to master and man, yet all were met by cheerful faces, their curiosity gratified, and questions answered, however frivolous, and the greatest civility extended in passing through the various departments. Some one was ready to show all that you desired to see.

Mr. G. Greatrake, by personal exertion in the freshet of '22, impaired his constitution, and became the victim of a disease of the lungs, and in a few years died at the south, whither he went to recruit his health. From his knowledge of the business, and popularity with the workmen, his death was a great loss to the establishment. But the business being changed and the estate having fallen into other hands, everything was soon on the wane; and we lament to note the decline and fall of an establishment of which this town could once boast, as unrivaled in its order and pleasant scenery, and the delight and amusement of distant friends in their walk to view the operations at the old paper-mill.

How old things have changed! The buildings are now cotton mills with additions. The beautiful trees and tasteful ornaments are laid low in the dust. Like the elder members of this hospitable family, they are mingling with the earth.

We will now pass on to a place of great notoriety, though of more recent growth, and continue to mark things and incidents on our way, as tea-parties and pic-nics often assembled here. We will describe a select one, in the words of a departed friend, after naming the young persons who had walked up the banks. "We rode to the paper-mill, where we alighted, and bore the provisions to the destined place of entertainment. We were soon joined by the company, and procured a sylvan retreat just above the mills. The seats on the rocks were arranged in convenient order to receive us, the rocks rising behind to screen us from the world, and affording a rural retreat beside the cold clear stream. The weather was enchanting. The opposite forest was beautifully painted by the finger of reflection, on the calm surface of the Brandywine. Every face beamed with youthful pleasure; soon the baskets were opened, and a limpid spring afforded its aid for our gratification. A huge pitcher of cold lemonade was followed by cake, and never did it more refresh the spirits. The three musicians bounded with elastic steps over the rocks, and placed themselves amid a green bower above us. There the flutes played, and the rocks reverberated their sweetest notes. We had a feast of melody.

"A second supply of lemonade and cake was handed round; conversation varied the entertainment; some with hook and line sported on the margin of the stream. The whole scene was picturesque and beautiful. The figures of our musicians, perched on an elevated rock, rendered darker by the rich foliage that nearly surrounded them, formed a fine contrast with the white robes and sylph-like forms of the young ladies, some standing on the green turf, others resting on the rocks, and others again bending over the stream. The sun declined gently and brilliantly, the breeze of evening played upon our faces, and we had a most enchanting walk home.

"I was struck by the romantic beauty of the cottages on the the Brandywine, all yellow-washed, with white doors, &c., and ornamented in the most tasteful manner with vines and various shrubbery.

"Thanks to the kindness of Mr. Gilpin, our New York guest was perfectly enchanted, and all professed themselves highly delighted. M. and his fair cousin left us at nine, much gratified. The gentlemen dreamed of rocks, cascades, and ladies fair. Even I was wandering in dreams over the fairy scene. The water-fall was a fine natural accompaniment to the flutes. We reached home at eight o'clock, the appointed hour."

Here is a natural curiosity, a flat blue rock of Brandywine, famed for solidity, and high upon it is a flat space, worn by pebbles, so as to leave the distinct shape of an overgrown human foot; that is called the Giant's Rock.

Another flat rock claimed notice in days gone by. A student of Doctor Way's, from South Carolina, who had spent years here, and associated with the best society, in September left here to attend the medical lectures in Philadelphia; sincerely regretting his change of home, was induced to make an early visit to the friends he loved. He rambled up these banks with his friend, E. Thomas, Sen., to enjoy the beauteous evening scenery. He observed he was taking his last look of the spot where he had whiled away so many happy hours. They crossed and re-crossed streams till wearied, and sat down on a rock musing in sadness that they so soon must part and meet but once more to bid a final farewell.

The doctor had his flute, and played Burns' Adieu, accompanied by E. T.'s voice, who sang well. While conversing, the doctor cut his name in the rock (" William H. Kenney, departed—"). He left a space for Wilmington, in which E. T. cut "this life, in October 1794." After his return to the city he was suddenly attacked by a violent fever, and died in a few days, in the same month, much lamented here, and to the great grief of his father, for he was an only son. "But I said truly, this is a great grief, and I must bear it."

During the speculative mania that raged to an alarming extent from the year 1812, many sober-minded men caught the epidemic, and it seemed to turn their thoughts back to days of yore, when Blackbeard hid his booty on the border of streams. For by fancied clairvoyance, they saw hidden treasure 'neath this barren rocky spot, and paid forty thousand dollars for a few acres. This was truly scattering to the wind; sowing on rocky ground that yielded no fruit, but verified an old proverb, that nothing is lost.

The folly that empties one man's purse goes to fill the purse of another. The original proprietor, Job Harvey, was a wealthy and far-sighted man, who gathered in a rich harvest by this speculation.

The next place to note is an old establishment formerly owned by a respectable inhabitant of early days, Vincent Gilpin, who knew Wilmington as a village in its simplicity, and beheld it rise to the glory of a borough; and amid all the changing scenes, he sustained his integrity as a worthy man; when full of years he ended life's pilgrimage, leaving to his heirs this property, which was a good old-fashioned house and grist-mill. They were sold to Lewis McLane, Esq., more than thirty years ago, who established a cotton manufactory, and called the place Rokeby.

The wire bridge across the stream is near, and also several factories; but Hageley was the oldest building, and most improved grounds. For many years it was a summer retreat of Rumford Dawes, a wealthy merchant of Philadelphia, whose family were residents here in village days, incidents of whom, as we proceed, will help to swell our narrative.

Some of our neighboring citizens in fashionable life no doubt yet remember the hospitality of the owners of this mansion, where they spent weeks enjoying the rural and lovely scenery at Dawes' slitting mill. This was purchased of Mr. D. by the Messrs. Dupont for fifty thousand dollars, to erect powder mills.

In the last century, these banks looked like a howling wilderness, studded with rocks, so unfitted for tillage, that, apparently, no art of man could change the face of nature. Rattlesnakes and copperheads, it was said, flourished here in countless numbers, when Jacob Broome, Esq., in 1795, selected the only eligible spot for a cotton manufactory—the first in this region. It was deemed a wonderful enterprise. Soon after he built a mansion, spacious for that day, on the hill now occupied by Dr. Smith. In the summer of 1797, Mr. B.'s family spent some weeks there; and I remember the spot, when I was on a visit to his daughters.

The mill was not long in operation ere it was burnt down, and remained a heap of ruins.

In the year 1802, we passed a balmy Indian summer in Brandywine Hundred, and my delight was to wander round and through the wood with an elder female, who loved to tell legends and early recollections of her birthplace and youthful home. Her ancestors were Swedish colonists, one of whom cleared and tilled a part of this region, and fitted up his cabin amid the red men, near their wigwam; and by precept and example convinced them that the white man who walked humbly with his God was their friend and neighbor. Here he was content to dwell and enlarge his borders, improve his grounds and tenements. In old age he set his house in order, trimmed his lamp, and waited for the messenger to guide him to a peaceful home.

The battle of the Brandywine, and many a link in that eventful chain was bright in the memory of this ancient female. The highway crossed her father's land, and his house was near. On that memorable day, she stood at the gate sorrowing over the hard fate of the retreating army, hastening on "faint, yet pursuing."

An officer, without a coat, and a bundle on his arm, stepped aside, and piteously asked her to wash a vest. "Most willingly," she said;

"but can you wait for it to dry?" On hearing it was drenched with the blood of the slain, as he handed it, she trembled, turned pale, and shrunk from the sight.

There was a draw-well at hand, and he implored her to lay it in water, and what she was about, to do quickly, for time was precious. This vest was the only relic of his valued friend, a pure patriot, and brave soldier, who had fallen on that day, by his side, and the sight of it was too grievous to retain longer in that state. His blood-stained garments were sprinkled by the noble fellows who fell on his right and left, while he escaped unscathed. His desire was so intense to preserve this memento, he seized it dripping, and ran, throwing her a silver dollar. She was indignant at the offer of reward. He was gone, and the precious metal was so rare in this region, that she laid it aside till peace was proclaimed.

This female, now in her eighty-ninth year, is a remarkable woman. Prosperity and adversity have fallen to her lot; joy and sorrow have been mingled in her cup. She is now alone. The chastening hand of the Almighty removed her worthy husband in the prime of life; having then an only daughter, who was the staff of her declining years. In all this, she murmured not, but fell down and worshiped, saying, "The Lord gave, and the Lord hath taken away; blessed be the name of the Lord." Dependent on the bounty of friends; living in an upper chamber, she provides for herself and keeps her room neat and in order. Previously to this year, she did plain sewing for the tailors. She goes to market, and regularly attends her church and religious duties, contented and cheerful. She feels no want, and says she hath faith to believe that her bread and water are sure, and when her strength fails, the Lord will not forsake her.

Once during this season it was proposed to cross the creek and extend our walk on the opposite side. There seemed no doubt of her finding the boat-way. But we were warned of difficulty, and my mother reluctantly yielded her consent to this pedestrian excursion. The sun shone auspiciously on a delightful morning, under a pure cloudless sky. We sallied forth at leisure, admiring the richness of the scenery as we went on. The foliage had changed its verdure into diversified hues; and the whole forest was decked in brilliant colors. Imperceptibly we entered a wild, rugged and almost trackless way, that turned my thoughts to a backwoods scene of a terrific wilderness, where naught was heard save an Indian whoop, or roaring of beasts prowling for prey. Our fears were aroused lest the footstep that put in motion the withered leaves might turn up a nest of rattlesnakes.

Hemmed in by rocks, we lost our way. Not knowing whither to go, we began to feel our excursion more romantic than pleasant. We were hedged in too by bushes, and entangled among briers that clung to our dresses and dragged us back as we scrambled over the rocks, with the twigs flapping our faces and scratching our limbs. There was no way to retreat; we must struggle through and progress slowly with no brighter prospect. My courage was on the wane pretty soon; and now the little stock was gone. We screamed for assistance, but our voices echoed in vain. A nervous tremor seized us, to laugh at one moment, and the next cry in fear.

After passing more than two hours in this sad predicament, we found that we were descending a steep hill, and soon heard a gurgling sound, and caught a glimpse of the stream. We pushed on with renewed vigor to reach the margin, where the sight of a man crossing in a boat cheered our drooping spirits. He ferried us over safe, but could not give us any information, for he was a stranger here.

In loneliness and weariness, we sat down on a mossy rock to rest, and to meditate on our adventurous ramble, "and what will ye do in the end thereof." A broken road was near, and hope buoyed us up that some one might thither direct their steps. We no more desired to try our luck in devious ways; steadily watching, at length we saw the shadow of a carriage, and called to the driver, who obligingly stopped to answer our questions.

The sun was in the meridian, and poured down on the road in extreme heat, so he advised us to pass through the wood carefully. The path was intricate, overgrown with brambles, and a harbor for snakes, and looked as if never trod by footsteps; we thought it more tolerable to endure a scorching sun, and preferred the road. This man was Mr. Davis's coachman, who, recognizing me, said he had no immediate duty at home, and could take us the two miles. His civility was gratefully accepted, and we stepped into the carriage with light hearts, and soon arrived at the place of our anticipated visit, rejoicing.

About the year 1800, the Messrs. Dupont & Co., made their first purchase here, that caused rumors to float through the country. The farmer was at his wit's end to conjecture what schemes were in view. To buy a barren tract of rocks! why, to expend cart-loads of money would not fit it for tillage. Others pitied the strangers for wasting their substance in wild adventure, and when the blasting of rocks commenced, said, it will surely exhaust a mint! Yet many of those farmers lived to witness mighty obstacles surmounted; and their wise predictions to fail. Neighboring estates have been enhanced in value; neither has ruin befallen the projectors.

There was no house to be had near, and Mr. Dupont fitted up a cottage for the family, in which they resided. It was as common for snakes to crawl to and drink out of the water bucket as it would be in a backwoods cabin. What a transition to those persons, from the beauties and refinements of France, to the rugged woody heights and snaky rocks of Brandywine!

It is said that Mr. E. J. Dupont's house was built of the stone from a single rock, on the spot where it stands. This house is beautifully situated on the brow of a hill. As you descend by the road, suddenly it bursts upon the sight, adorned by clusters of forest trees left on either side. From a balcony you overlook the powder-yard and mills. Here hundreds of men are as actively engaged as the little busy bees providing their winter stores.

Those men so industriously employed are no doubt buoyed up by the hope of providing stores for the winter of life. When no one dreams of it, a fatal explosion may take place, and in the twinkling of an eye many may be cut off in the midst of labor. What a shocking spectacle of mortality does such a scene exhibit; confusion and dismay seize the multitude; the vicinity is thrown into a panic. Men who cheerily left their abode full of life and hope at morning dawn, ere the evening shades have fallen, have become a terror to be looked upon by their dearest relatives.

However feeble the effort, we will attempt briefly to portray the explosion in March, 1818. About ten o'clock, the town was thrown into consternation. The noise burst upon the ear like the report of a cannon, and the earth shook! At the moment crossing King and Second Street, my attention was fixed on passengers hastening on to the steamboat. The earth trembled, my ear was stunned, and I involuntarily exclaimed, "The steamboat!" Many voices echoed, "Yes! Milnor's boat full of passengers is blown up!" Men and women ran to and fro. My steps were bent to a store in Second Street, where a friend was waiting for me. This family had assembled in the store, and said it was an earthquake, the windows shook and the door bell rang aloud.

We hastened homeward almost breathless, hearing on the way it was a magazine in rear of our dwellings, opposite the Town Hall. A second tremendous report seemed to lift us from our feet. Now we ascertained it was the powder-mills, by the dense black smoke rising in piles of clouds, and gathering into a column, fold upon fold, and twisting into a cork-screw shape, varying in lights and shades, stretched over our heads and seeming to totter as if ready to fall and crush all beneath. Some of the dark folds appeared bespangled with stars, others looked like brilliant clusters suspended and enveloped by a thin mist, shooting out and twinkling as they fell, till lost in the blaze of noonday. This scene was too magnificent for ordinary powers to portray.

Nearer home a horseman passed in full gallop, shouting "Raise your windows!" Another followed as rapidly and cried, "Abandon your houses, the grand magazine will soon explode." Every dwelling was quickly deserted, even by the domestic animals. Being about the hour to prepare dinner, some had meat on the fire, others had it spitted, and in the general confusion much was thrown on the floor, where it lay untouched for three hours at least.

Friends had assembled for worship, when the messenger gave the alarm; and as a rare occurrence they left the meeting-house in a body, and walked up the middle of the street. From the lower part of the town, not a few women and children fled across the Christiana. Men and boys, with some women, ran to the fatal spot. But a very large group of women and children, of every age, class, and color, mingled on a vacant square on Market Street. Invalids who had not been out of their house all winter, and the aged and the infirm fled for shelter to a school-house with no chimney. The March wind blew keenly, yet none of these caught cold, so intense was the excitement.

Amid this great consternation, it might truly be called a noiseless day! Every voice was hushed, and all spoke in a whisper; no noisy mirth or crying of children disturbed the quiet sadness of the mixed multitude. The dog was subdued and ceased to bark, and so softened into sympathetic fear, couched at his owner's feet. Pacing of horses and footsteps were the only sound to interrupt the awful silence, while memory was refreshed with the descriptions read of earthquakes in by-gone days, when danger threatened; the people were seized with despair, and in profound silence awaited the sad doom to be engulphed in the bowels of the earth.

Intense anxiety was depicted in each countenance to hear the true statement. At one o'clock, the thrilling story was told that instantaneously forty souls were hurled into an unknown eternity; and fragments of their mangled bodies were scattered over the face of the earth, or lodged on the tops of trees; that widows and orphans rent the air in wailing and lamentation, as they stood shuddering over the spot of this appalling tragedy.

By throwing a quantity of powder into the water, much destruction was arrested, and many lives preserved. It was extremely perilous to those engaged, and those whose foresight and energy had proposed it, among whom was Marshal Grouchy, on a visit to the family. Of all the explosions, this one was the most terrific and fatal.

The bereavement of the widows awakened the sympathies of E. J. Dupont, Esq., and it was not a momentary impulse. He, with noble generosity, allowed to each one an annuity during her widowhood, and this benevolence was faithfully fulfilled, and continued to the few who remained after he lay mouldering in the dust.

Fine mansions now adorn this rocky spot, clusters of cottages, and hamlet after hamlet rises upon the view, while this region, more than others, exhibits a bustling active life on every hand. The growing establishment is a stong evidence of the ability of the managers, and of the spirit which influences them. Those energetic operations in the immediate vicinity of Wilmington have, no doubt, added to its prosperity.

In the year 1825, Gen. Lafayette made a visit of a few days to the Messrs. Dupont; and with those gentlemen, reviewed the battle-ground, Chad's Ford, of which he bore the mark of a brave man. A public dinner was given to him on the spot, where he remarked the astonishing change in the whole region. On his return to the mansion, he wrote in the album of Miss E. Dupont as follows:—

"After having seen, near half a century ago, the banks of the Branywine a scene of bloody fighting, I am happy now to find it the seat of industry, beauty, and mutual friendship.

July 25th, 1825. LAFAYETTE."

Here the Messrs. Dupont, Sen., in life were highly esteemed, and in death lamented. The sudden departure of those gentlemen were singular coincidences, alike in character and place. E. J. Dupont died in the autumn of 1836, and his remains were borne through the town, on the eve of an important election. The political storm was calmed, at least for the moment, and the mingling of parties to pay their last respects to so useful a character was expressive of the loss the community had sustained, and numerous friends sympathized with the bereaved family. One who cared for the widow and orphan was gone. "Behold he taketh away; who can hinder him."

On these premises is a large school-house, and a flourishing Sunday school has been opened for years, under the superintendence of Madam Bauduy, eldest daughter of E. J. Dupont, and we trust, from this little source, the waters of life have flowed. Here, too, the Gospel is regularly preached on Sunday afternoon.

Young's establishment will conclude our notice of the Brandywine.

In 1793, William Young, a worthy Scotchman, for years in the book business in Philadelphia, erected a paper-mill in this region.

As soon as Mr. Young became interested in this rocky tract, he built a house for public worship, in a romantic spot, and it is really a novelty. The floor is a solid rock, and the crevices filled with mortar and the rough places are plastered. "I will liken him unto a wise man, who built his house upon a rock." Being eminently pious, he took care to provide a pastor to feed the flock, and guarded well the sheep of his pasture.

A fine mansion was also put up in the last century, and improvements made from year to year, and the numerous cottages soon changed the face of this district. Mr. Young was one of the first directors of the steamboat to ply hence to Philadelphia, and firmly opposed traveling on the Lord's day, and during his life it lay at the wharf on Sunday. His place was called Rockland. In the midst of usefulness, death summoned him to leave a large family and numerous cares. He too was lamented as a public loss.

"Whosoever shall confess me before men, him will I confess also, before my Father who is in heaven."

The old mansion of James Brindley, on this side of the Brandywine, claims our passing notice, because here Gen. Washington took his breakfast on the morning of the battle of Brandywine, walking the floor in deep thought, or standing with his cup of coffee in his hand, eating little, and soon hastening on to Chad's Ford. James Brindley, Jr., who resides here, possesses a valued relic, a lock of Gen. Washington's hair; also a lock of his lady's.

Part of this farm was owned by a Swede, T. Stidham, who lived to a great age, the life of a hermit, and for one hundred acres of arable land, paid the proprietary agent one bushel of wheat yearly, quit rent.

The Stilley's lived to a great age; they were descendants of Swedes. One female of this family regularly attended the old church in her eighty-fourth year, and walked more than three miles. There are many families in this district whose ancestors were Swedish colonists—Hendrickson, Armstrong, Poulson, Springer, &c. Some of those farmers retain much of the ancient simplicity of the fathers, and we add with pleasure that they are respected by the community for integrity of character and honest dealing. One evidence of similarity between father and son is very strongly depicted by a recent incident. At the close of the year 1849, this parish was visited by a Swedish minister just eight years from home. This was the Rev. Mr. Unonius, the first Swede who preached here since the Rev. Lawrence Girelius left Wilmington in 1791.

This gentleman's attention was arrested in Trinity Chapel by seeing an old member of the congregation, and a wealthy farmer, walk up the aisle to his pew. Mr. Unonius thought his whole appearance precisely such as he had been accustomed to in his fatherland—dress, manner of laying down his hat, and fixing his whip. Beside, he said his overcoat must have been made in Sweden, for it was their exact pattern for centuries past, and even his collar was fixed as they were worn. He became so excited that he could scarcely retain his seat, as he felt himself indeed among his brethren.

The settlements of the Swedes on the Delaware preceded those of the English by many years, and the emigrants who came were remarkable for an amiable character and an integrity which very much descended to their posterity; there were four churches, which were for a long time under the government of the diocese in Sweden, and ministers were appointed from there. The Swedish churches were this Trinity Church at Christiana, and the three old Swedes churches in Pennsylvania—at Philadelphia, at Moyamensing, and at the Swedesford on the Schuylkill.

CHAPTER IV.

King's Road—Bancroft Woodcock—Dr. James Tilton, Sen.—Old Letter—Cæsar A. Rodney, Esq.—Dutch Dolly—Fine Scenery—Col. Townsend—Carl Christopher Springer—Old Cottage—J. Springer—Introduction to the Sixth Generation of his Pastor.

WE now leave the Brandywine, cross the small bridge, and walk up the "Old King's Road." On the left is the new cemetery, extending to the Kennett turnpike, in which are many interments, and some improvements in trees and shrubbery. Yon new house at your right, pleasantly situated on rising ground, belongs to Mrs. Lovering, a daughter of Joseph Shallcross, who was a true patriot in the day of his country's trial. A century has passed since he bought this farm for five hundred dollars. Our notice of him will be included in the revolutionary part of our narrative, therefore we pass on and view the fine prospect.

Here hills over hills arise; well improved farms, with good buildings; entering the town by the Kennett road as the sun descends beyond the western hills, with its dazzling beams glittering on the windows of houses towering over others, we have a most magnificent sight, exceeding any illumination, for fine and extended scenery is added to it.

Yon stone edifice towering so high, with a copse of evergreen on the south side, was once the hospitable mansion of Doctor James Tilton. But it seems in place to notice his predecessor, Bancroft Woodcock, of whom, I believe, he purchased it—it was then called Bancroft's or Federal Hill. This person was a remarkably plain, stiff looking Friend, reminding one of bones and sinews, yet famous for his agility. In skating he excelled the youths of his day; no one could equal him. It was a novel sight to see such a person flourishing on the ice, and mid boys and youths, performing feats to the amazement of beholders. He was celebrated for this exercise, and often displayed his skill and graceful movements on the Delaware, opposite Philadelphia. He was also famous for walking. He lived to a very old age, and was so thin that old people used to say he would evaporate.

Long before the Revolution he was a noted silversmith here. In 1774, he made plate for my mother; his workmanship was superior. Half a century ago he removed to Redstone, then called the backwoods. Years after this, Mrs. Lea, returning from Pittsburg, was recognized by him on his way from monthly meeting, to and from which he walked seventeen miles in one day every month. Then he was a mere shadow. He afterwards more than once walked to Philadelphia, and died about thirty years ago.

When Doctor Tilton became owner of this farm, it was called Federal Hill, then Tilton's Hill, next changed to Bellvue, as the view is commanding; it overlooks the city, rivers, and fine meadows on the east, with the surrounding country for miles. From the top of the house and from the adjoining farm there is a distinct view of four States; and from the chimney, as the sun sets, Christ Church steeple in Philadelphia, nearly thirty miles distant, can be plainly seen with the naked eye. When the Doctor enjoyed good health, he had an excellent garden and abundance of choice fruit, and freely shared it with his friends. To pass so prominent a character would be inexcusable; yet to describe one so original, and to do him justice, exceeds my powers for description.

In making the experiment it would be cause of regret were any other impression given than that he was a Christian, a scholar, and a gentleman; though if I may be allowed the expression, I will say the latter without polish. His person was above six feet; dark hair; keen black eyes; very dark, swarthy complexion; loud, quick, and coarse voice; an unwavering patriot; well tried, and faithful to his country's cause—an old bachelor of the fisst order; finished in the art of chewing tobacco, yet always in pleasant humor; no misanthrope; he loved the society of ladies, and they enjoyed their visits to partake of his fruit, and many well remember his baked pears and milk, which he called his " Virgilian suppers;" neither tea nor coffee was used at his establishment; a professed democrat of the old school, carrying out fully his views; living on the produce of his farm; wearing homespun (so called); admonishing others to do the same to encourage and protect domestic manufactures.

As a practicing physician, he was justly esteemed; with nervous persons he was eminently successful in arousing their depressed spirits by his eccentricities; advising delicate females to lay aside their lady airs, and learn to spin on the big wheel stocking yarn for the family, or go to a farm-house, milk cows, and attend to the dairy—making themselves useful was the only remedy for their restoration to health. In the Revolution, Dr. Tilton was a surgeon—in the last war, surgeon-general.

The evening of his return from Washington, with his commission, Mrs. E. Massey and I walked to the hill, met him in good spirits, and were much amused at his description of a visit to the White House. He said, on entering, he was surprised to be an object of notice, for he soon observed the ladies were in a broad grin, and the drawing-room was crowded. He could not imagine why he attracted their attention, being well dressed, in that handsome thunder and lightning coat you ladies (meaning us) have seen me wear to church.

We both exclaimed, "Not that coarse tow linen coat, doctor! Why, it is only fit for a floor cloth." "Yes, surely." "Can it be possible, doctor, you went to the President's in that dress? Why, they have taken you for an Indian chief!" Then his tobacco quid flew the whole length of the hall, with his head thrown back on his chair, and such a loud roar of laughter, not exactly like anything but himself, he replied, "There is no doubt the jades did."

Next day he dined with Mr. Madison, " met the foreign ministers all the secretaries and officers of the army and navy, dressed in British cloth, and buttoned up to the chin, bedizened with gold lace, puffing and sweating, the blockheads; while I with my handsome thunder and lightning coat, was cool as need be. 'Why, doctor,' said, they, 'you do not appear to feel the heat,' 'Neither would you, if dressed as you ought to be, in such nice homespun as this,'" tossing up the corner of his coat.

By some means, the doctor hurt his knee, during the last war, and it became very painful; then a white swelling ensued, and after a prolonged state of great suffering, his limb was amputated, which he bore with Christian fortitude.

When the wound was healed, he directed a cradle made of enormous size to rock him in for exercise, and a wagon, drawn by a strong man, was his only conveyance to and from town, visiting his friends in this vehicle.

The doctor was likewise a member of the olden Congress, when none but honorable men, or those whose capabilities had been tested, were thought of, to make laws and manage the affairs of State, and when riotous scenes and displays of valor were never witnessed in the legislative halls. "When good men are in authority, the people rejoice." When others rule, "the people mourn." "Remember, O Lord, what is come upon us, how many may say we are orphans and fatherless. Our mothers are widows, because of the sword of the wilderness." "Turn then us unto thee, O Lord, and we shall be turned, and renew our days as of old."

The following is a letter from Doctor Tilton to Hon. G. Bedford:

ANNAPOLIS, *Christmas day*, 1783.

DEAR SIR:—You will have published at large the General's speech of resignation, with the President's reply, &c. I will endeavor to give you some sketch of the manner in which this business was conducted, and assist your imagination, if I can, to finish the picture which the next newspapers will probably present to you, by the time this letter arrives.

The General came to town last Friday, and announced his arrival, by letter, to Congress, requesting to know in what manner they chose he should resign his authority, whether by private letter, or public audience. The latter was preferred without hesitation. Some etiquette being settled on Saturday, a public dinner was ordered on Monday, and the audience to be on Tuesday.

The feast on Monday was the most extraordinary I ever attended. Between two and three hundred gentlemen dined together in the ball-room. The number of cheerful voices, with clangor of knives and forks, made a din of very extraordinary nature, and a most delightful influence. Every man seemed to be in heaven, or so absorbed in the pleasures of imagination as to neglect the more sordid appetites, for not a soul got drunk, though there was wine in plenty, and the usual number of thirteen toasts drank, besides one given afterwards by the General, which you ought to be acquainted with. It is as follows: "Competent powers to Congress for general purposes."

In the evening of the same day, the Governor gave a ball at the State House. To light the rooms every window was illuminated. There the company was equally numerous, and more brilliant, consisting of ladies and gentlemen. Such was my villainous awkwardness, that I could not venture to dance on this occasion. You must therefore annex to it a cleverer idea than is to be expected from such a mortified whelp as I am.

The General danced in every set, that all the ladies might have the

8

pleasure of dancing with him, or, as it has since been handsomely expressed, "get a touch of him."

Tuesday morning Congress met, and took their seats in order, all covered. At twelve o'clock, the General was introduced by the Secretary, and seated opposite the President, until the throng that filled all the avenues were so disposed of as to behold the solemnity. The ladies occupied the gallery, as full as it would hold; the gentlemen crowded below stairs. Silence ordered by the Secretary, the General rose and bowed to Congress, who uncovered, but did not bow. He then delivered his speech, and at the close of it, drew his commission from his bosom and handed it to the President. The President replied in a set speech; The General bowed again to Congress; they uncovered and the General retired.

After a little pause, until the company withdrew, Congress adjourned. The General then stepped into the room again; bid every member farewell, and rode off from the door, intent upon eating his Christmas dinner at home.

Many of the spectators, particularly the fair ones, shed tears on this solemn and affecting occasion. Sir Robert Eden and Mr. Harford attended very respectfully. They were also at the public dinner and the dance; and Master Harford was so gay as to say that he would show away if the *State* would give him anything to do it with.

Before this comes to hand, President V. Dyke will make you acquainted with an express, sent by Congress, to the executives of all the unrepresented States to the eastward, viz., Jersey, New York, and Connecticut. President V. Dyke was addressed among the rest, because Mr. McComb informed Congress he could stay no longer than until next day after to-morrow, when we shall not have a Congress.

As soon as you arrive, Mr. Ellery* proposes to demonstrate that the story of the Isle of France is an arrant falsehood, and that both latitude and longitude have been discovered in Delaware. For the honor of the State, then, make haste.

    I am, dear sir,
      Your friend and humble servant,
        JAMES TILTON.

Hon. G. Bedford.

As so lively an interest is felt in all the incidents and anecdotes accompanying the career of General Washington, it may be acceptable

---

*William Ellery, a Senator from Rhode Island in the first Congress.

as a part of these reminiscences to insert from the original the address of the burgesses and citizens of Wilmington to the General on his passage through the borough towards Mount Vernon, after the revolutionary contest had ended and peace and prosperity had been thus renewed to our country.

The address is unrivaled as a composition; and having never before appeared in print, may be duly estimated. It was probably written by Jacob Broom, Esq., who was an eminent and talented citizen of the State of Delaware, and has been loaned for this purpose to the author by her friend Thomas Gilpin, who has the original. General Washington's answer to this address is also given from the original, and is consistent with that dignity and modesty which always accompanied his services and character.

> *To His Excellency, George Washington, Esq., General and Commander-in-Chief of the Armies of the United States of America.*
>
> MAY IT PLEASE YOUR EXCELLENCY—The Burgesses and Common Council of the Borough of Wilmington, in behalf of themselves and the inhabitants thereof--
>
> Being penetrated with sentiments of the most perfect respect, beg leave to approach and to be permitted to congratulate your Excellency, that your glorious endeavors to rescue our country from a determined plan of oppression have been not only attended with the most brilliant success, but crowned with the noble rewards of liberty, independence, and the final accomplishment of an honorable peace.
>
> When we reflect on the magnitude of the object for which we contended, and the greatness of the power we had to oppose, the boldest among us have sometimes shuddered at the prospect, while your magnanimity was our invincible shield on the most gloomy occasions.
>
> Convinced that our humble talents cannot express in language suitable to the subject, either the grateful sensations we feel in the contemplation of your great and eminent services, or the love and admiration of your many amiable virtues which fill the bosom of the friends of freedom in America and in distant nations, yet, rather than wound that delicacy which would receive with reluctance even less than our duty and inclination prompt us to mention, we will conclude with embracing this opportunity of joining the general voice of America, which hails you as "the deliverer of our country;" and we flatter ourselves you will believe that our most fervent wishes will

accompany your illustrious and long meditated retirement, with the enjoyment of health, tranquility, and every other felicity.

And permit us to indulge the pleasing hope, that even in the serene enjoyment of that retirement which will astonish mankind little less than the splendor and greatness of your services; that with a parental consideration, your excellency will occasionally contribute your advice and influence to promote that harmony and union of our infant governments which are so essential to the permanent establishment of our freedom, happiness, and prosperity.

Signed by order of the burgesses and common council.

JOSEPH SHALLCROSS,
Town Clerk.

DECEMBER 16, 1783.

To the Burgesses and Common Council of the Borough of Wilmington.

GENTLEMEN:—I earnestly wish to convince you of the pleasure I take in reciprocating your congratulations on our glorious successes, and the attainment of an honorable peace.

Although the prospect of our public affairs has been at sometimes gloomy indeed, yet the well-known firmness of my countrymen, and the expected aid of Heaven, supported me in the trying hour, and have finally realized our most sanguine wishes.

In the course of your address, you have sufficiently convinced me of your ability to excite very pleasing emotions; and you must permit me to say, that the genuine approbation of my fellow-citizens is far more satisfactory than the most lavish econiums would be.

Under a deep impression of your generous sentiments and wishes, I return to a long meditated retirement. And let me assure you, gentlemen, though I shall no more appear on the great theatre of action, the welfare of our infant States can never be indifferent to me.

GEORGE WASHINGTON.

WILMINGTON, *December* 16, 1783.

The stone house on the brow of the hill, called Cool Spring, was the country seat of Cæsar A. Rodney, Esq., a name well known in this State, as affixed to the Declaration of Independence, by being an uncle to this gentleman of whom we speak. Mr. Rodney commenced his youthful career in this town, and was a successful lawyer. His popularity advanced him to a seat in Congress; and being noticed by those in power, he was soon appointed to higher honors. The first was U.

S. Attorney-General, when arrangements were made to remove his family for part of the year to Washington. A frail vessel was chartered and loaded with furniture, his valuable library, and many expensive articles, and sailed from Brandywine, he waiting to hear of their arrival before his family left.

On Sunday morning at the breakfast-table, Mr. R. observed that day he hoped to hear from the captain; Mrs. R. replied, "You will hear of his vessel being wrecked," and then went on to relate her dream the previous night. He entreated her not to notice such follies. However, she was but concluding, when an express entered the house to inform him that the vessel was on shore near Chincoteague. Their goods were partly saved, but in a damaged state. This disaster prevented their removal.

Mr. Rodney was a prominent politician, a democrat of the old school, and an advocate for the establishment and protection of domestic manufactures; though his views did not extend to the *table*, as did his friend's the Dr. He enjoyed the luxuries of life; and was equally hospitable in sharing his dainties with his guests; and sustained the character of a kind neighbor and benevolent man.

He was appointed on a special mission to South America, accompanied by Dr. Baldwin, a respectable botanist, and returned in a few months having been successful in his duties. His last commission was minister to Buenos Ayres. He sailed from here with his family, in the frigate Congress, Com. Biddle, arrived safe, and was most graciously received. His feeble health was not improved by a long sea voyage; however, change of climate in a few months seemed so favorable that he gained strength, and was much encouraged.

Preparations for a large evening party were made, and the family anticipated much pleasure, pleased to acknowledge the compliments paid to them in a strange land. As the setting sun withdrew his rays, every heart was gay and joyous. The music and the dance soon enlivened the brilliant assembly.

But oh! what a thrilling scene chills the heart to relate. Amidst the festivities of the night, an unexpected messenger arrives, like a bold assassin; lays his icy hand of death on a beloved father; and the morning sun arose, and threw its light over the inanimate form, but the buoyant spirit had fled forever; and a mantle of gloom cast over the abode, and the bereaved family shrouded in sorrow. "The joy of our heart is ceased; our dance is turned into mourning; the crown is fallen from our head." Alas, how agonizing! what a melancholy change in the short space of twelve hours, with the decorations of the preceding evening in full view. The last sorrowful arrangements were preparing for the funeral solemnities. An affectionate husband, a fond father, cut off so suddenly to mingle with the dust in a foreign soil, and there be left to slumber in the tomb, by a widow and eleven fatherless children, far from friends and home, a vast ocean rolling between.

Thus ended the earthly career of a public character, deserving of remembrance. His remains were interred with all the respect and honor due to himself and the nation he represented. The family in a few days embarked for this country, and arriving safe in 1824, were affectionately received by kind friends, who did sympathize in sorrow with those among whom they had so often mingled in scenes of joyous pleasure.

On the borders of Cool Spring, there is yet a relic of antiquity, a log cabin, built by one of the early settlers, Hance Naff, from Switzerland, who died here in old age, and his widow died in this cottage at the advanced age of 95.

On the Kennett road, opposite, was the last earthly dwelling-place of his son Hance Naff and wife, a respectable pair, who lived a long life together, in great harmony. And Mrs. Mary Naff, will be long remembered as a good neighbor, a kind and faithful friend in sickness and sorrow, as they lived, the one to the age of eighty, and the other to eighty-four. "They came to their grave in a full age, as a shock of corn cometh in its season," leaving many descendants to mourn.

The old time-worn stone house below was long the homestead of Joseph Shallcross, whom we before noticed. On this same road, near Rodney's gate, is an old shanty, occupied not many years ago by an English woman, Mrs. Russel, whose only companions were her dog and cow, both useful members of the family. But poor Piedy had double duty to perform; her mistress raised some vegetables, which she cultivated with her own hand, and a few apple trees grew near, which bore pretty good fruit; with these she attended market in a small light cart. Wednesday and Saturday, the little old cow was fastened with ropes to the vehicle, and the trio jogged down Market Street side by side, when they took the stand, and sales began; Piedy was milked, and this dainty sold to those who chose to buy.

Mrs. R. and dog were regular attendants at Trinity Church, and whoever accommodated her must admit her little friend, not always a pleasant neighbor. If the sexton, never too amiable, by chance met them at the door, and gave the dog a kick and refused him admittance, an affray would ensue; for the old lady, with her stick, was ready for defence when her pet was assailed, and would not enter without him. Some one had always to go forward as a peace-maker.

A stroll along this western way will recall to memory many of the olden ones of the last century, who passed away as the morning cloud or early dew, and those, too, who stood on high places, and are remembered in the annals of their country; all will have a passing remark who were useful in their day, whether they filled the chair of State or won laurels in the field to advance their country's glory, or tilled the land to produce bread to feed the hungry, or by professional skill healed the wounded or relieved the sick, or labored in the garden to supply the table; all were useful members of society, whose industrious habits contributed much to their neighbors' comfort.

The occupant of that decayed frame on your right cultivated a most excellent vegetable garden. Half a century is passed since Mrs. K. regularly supplied the market with her produce, finding ready sale, for it was the best of its kind, and impressed by a good name with few to rival her in business. She pursued it with spirit and success.

B. S., also on the Newport Road, served the market with excellent vegetables for a long period. But Dutch Dolly was a formidable rival, living in town, and her garden on the corner of King and Hanover Streets had the precedence, as persons could send there any time of day and have fresh articles to order. All the old and middle-aged persons who have lived in this vicinity remember little old Dutch Dolly, with her quilted calico cap, and basket upon her head, filled with radishes, lettuce, &c., and her steady quick step, passing through the streets as she daily served families, and was sure of a hearty welcome, for the market was not plentiful as at present. Many vegetables now used were then unknown, such as the tomato, egg-plant, and a variety of others introduced here since, and raised by the French emigrants. Dolly was a dignified little woman in her own way, as you will be informed.

After knowing her during a long life by no other name, how amazed was I on hearing she was really Mrs. Anna Dorothea Vertz. Frederick Vertz was a tailor, and followed his trade, sat on a table opposite a window, with a bag of onions hung over his head, a cup of salt, and a loaf of bread at hand. When hungry, he would cut and eat these for his dinner, but Dolly provided plentifully for breakfast and supper. They had no children and left a handsome property; and although he was not Frederick the Great, his title was once Frederick the Great, Fortune Teller, who predicted events by astronomical signs.

And as Mrs. Vertz was the better half, she would not allow her house to be disgraced by this black art; and the young people, ever ready to be informed what should befall them in their later years, waited patiently till she passed on with her basket, then one stood sentinel, and if she came home unexpectedly, there was a scampering over fences, and out of windows to escape, and as the last resort, even to play bo-peep under his table as she went through to her garden. An old lady, often one of the company in her youth, described the scene as very amusing. This folly was declined long before his death.

Dolly had descended from a family of consequence in Holland, and brought over many valuable articles of clothing, &c., and some money. When figuring as Mrs. Vertz in her holiday dress, she was the admiration of the rising generation, for many had never seen such splendid equipments. A black silk velvet hood, and boddice of the same, her petticoat a superior deep blue cloth, the whole dress trimmed with rich gold lace, and two rows of gold fringe on the skirt, left no trace of little old Dutch Dolly in her calico cap. She died in good old age, and was interred in the Swedes Cemetery.

Although these persons moved in an humble sphere, and died in old age unheeded, naught could be said against their fair reputation. How much more useful are such members of a community, and think you not more honorable and happy than many young men high born and well educated, who spend a listless life, waiting for an inheritance on the death of a relative; or bowing to the powers that be for a lucrative office, or hanging on to the wheel of fortune, hoping the next turn may toss them to top; or still worse, aiding in election frauds to obtain a place which merit has denied, and when those airy castles have crumbled into dust, and all visionary schemes vanished, too often resort to the gaming-table and to intemperance?

Yes, we have heard of those who once promised fair to be an honor to their friends, after disappointed hopes, and every evil resort had failed, filched their neighbors' pockets by some dishonorable act, and, even more horrid, raised the assassin's dagger, ending their mis spent life within the gloomy walls of a prison, or mayhap a cheerless dungeon.

Alas, we know nothing of ourselves; remember, when the prophet looked upon Hazael and wept, he said, "Why weepeth my Lord?" "Because I know the evil thou wilt do to the children of Israel." And when he had foretold all, Hazael said, "What! is thy servant a dog, that he should do this great thing?" Yet it all came to pass.

"Therefore, trust in the Lord with all thine heart, and acknowledge him in all thy ways, and he shall direct thy path."

Along this ridge the view is beautifully varied with its hills and dales, improved farms, overlooking the little "city built on a hill," containing fourteen thousand and more inhabitants, extending from the Christiana to the Brandywine, with many places of public worship, and its wharves, vessels loading and unloading, as they proceed to sea or return from a long voyage; others in building; then bridges; and for miles you can see the famous river Delaware, and other navigable streams, bearing on their waters fleets, from the noble ship of the line Pennsylvania, the largest war ship ever built, to the most trifling craft that floats.

Extensive meadows, affording rich pastures for grazing numerous herds, here and there interspersed with lots of luxuriant grain, steamboats and railroad cars in constant motion; the noted Brandywine mills, factories, and foundries, the old ferry, the only way to cross the Christiana in days gone by, and the once famed rocks, the first settlement of the colonists. Then the old Swedes church, though last, not least cared for; and its more ancient cemetery, where lies the infant of days, and the man of an hundred years; now an extensive chain of Jersey woods, like the blue mountains, bounds your prospect on the east, all contributing to ornament this unrivaled landscape in variety of scenery.

The white house on the right was built by Judge Way; it is beautifully situated, some distance from the Lancaster road; on the right is a stone house, that was once the residence of Col. Ann Louis De Tousard, a distinguished French officer, who served in our revolution, and lost an arm. He purchased and removed to this farm in 1793. Finding the walls damp, he had frames made with canvass drawn over, and let into the plaster. Some of his distinguished guests amused themselves by painting landscapes, birds, and flowers, very beautifully, sufficient to cover the walls of three rooms. The work being varnished very highly, was preserved well; it was there a few years since, and may be still, over fifty years' standing. Madame De Tousard died in the year '94 on this farm; she was cut down in youthful bloom, leaving a young family to lament the loss of a mother, and a most worthy and accomplished lady. She was interred in the old Swedes cemetery.

The lane above leads to an antique log cabin, which has stood more than an hundred and twenty years. Long after it was inhabited, a room was added of stone, by Joseph Springer, who was born and died here. He was a descendant of Carl Christopher Springer, whose history is very romantic. It appears he went to London, in the suite of the Swedish Ambassador, and resided in his family. On riding home one evening, he was siezed, put on board a vessel, which sailed for Virginia, where he was sold for five years. After serving out his time, he came among his brethern here, where he was most graciously received as a well-educated man; was promoted to trusts of consequence with the colonists.

This descendant was a plain honest farmer, and his wife so great a manager that they supplied the market with excellent provision; leaving ample for family use, and to entertain a host of guests, enjoying society, and providing bounteously; they secured to the old time-worn tenement its share to overflowing. The old lady had a passion for flowers, with skill and taste to cultivate plants successfully; and on her visits to Philadelphia, would purchase rare flowers to ornament her garden, and they were beautifully and tastefully arranged.

Having no children, they brought up many orphans in industrious and useful employments, and to those they bequeathed their estate. The old lady lived over eighty years, and few, indeed, passed through so regular a life; no changing events ever seemed to disturb her repose, till she went the way of all the earth.

Mr. Springer long survived her. Some months previous to his death, Mr. Monges, accompanied by his sister-in-law, Miss L. G. and myself, rode out to this relic of ancient days, and, having the pleasure to preside on this occasion, I thus addressed the sire: "We are pleased to introduce to your notice this infant, Cora Monges, the sixth generation in a maternal line from your once worthy rector of Trinity church, the Rev. Petrus Trauberg, whom you remember."

On receiving her in his arms, the old man's eyes flashed with joy; and, with the most expressive pleasure, he thanked us for such unexpected attention, and, with deeply excited feelings, related events of olden times; how, in the midst of the winter frosts and heavy snows, his mother would mount one horse, and his father another, with him behind, plunge through the deep snow to church, where no fire was seen, and listen to a long sermon, then ride home two miles, ere they warmed. Well he remembered Mr. Trauberg's pastoral visits to the family.

Saying, "There," as he pointed to an immense fire-place, "stood at each corner a block cut from the stump of a tree, planed smooth and scoured every day;—if it was damp weather, Mr. Trauberg sat on one of these to dry his feet, and my father on the other, and in the Swedish language talk about their fatherland." Mr. S. lived ninety-two years, and died an "old man full of years," and was gathered to his fathers in the Swedes Cemetery.

CHAPTER V.

Almshouse Inmates—Of High Order—Mr. B.—M. Martel—Mrs. B.—Burnt March 25th, 1804—Tamar Way—Frederick Craig—Mantua—Delamore Place—Col. Davis—Tusculum—J. M. Broom, Esq.—Dr. Read—Dr. Martin —Richardsons—Latimers—Swedish Families—July 4th, 1794—Celebration.

AFTER our long rambles and enjoyments of pleasant prospects of land and water, the rural, the busy, and the gay, we have come to a resting-place, where we will tarry a season, and improve the time in conversing of the changing scenes of life, which some of the inmates of this useful establishment have passed through.

To many this has been a happy home, whose humble pilgrimage never led them to soar above things within their reach, and here, supplied with food and raiment, they were content. The necessaries of life are amply provided—physicians and nurses for the sick and afflicted. An excellent house kept with cleanliness, and well ordered by a kind matron. The situation is healthy; a fine vegetable garden, and cultivated farm add much to the comfort of the dependents. All the beautiful scenery described is presented to your view; so we may exclaim with the psalmist, "Thou, O God, hast prepared of thy goodness for the poor. Thou waterest these ridges with soft showers, so that the little hills rejoice on every side. The pastures are clothed with flocks, the valleys also are covered over with corn."

And there have been those here, too, who in the morning of life never thought that the evening close should pass in an almshouse. Their day-star rose with a cloudless sky, and the sun in splendor gilded their noontide with honor, riches, home, and friends. But, alas, as the sun declined in the horizon, all their earthly grandeur and comfort were overshadowed by the dark cloud of adversity. Not even a home was left to shelter their defenceless heads, when the cold hand of charity tendered this asylum wherein to end the night of their weary pilgrimage.

Three such persons, inmates of this dwelling, were personally known to me, two in the last century, and one early in this. The first was a sad reverse of fortune that rarely occurs. Somewhere about 1789, an aristocratic English family flourished in this town; luxurious plenty crowned their board, enlivened by cheerful guests. ——— was a merchant in London, where he married a lady of a noble family. The connection was offensive to her relatives, which induced them to emigrate. Wilmington at that time being a place of some commerce, they chose it for a residence. ——— was a shipping merchant here for years, and had under his special care a relative of his wife, the son of a lord, heir to the title, and a very large estate. Being a reckless youth, his father hoped to reclaim him, and during his exile allowed him two guineas a day; towards the close of his sojourn here it was reduced;—all was unavailing.

In a few years this unhappy youth returned to the land of his nativity with Captain T. Mendenhall. On the second voyage to Liverpool, Capt. M. visited him in prison, where his agonizing distress so interested the sympathies of the captain that he went to London to solicit relief from the youth's father, and had an interview with the noble lord, who declined all intercourse with his wretched son, whose feeble frame could no longer sustain the weight of grief, and his sad career was soon ended within the prison walls.

"Rejoice, O young man, and let thy heart cheer thee. Walk in the ways of thy heart, and in the sight of thine eyes. But know thou, that for all these things God will bring thee to Judgment."

———'s houshold was most expensive; a train of servants attended, and three nurses waited upon the children. Two incidents are fresh in memory that portray prosperity and adversity—in the style of dress at each period.

Being at their house when a child, Mrs. ———'s dress was my admiration. A light blue satin gown, gauze apron and handkerchief;

a high crowned cap; blue silk shoes worked with white, and high French heels, was her daily attire. Soon after this they returned to England. On the eve of their departure, one of their children died. It was shrouded in fine flannel; and the coffin was a straight box covered with black cloth, the first perhaps ever seen here, and bound with silver, the age and name inscribed on a plate. It was a young child, and interred in the Swedes cemetery; and Mr. Girelius was the officiating minister.

Some years after, they came to reside here a second time; and during the prevalence of the fever, in '98, being in a house high up town, a female entered the back gate, and inquired of me for the host. Her dress was a calico short gown, dark worsted petticoat, and coarse shoes; a man's hat on her head. Her manner was so like a lady that I inquired who she was. The answer startled me. Don't you know Mrs. ———? Never was I so amazed. The contrast of the two figures, even now, is present to my imagination.

Governor Dickinson was a kind friend in their poverty, and often expressed regret for their extravagant habits. When the lowly cottage was obscured by the clouds of adversity, known only by the charitable, who came to supply their scanty fare, or to soothe the sorrows of declining years. The old gentleman died in this almshouse. No immorality caused this extreme penury. "Happy is the man whom God correcteth." "We are but of yesterday, and know nothing, because our days upon earth are sorrow."

The second character was a distinguished individual, who fled from France during the tragical days of the Revolution of '89, '90, and in this country sought an asylum. His pre-eminent knowledge of language—a proficient in fifteen—with a wonderful facility to communicate what he knew, acquired a fame for teaching that had never been equaled in Boston or New York, whither he came from to seek rest from his great labors in this quiet little town.

Many of the honorable in all these places were his pupils; and here likewise he taught persons of every age, and numerous applicants daily were dismissed. Amidst his usefulness, paralysis seized him, from which he never recovered. He forgot every language except French, which was so great a difficulty to persons with whom he boarded, no one was willing to undertake the charge, consequently he was removed to this institution.

It is proper to state, in justice to many young gentlemen who were his pupils, that all his comforts were regarded with strict attention.

Having been preceptor to Miss Theodosia Burr, and the intimate friend of her father, he had taught this lady five languages, and to her dedicated his works. During his affliction, Col. Burr, Vice President of the United States, in the zenith of his glory, was on a visit in town.

Two young gentlemen deeply interested for this destitute stranger, called upon the honorable sir to present Michael Martel's sad condition. His answer was, "I know him not." He observed their surprise, and saw his own letter of introduction in their hand, then said, "I own I wrote that letter when I knew him; but I know him no more." How little we know what a day may bring forth; for the same epithet was very soon applied to Col. Burr. Those who honored him then knew him no more.

M. Martel was regardless of money. When he received a sum would throw it aside carelessly, or give freely for charity, refusing none; he took no care for the future; trusted all to the honor of his pupils, and kept no account; and this indifference to business matters left him penniless. He compared his fondness for teaching to the love of persons for cultivating flowers; and often remarked that he would rather pay young persons fond of study for the pleasure of teaching them than for any sum to teach an idle stupid youth. In old age death summoned him to the tomb, leaving no one to mourn.

> "A homeless exile here his poverty bespeaks,
>   And hoary locks proclaim his lengthened years,
> For many a furrow in his grief-worn cheek
>   Has been the channel to a flood of tears."

The last one of the three named was an only daughter of a professional gentleman of great acquirement, and of a noble Scotch family. She was well educated, handsome and refined; of course a belle; and previous to the revolution married a colonel in the British army. While New York was in possession of the enemy they lived there in the midst of gayety. Soon after peace, he died, leaving her a competency. But on his grave the sun of her prosperity set to rise no more.

Feeling her isolated condition as a lonely widow, she turned her thoughts to the home she had left with an affectionate husband, surrounded by worldly affluence and pleasure. Years had rolled on, when she engaged in a second marriage with a dissipated man, every way her inferior, who soon squandered all her substance within his grasp, and died, leaving her poor indeed, with only a scanty annuity, not in his power to touch.

To aid her future support, she proposed to do plain sewing, and came to reside in this town. Her dwelling was in our neighborhood, and she was an acquaintance of my mother's in early days, who was a guest at her first wedding. Several times she called at our house to solicit mother's interest to procure work, without making herself known. Years had glided them down the stream of time, and each one had passed through many trials and vicissitudes in life, with its sorrows and cares, now overtaken by the infirmities of age, no traces of her youthful beauty being left.

But mother seemed to have a presentiment that the old lady had seen better days, and would express much anxiety to know more of her; and say, "Who could that person be?" and look so sad; some time had elapsed without seeing her. Mrs. Roache called, and in conversation, said, "Mrs. M., do you recollect Miss ———?" "Perfectly," was the reply. She then related her story, ending at the almshouse.

"For months she was your neighbor, and resolved to inform you of her situation; with that intention called upon you ofttimes, but feeling so sensitive it was still deferred, your kind manner, always treating her like a lady, and the sadness that clouded your brow, as she solicited work, was so touching, that she felt as if her heart would rend unless she retired to give vent to her agitated feelings."

Mrs. Roache was a stranger to her abode, till accidentally they met at the almshouse. This was deeply affecting, and it was much regretted by those ladies, that one who once was esteemed so lovely and attractive, brought up in the lap of indulgence, known in the bloom of youth, midst affluence, should now in sorrow and poverty be within their reach and receive no relief. Soon after this interview with Mrs. R——, her faculties were benumbed, and reason left her forever. "Cast me not off in the time of old age; forsake me not when my strength faileth." "I am old and gray-headed, O God." "Thou who hast showed me great and sore troubles, shalt quicken me again, and shalt bring me up again from the depths of the earth."

This almshouse was built in 1792; the land attached to this establishment was presented by John Stapler, a Friend; the first building was about the size of one wing, and was burnt down March 25th, 1804, then rebuilt and enlarged. Within a few years, two structures have been added; one for the insane, another for the colored population.

Half a century has glided on the stream of time since an insane woman, of great physical strength, confined in one of these cells, would by some means loose her chains and escape to town, and do incredible acts of destruction before she was caught; always commenced by breaking windows, next unharness horses, and unload heavy wagons; cut the rigging of ships, loose them from the wharf, and throw overboard everything within her grasp. Her flight was as swift as the wings of an eagle, none could equal her speed; she was never caught till exhausted by fatigue. This woman was a living terror to the children. Indeed, her visits were so dreaded by all the inhabitants that it was common to close the doors and windows when Tamar Way appeared.

Frederick Craig managed this house for years with great propriety and good order. He was a printer here in early life, then engaged in commerce. Death spared him eighty-five years in possession of his faculties; with a most astonishing memory, he was the chronicle of past events, and considered a loss even in advanced age. Through all the changes of life he was esteemed a respectable townsman. "Remember the days of old, consider the years of many generations; ask thy father, and he will shew thee; thy elders and they will tell thee."

Opposite to the almshouse was the estate of Hannah Stalcup, the descendant of a wealthy Swede. She was long deranged and confined in her hwn house, but at times would make her escape, to the terror of the children. Though mischievous, she was inoffensive compared with Tamar Way. Her paternal inheritance was valuable, and it was supposed that riches caused her insanity, which continued to her death. A part of her property is now owned by Rev. S. M. Gailey, a Presbyterian clergyman, who has a respectable classical school there, and calls his residence Mantua.

A little beyond this, on rising ground, a property was purchased by John Warner, who built a fine mansion, which was sold in an unfinished state, and is now owned by Col. Samuel B. Davis, who commanded at the defence of Lewistown, Delaware, in the last war, and was presented by the legislature with an elegant sword for his services. This is beatifully situated, and called Delamore Place.

The gate below is the way to Tusculum. This mansion was built by James M. Broom, Esq., for his residence. At an early age Mr. B. was elected a representative to Congress, by an undivided vote of the electors of his district. His ancestors were here in olden times, and his father was engaged in commerce for many years in Wilmington, and represented this State in framing the Constitution of the United States. As Delaware was the first State in the consummation of that great event, we trust she will ever hold fast those principles which entitle her to as high honors as any of her overgrown sister States; and though she be small in territory she may be gigantic in noble deeds.

This house is modern, handsome, and well situated. Part of the forrest trees are left on two sides with great taste; amongst these are the dogwood of unusual growth, which, when in blossom, are magnificent. You have there all the fine scenery that is presented on this ridge, and it could scarcely be rivaled in beauty were it highly improved. Mr. Broom practiced law in Delaware, and honorably represented the State; his family were of the old Federal party; he is now ranked among the most able and respectable lawyers of Philadelphia, whither he went more than thirty years ago.

Tusculum was purchased by Dr. Martin, a most estimable man, an adopted son of a worthy Presbyterian clergyman, Dr. T. Read, who officiated in his profession in this town for many years, and was beloved by all who knew him. One of Dr. Read's peculiar traits of character was to speak evil of none; if another dared to do so in his presence, though what they said might be the truth, he could find in every one some good as a set-off. In his religious views he was opposed to controversy, and said he had never seen other than evil arise from it.

During the last war, when the British made an attack upon Lewistown, an express was sent here for aid, which threw this quiet town into a state of commotion, and as a number of the men obeyed the call, leaving here on Sunday morning, the churches were left empty. In the afternoon Dr. Read preached an excellent sermon, from a very appropriate text, "And the messenger came to Saul, saying, haste ye and come, for the Philistines have invaded the land." He died full of years, and at peace with all mankind. By example following the precept of the Apostle Paul, "If it be possible as much as lieth in you, live peaceably with all men." Dr. Read was the first Presbyterian missionary in the lower counties of Delaware.

Some time after his death, this place became the home of his widow, who lived with her beloved adopted son. Afterward her son-in-law, John Connel, Esq., purchased it, and she continued there with her daughter to the end of her long life, (eighty-three years). It may seem useless to speak of a person so well known and recently departed; yet a small passing tribute is due to the memory of a friend, whom we knew well, loved much, and passed days and weeks with, and feel that we had an interest in her prayers, and a place in her affections, and always instructed by her holy life.

Mrs. Read, though long in feeble health, was very active in the performance of domestic duties; with cheerfulness adorning the Christian life by her labors of love in the cause of her Redeemer, giving a word in season with such meekness and affection as to leave an impression kindly received and long remembered. No one was above her reach nor beneath her notice. She felt that each one had an immortal soul, winging its flight to eternity, and used to say she was a missionary in her own house, and must give a word in season to her numerous guests.

To the Hon. Henry Clay she once observed, "You, sir, I presume, are seldom approached on the subject of personal religion; as I am advanced, and feel it all important, permit me to entreat you, who have so long devoted your talents to the good of your country, and so nobly and recently resigned your crown of honor to a friend, to spend the remnant of your days in your Heavenly Father's service, and be zealously affected in searching the Scriptures, and preparing for that better world to which you are fast hastening, to secure the crown of righteousness which fadeth not away." His kind reply was soothing to her warm heart. A year afterwards she received the most gracious message from him on the remembrance of her excellent advice.

A singular incident in the life of Mrs. Read was sensibly impressed on her mind, and in conversation with me she often reverted to it. Living on Bohemia Manor, she was subject to chills, and was sent to board at a farm-house near the Brandywine Springs for the benefit of the water and a change of air. Every day she rode on horseback with young company boarding there for the same object. Being gay and thoughtless, in riding through the country, they often entered these woods, and she thought the very spot where her house stood was an opening. The scenery so enraptured her, that her companions would often have to force her away, saying, "You must think it Paradise;" her reply was, "Yes, Paradise enough for me, were it my dwelling place."

At the close of summer, she arrived at home with renewed health, and married Dr. Read, who lived in the lower part of New Castle county. In a few years they came to Wilmington, where he died, and in this favored spot her days were ended, and with the Psalmist, she could exclaim, "This is my rest, here will I dwell, for I have desired it." "I know thy works and charity, and service, and faith unto death, and I will give thee a crown of life."

More than fifty summers have winged their flight since the fourth of July was celebrated in these woods, not by a political clique, but as a national day of joy, on the anniversary of a great event. This is an ancient custom on record, "The Jews assembled at Shushan, and rested from their enemies, wherein the days were turned unto them from sorrow to joy, and from mourning to a good day; and they ordained that these two days should be kept yearly without fail, throughout all generations, as days of feasting and joy, and of sending portions one to another, and gifts to the poor, as a memorial of the noble resolution of Queen Esther, saying, 'If I perish, I perish,' on presenting her petition to the King, to interpose his authority, and rescue the devoted people from the impending slaughter."

Modern record states that our Congress rested at Annapolis, in Dec. 1783, and received the resignation of the noble defender of their rights (Washington) with feasting and joy, after seven years' war, wherein many of the flower of the nation had fallen, and others had been led captives to foreign lands. Now peace was confirmed, the prisoner released, and the weary soldier at rest. Then it was proclaimed that the fourth of July should be kept yearly as a day of feasting and gladness, to commemorate the deliverance of this nation from foreign aggression.

1794, July 4th. The morning was bright and promising; in those days ladies were guests, and after dinner children united in their festivities, and the gleanings were left for the poor of the land. All went on merrily, amid the roar of cannon and din of military music, till the banquet was announced; then cheerful faces and keen appetites surrounded the plenteous board, and did justice to the choice viands suited to every taste; patriotic toasts were given, and the dinner concluded with national songs.

When about to rise from the animating scene, as the sun was declining in the western horizon, a black cloud rose, that soon spread, and wrapt the whole firmament in darkness; distant rumbling thunder came nearer and louder, with vivid lightning most terrific; then a mighty wind, sweeping everything around, scattering the fragments of the dinner, uprooting trees, with their broken branches flying in every direction, threatening desolation. Many thought it was the last day, and that time was to be no longer, while the convulsed elements proclaimed the majesty of an Almighty Power. Torrents of rain fell, and each one had to seek shelter for himself.

The poorhouse was only one-third its present size; Crip's house was not large, and one room occupied by H. S., and a small barn well filled with grain, were the only buildings near. Many bent their way home, when they came to a run, where there was a log on both sides to pass (now an arched bridge); the water was too high, they could not cross. A few daring spirits, however, found the log, and held on to the frail fence, while men swam over with others holding on. The greatest number remained, until assistance could be brought from town. Unfortunately for the ladies, paper hats were worn, resembling in material the Navarino of later days; all those came home bareheaded—still worse, many who had light kid shoes returned without any. The whole road was strewed with torn hats, ribbons, and shoes. Thus ended this glorious day.

The next farm is called Quincy; this is beautifully situated. A large stone house was built by Joseph Robinson, deceased. It is now the property of James T. Bird.

On the Newport road are many fine farms; here are the Stidhams, Lynams, Brynbergs, Walravens, Justices, &c., all descendants of respectable Swedish farmers; then the Richardsons of the Friends Society, and of olden times, respectable and wealthy. Here is Richardson's mill, an old establishment. I have heard Major Jaquett say that when a boy, he used to take wheat from his father's farm there to be ground, and always went in a boat. Then comes R.'s Hill, long known for its rugged and steep ascent, though now much improved; and R.'s woods, often the haunt of troublesome people, secreting there to escape justice.

That house so handsomely situated on the Christiana side was built by William Warner, then a wealthy and respectable citizen, whose family were old inhabitants.

It was purchased by Robert Andrews, who expended much in improving the grounds, and sold by his heirs to the present owner, John R. Latimer, who has wealth to enable him to gratify his taste, and who spares no expense in ornamenting this beautiful spot. Though the view is not so extensive as those described, yet it is very attractive and some persons even prefer this situation. It is decidedly the most improved of any in this section of country. His ancestors were here in by-gone days. Dr. Henry Latimer was a surgeon in the revolution —after that event he was Senator to Congress. An elder brother,

George Latimer, Esq., was long collector of the port of Philadelphia, when party services alone were not sufficient recommendations for office, and defaulters seldom disgraced high places.

Their ancestor, James Latimer, settled in early life, in a small village on the Christiana, three miles south of this, and carried on an extensive business in flour, brought from Lancaster in wagons to Newport, thence to Philadelphia in sloops; he died there in good old age. "Because he hath known my name, with long life will I satisfy him, and show him my salvation." Newport was then a flourishing village, and contained many respectable inhabitants.

Captain Henry Geddes married Miss M. Latimer during the revolution; Mrs. G. lived to the age of eighty-five, with unimpaired faculties, and sat and walked erect. Her stately figure was a true representative of her strong intellect and fixed principles that never wavered. She was an affectionate relative, an unchanging friend, and a kind neighbor. Her traits of character were as noble and majestic as her person. Mrs. Geddes was long a professor in the Presbyterian church and a practical Christian, therefore we do not mourn her departure, only say, "Let me die the death of the righteous, and let my last end be like hers."

Mrs. Ann Latimer, widow of Dr. L., died within a few years; she was an excellent and charitable lady, whose loss many a poor widow has cause to mourn. Her purse was always ready to relieve the necessitous; for she was truly a cheerful giver. Her eldest daughter, Sarah Latimer, was suddenly removed by a most mysterious Providence, in the prime of life, and engaged in the most active benevolence, constantly seeking and relieving objects of charity, and we can truly apply the words of the evangelist to this worthy and useful lady:—

"Come, ye blessed of my father, inherit the kingdom prepared for you. For I was an hungered, and ye gave me meat; I was thirsty, and ye gave me drink; a stranger, and ye took me in; naked, and ye clothed me; I was sick and ye visited me."

CHAPTER VI.

Long Hook—Major Jaquett—His Father—Whitefield—Major P. J. enters the Army—Description—Visit of an Old Soldier—The Avenue—Night Walk—Blackbeard—The Alarm—Surrender to Bull Frogs—Solomon.

OPPOSITE the town, a curvature of the Christiana forms a point of land called Long Hook farm, the patrimonial estate of Major Peter Jaquett. Here the day dawned on his birth, and the night of death closed his mortal career, at the age of eighty-three years. He was borne hence to his grave, in the old Swedes cemetery, over two miles, by sixty young men, as a tribute of their respect for his revolutionary services, and we record it as a tribute of ours for their national feelings.

His father was one of a little band of French protestants, who fled from the persecutions in the land of his nativity, and pitched his tent in the wilds of Delaware, with a few Swedish colonists, and the red men of the woods, where he was content to dwell. "Oh! that I had in the wilderness a lodging-place of way-faring men, that I might leave my people and go from them." Delighted with the fertility and freshness of the soil, as it came from the creative hand, he adopted it for his home, and became an owner of this tract, and a tiller of the ground, felling the logs and fitting up his cabin, which remains to this day a relic of olden times, attached to the present mansion, built by him in after years.

Now settled in this rural retreat, believing "it is not good that man should be alone," he paid his respects to a Swedish family, and interested one of their fair daughters to share his comforts and his cares.

On a visit of the celebrated Whitefield to this region, he was numbered among his converts; and when a hoary-headed sire, he ended his life's pilgrimage in peace.

As Peter entered his seventh year, his father, alluding to the stately buttonwood trees which he had planted on the creek side, said, "My son, if you foster these trees in youth, they will grow with your growth, and shade you in declining years; when these hands are motionless in the grave, and our frail bodies have returned to dust, they will long survive, and annually renew their verdure." They were cared for in Peter's youth, and venerated in his old age. He approached manhood, and the trees were in full vigor, at an important epoch in our national annals.

Redress of grievances long borne had been sought in vain by petition to the mother country, and the spirit of the nation was aroused to resistance. A call was made to arms. Many young men from the plough responded, among whom was our hero, Peter Jaquett. On the first day of January, 1776, his services were enlisted as ensign. Sage patriots had viewed the rising clouds which threatened to overshadow the land; while skilful husbandmen most assiduously prepared the soil as when "an overflowing shower and a stormy wind shall rend it."

On the fourth of July, by acclamation, the liberty tree was planted, and the hurrahs resounded from the Atlantic shores to the western wilds. "I am pained at my very heart; my heart makes a noise in me, I cannot hold my peace, because thou hast heard, O, my soul, the sound of the trumpet, the alarm of war." As this was an experimental scheme, it had many opponents. There were some who were attached to the old paths wherein they were taught to walk, timid ones, too; while there were others who stood on high ground, carefully watching events, ever ready to fall into the ranks of the stronger party.

Foes within and foes without were to be met by mental and physical energy; free-will offerings were required to sustain and rear this tree, on the prosperity of which sanguine hopes were founded, for the good of the human family. If it drooped and died, this fair portion of the earth would be stained by the blood of martyrs. Endurance through winter's frosts and summer's heats, harassed by fatigue, hunger and thirst, was borne for seven years, meanwhile this tree had taken root, and was soaring upwards. Now the jubilee was proclaimed with feasting and gladness. The land had rest, and the weary soldier returned with the laurels on his brow.

The roar of cannon and din of military music were changed to joy and peace.

In Philadelphia, great preparations were made for splendid fireworks, at the intersection of Market and Sixth Streets, then the residence of two distinguished patriots, Governor Dickinson, and Robert Morris, Esq. A triumphal arch was thrown across the street, and a wire extended above; from this wire the goddess of liberty and queen of peace were to descend, and with the trumpet of fame illuminate the arch; and under it, I think, was fixed the genius of America. Transparencies had been placed there with great care, and thousands had assembled to witness the magnificent spectacle, when, oh, shocking! by some mishap, just at the interesting moment, the whole took fire and exploded, most terrific to the heedless mass, rushing on each other in their fright, believing that time was no longer. To many, it was their last night; others were carried into houses with broken limbs, or mangled by being stepped upon. Vast numbers were seriously injured.

Though we feel that honor and praise are justly due to the great and brave men who guided the affairs of state, or wielded the sword in their country's defence, and brought it to a happy consummation—"O! Lord, I know that it is not in man that walketh to direct his steps"—and that the Almighty Disposer of events overruled all by his superintending providence for the benefit of his creatures. "For thus saith the Lord, Behold I will bring them from the north country, and gather them from the coasts of the earth, and with them the blind and the lame. A great company shall flow together to the goodness of the Lord, for wheat and for wine, and for oil; I will comfort them, and make them rejoice."

Now the varied seasons, of all the years allotted to man, have passed over this tree, which is in its meridian glory, shadowing forth its boughs from the remote mountains to the ocean, and shedding its refreshing dews on millions of the human family, from every clime and every age. The gray-headed cripple, and the infant of days, have dwelt under its shade, while it fertilizes the land so as to yield bread enough, and to spare, for ages yet unborn. "As the earth is the Lord's, and the fulness thereof," we them welcome; all who may come with industrious habits, and peaceful lives, we wish them granted all the privileges their merit may deserve. We only claim one proviso—that they meddle not with the affairs of state, but leave those things to be managed by the natives of the soil.

> Wanderer, whither wouldst thou roam,
>   To what region, far away,
> Bend thy steps to find a home
>   In the twilight of thy day?
>
> In the twilight of my day
>   I am hastening to the West;
> There my weary limbs to lay,
>   When the sun retires to rest.

> Thither, thither, would I roam,
> There my children may be free,
> I for them will find a home,
> They shall find a grave for me.

Tracing the environs of the town, and led to this point, Long Hook, we should pass on were it not the domicil of a patriot of 1776, who is "now no more." As we linger here, the shadow rests on the hearts of many with whom we associated, and spent happy hours, who are now slumbering in the tomb. Imagination loves to sketch the incidents of the primitive family abode, and dwell on the tender recollections of early friendship and affection. It awakens a pensive train of thought, and reviews in memory the deeds of those passed away, to see at this time the deserted home, and the silence of death now brooding over the spot where once the social circle were seated, enjoying the cool breeze and refreshing shade of these majestic trees.

To these, the kind hostess, often involved in domestic cares, devoted her early attention, by having mounds thrown up around their base, decorated with gay flowers, and vines to entwine their noble trunks; not a broken branch or fallen leaf lay there to mar the green sward beneath, where seats were arranged in order. To her industrious habits and good taste, many of the useful and all the ornamental improvements were due.

There, in martial array, and in the pride of manhood, once trod the warrior! Here stood the statesman and venerable prelate; here we have witnessed the sprightliness of youth, and the wisdom and solemnity of age, mingling with sportive childhood, whiling away hours in careless joy, where refreshments of olden times, syllabub with its accompaniments, were not forgotten.

The sportsman and angler often rested their weary limbs here; lovers of music, with their melodious notes, sometimes enlivened the scene, and conversational parties assembled to talk over tales of the Revolution.

Here the greatest man of the nation, Washington, has sat, with a Lafayette, and our venerable Bishop White, and many other worthies, who admired and enjoyed the shade of those trees. Then shall we not commemorate them? Often have I seen children listening with intense interest to anecdotes of the war, and seem to echo these lines,

> "Major, now tell us all about the war,
> And what they killed each other for."

He, so excited, would exhibit his diploma with Washington's signature, and the sword and the gun presented, and the one used in the Revolution, and other relics; then to promote their pleasure, order the cart and horse harnessed, and with his youthful guests, hie to the woods for nuts, return in full glee, slip out the tail board, and out the little urchins would pop on the grass much to their amusement. At other times fit them out with fishing-tackle, and away to the inlet. Such was his fondness for children even in old age.

The lawn in front was large and surrounded by lofty poplars, the middle interspersed with a variety of most beautiful evergreens, kept with extreme neatness. At the wicker-gate in the front of the yard stood an immense weeping willow, with a hanging bird's nest deep and narrow at the extreme end of a twig; this was quite a curiosity. On this side of the house a small portico, with boxes for wrens, sheltered whole families, so tame as to hop around and light on your head; and the sweet notes of the robin sounded in your ears. The ivy that covered this side of the dwelling was a resting-place for birds. It sprang from a very small sprig sent by a gentleman in a letter from New York to Mrs. Jaquett. He gathered it from the castle where Mary, Queen of Scots, was imprisoned.

The first Champney rose in this region Mrs. Jaquett put down against the old fabric, and when in bloom it was a beautiful contrast to the ivy; it entered through the eaves to the attic, and there bloomed the whole winter. A fine garden on the south side was ornamented with choice flowers; the magnolia and honeysuckle regaled you with their fragrance. Thirty summers these flowers have bloomed and withered; since, on removing the roof of this old cabin, the workmen found an incredible quantity of honey under the eaves. Here the industrious bees had labored for years.

We now give our valedictory address to the home of bygone days by reciting an animating scene that occurred just before the major's death. Being on a visit, we were sitting at tea in the hall that connected the two buildings, having a door opening to the road. I saw an old man walking slowly up the lawn, apparently lame; he came forward and inquired for Major Jaquett. The good lady desired him to take a seat at the door until the Major was disengaged. Hearing his voice, he advanced, saying, "Impossible, madam, to seat myself when I hear my old captain's voice once more. My—my brave officer, don't you know your old soldier, John Turner, of Sussex, the first man you enlisted, Jan. '76?" The Major then jumped up, and in ecstasy exclaimed, "John Turner, my brave fellow! is it possible this can be you?" Never had I seen such expressive joy. Water was ordered for him to wash; and to his wife he said, "Eliza, set the best you have in the house for this brave fellow. He deserves more than you can give. He never flinched from his duty, and served his country faithfully for seven years." This reminded one of the patriarchal age, of Abraham and Sarah's entertainment; it was in such simplicity and sincerity.

They commenced a recital of Revolutionary scenes, having been together in so many battles, and both escaped unscathed; the slaughter of their regiment at Camden, and many hairbreadth escapes. Then spoke of their hard fate in Georgia, living three days on green peaches, boiled, and nothing to season with, not even salt, nor a particle of other food.

> The broken soldier, kindly bade to stay,
> Sat by his fire and talked the night away,
> Wept o'er his wounds, or tales of sorrow done,
> Shouldered his staff and showed how fields were won.

Next morning, Saturday, the Major took John in his gig to visit Governor Bennett, who was a lieutenant in the same regiment, and a lady present gave an account of the scene acted over again there. Such greeting she never witnessed. The Governor gave his orders for the best dinner to be prepared. John Turner, a brave old soldier, was to dine—saying to his wife, "Kate, nothing you can get is too good." Next, the two old officers fitted him out with a new suit complete, and took him to church on Sunday. On Monday the Major went with him to New Castle, on his return to Washington. General Cass, then Secretary of War, had advised him to procure the signatures of these two gentlemen to his certificate, which would insure an increase to his pension, and in this he succeeded.

We next trace the way to town, then relate a nocturnal adventure on this road as a prelude to revolutionary incidents. From this gate to the bridge is an excellent road banked up through the meadows, high, and one mile and a quarter in length. Nearly the whole way, this avenue is shaded on either side by water-willows, adorned with thick foliage, that shields the rambler from the scorching sunbeams, and the birds of the air rest upon their branches, throwing their shadow into the meadows, and refreshing many a panting animal. Yet, strange to say, so various are the uses of terrestrial things, those tender boughs so cheering to the many, are made a traffic of, burned into charcoal, and then ground into powder to destroy the life they have gladdened.

On the outside are canals cut to drain the meadows; these are inhabited by numberless frogs of every age and kind, from the hop-toad to the most sonorous bull-frogs, with their thundering noise, making the whole welkin ring, when they join in concert. The borders are fringed with flags, water-lilies, and other aquatic plants, that shoot up out of the oozy soil, beautifully gay. Under these trees you see scores of gaudy butterflies flitting before you in various colors on the green sward, and seeming to paint in flowers the grassy pathway. The cattle are grazing, and lowing in the meadows as you pass, and the wind whistling through lots of green corn, give you rural sights and rural sounds.

Well, once upon a time, twelve females had spent a very pleasant day at Long Hook; the evening shades had closed, and gathering clouds admonished them to hasten home; no danger was apprehended, though the night was dark. A stout man, long in the Major's employ, was sent to escort us over the bridge. A few glimmering stars lighted our path, and we set out merrily. Entering the avenue, we were enveloped in total darkness, and for an instant a star would twinkle through the trees and vanish. Then we heard noises, the screech-owl and bull-frogs; though familiar sounds, the gloom made them appear strange.

Now a restless animal among the cattle bellowed most terrifically —approaching nearer, our escort said we need not fear him; the ditch was a sufficient bulwark; so we stept cautiously and timidly, afraid of the sound of our voices, and even the tread, lest it should crush the worm under our foot.

When Solomon broke silence, exclaiming, "Did you see that?" "No, what?" "That 'ar light." "Well, what of that?" "La, have you never hearn tell of the strange lights seen here, and you have always lived in these here parts? La, marm, have you never hearn tell of Blackbeard, as how in old times he used to come up this here creek and hide money? and that he killed folks, and buried them in these here banks? and as how, when men were digging for this money, Jack-o'-the-lantern would scare them away, just as they hit the box? La, marm, folks say, sometimes he would tote them off bodily."

"Do you believe all that, Solomon?" "Yes, marm, I do, for I have seen queer sights myself; and I don't like this walk of a dark night, nohow you can fix it." Then the bull-frogs bellowed, and we started. "Never mind the frogs, ladies, they won't hurt you; but look out for the lights. Howsomever, the frogs are very alarming sometimes; for I suppose you have hearn tell of that are kurnel in the old war." "No, what of him?" "Well, they say he was in about such a fix as this, only it was a swampy place, they couldn't run." "Well, a colonel would not wish to run." Well, he moughtn't be a kurnel, but anyhow he was a big bug, that did not do much, but made every fellow do as he chused. Well, as I was saying, in such a fix as this, only the red-coats were arter him, full tilt."

"Well, we may thank our stars they are not after us." "La! marm, I telled you that happened in the old war." What happened?" "Well, you know how brave the Delaware men were; that officer, now I hit it, was one on 'em. Well, they were creeping softly through the swamps, and one of them are creatures bellowed out, and the wind whistled through the corn, and they raly thought it was a musket-ball; then they halted—next the whole army of bull-frogs in the swamp gave a shout that rang through the corn like a volley of musket-balls. Then he ordered the men to lay down their arms, and surrender, shouting aloud, 'Sirs, we are your prisoners!'"

"What, a Delaware officer surrender to bull-frogs? Never!" "Yes, marm, I have hearn my father tell as how one of his kin was a soger that was with him; telled him the officer's name, too, and there was twelve on 'em."

At that crisis the whole company of frogs in harmonious concert made such a terrific roar, and resounded through the marshes, that we bounded over the pathway like deers, not seeming to touch the ground, or draw a breath until we reached the bridge that was lighted, leaving poor Solomon in the utmost consternation, thinking for a moment Jack O'Lanthorn had toted us off bodily.

CHAPTER VII.

Major Jaquett—Battles—Brandywine—General LaFayette—Bell McClosky—Colonel Hazlett—General Smallwood—Guilford C. H.—General Green—Camden—Baron deKalb—Delaware Regiment—Singular Incident—Virginia—Patriotic Lady—Return—Joseph Tatnall, Esq.—Mrs Jaquett—Bennet—Lord Cornwallis—Monckton Park—George Haines, Esq.—Robert Morris, Esq.—A thrilling story—Judge Bedford and lady—Mysterious events—Hays's family—An eventful day—General Washington, President of the United States—Eden Park—P. Bauduy, Esq.

MAJOR JAQUETT entered the army at the commencement, and continued in service during the war, only spending six weeks at home, to recruit his health, impaired by a southern climate, and consequent exposures of a camp. He was soon promoted to a captaincy, and major by brevet at the close. He was in thirty-two pitched battles, and many skirmishes; and though never severely wounded, had several hair-breadth escapes. At Princeton, when his commander, Colonel Hazlett, fell, he was at his side.

At the battle of Brandywine, when General Lafayette was wounded, he was near, and heard him call to General Washington, "General, I am wounded!" who answered, I am sorry for it, sir." "Sir, I am not sorry," was the reply.

A woman came, and with her scissors extracted the ball, put it into her pocket. Next came the Major, and after him the surgeon, who said all was done well. This woman lived to an old age; used to carry cakes in a basket to sell, with this relic of her revolutionary services always at hand. Her husband was a soldier, and she followed him in the army, where she was very useful in binding up the wounds of many who might have bled to death without her timely aid.

On General Lafayette's visit to this town, in 1824, a dinner was given at the town hall. When the guests were all assembled, Bell McClosky came, and asked for Major Jaquett, and said, "Major, I wish you to introduce me to General Lafayette; I feel an indescribable desire to speak to him once more."

"You shall be gratified, Bell, for you were a true patriot, and, I believe, saved many a poor fellow's life." Being presented to the

General, who recognized her, and expressed his deep gratitude for her prompt attention on the day of battle, she handed him the ball, saying "it had never been out of her pocket one hour since that memorable day."

As it seems in place here, I will relate an anecdote of Colonel Hazlett, a fine looking officer, on his way to join the army. At a hotel, well known afterwards as Captain O'Flinn's, south-east corner of Third and Market streets, an old Irish woman, who had lived here many years, had been his nurse, and left Ireland when he was a boy, heard of his arrival, and in the warmth of her heart, went rejoicing to see him, and was ushered into the parlor, where he was walking the floor in full dress, and a number of officers present. She instantly recognized him, and flew to him, and caught him around the neck, and kissed him, saying, "Och, dare John, and sure it's jest you!" The officers thought it was his mother, whom he did not choose to own. He exclaimed, "Woman! who are you—what do you mean?" "Och, dare John, arn't you my own dare wean? Sure these arms bore you mony a day; and sure it's jest me that knows all your fore-bearers in Ireland!"

As soon as he recollected her, he expressed the kindest feelings for her, and inquired where and how she lived. She replied by saying, "Will you come and see?" "Yes, most certainly." "Then you will find me dune the back street, jist above the big buttonwoods, and foreninst the ould oak, in the turkey's nest." "Well, if you live in a turkey's nest, I hope it is well feathered." "Then you will jist see! only ask for Granny Miller, in the turkey's nest, and ony child can direct you."

This place I long remember; it was a small shed-room adjoining a frame house, in Walnut street, and stood there in a tottering condition for years, until the day Col. Hazlett's remains were removed to Dover; it was then taken down—a singular coincidence.

Another revolutionary anecdote occurs to my memory that happened in this hotel. When General Smallwood's division was quartered here, he had ordered some horses driven into a clover lot, some miles above the town. The owners were Friends, and not very favorable to the American cause, and much displeased at what they thought a very unjustifiable act. The old lady came to town, inquired by whose authority it had been done; when informed, she went to the hotel, and asked if *Billy Smallwood* was there. They said General Smallwood was in that parlor.

As she entered, the General came forward, and hearing his name announced, when she accosted him: "Is thy name *Billy* Smallwood?" "Yes!" "Well, thee deserves small wood well laid across thy broad shoulders, thee naughty man, for destroying my fine pasture." The General was much amused with the appropriate salutation, and tried to appease her by promising payment at a future day, and often laughed at the joke.

At Guilford Court House, N. C., Friends were holding their monthly meeting. Our army was in great distress for clothing, no shoes to their feet, which were so sore that it was with difficulty they could march, leaving their tracks of blood on the ground, and expecting to meet the enemy, and have a battle. In this tattered condition they appealed to General Green for permission to enter the Friends' meeting, and furnish themselves with shoes, as their necessities were so great, and this was their only chance. The General replied, "I know your wants, my brave fellows, without the power to relieve them; say no more to me," and he turned around from them.

They then went into the house, and Captain See addressed the Friends most feelingly, showing the men's lacerated feet, declaring that nothing but the most imperious necessity could influence him to take his intended course; many of them most willingly gave their shoes, while others were forced.

Major Jaquett was on the women's side, to assure them they would not be molested. One old lady, with large feet and coarse shoes, insisted on his taking hers, and she gave them to one of the men herself, while others offered theirs. They took their horses too. And this little affair was of great importance to the army, though General Green never wished to hear of it, as he had great respect for Friends, being educated by his parents in their principles.

Previous to the battle of Camden, a council was held, and a close conversation between General Gates and Baron De Kalb, with respect to the time, place, and the force they would bring into the field. The latter officer seemed to be impressed that if an action took place then the result would be disastrous to the army and his pathway to the grave. Just before the first round was fired, he turned to Major Jaquett, and said, "If you survive, my brave young officer, have a care for my remains." In a few moments, he fell mortally wounded into his arms. Thus died a noble and brave officer, deeply lamented.

The Delaware regiment went into battle, eight hundred strong, and at the close could not muster one hundred men, the rest being either killed or wounded. Those fit for service joined the Virginia line, and after the war the State of Virginia gave a portion of land to each man who served in that regiment. Those from Delaware were included, and it may be strange to say, after so many years had elapsed, the day on which Major Bennett was elected Governor, each share was paid; his share amounted to the exact sum that he would have received as the year's salary for that office. He was a lieutenant in Captain Kirkwood's company; they were all paid on the same day, but only four were then living.

When peace was established, Major Jaquett was at the South, without money or clothes sufficient to bring him home. Gen. Green advised him to take charge of nine sick and wounded men. By so doing he would give him an order on each depot, where he could be furnished with supplies to proceed to Delaware. This he accepted, but was chagrined to find on his arrival every depot broken up. Burdened with those poor fellows, whom he would not abandon, he was obliged to beg his way.

They passed through Virginia in these distressing circumstances. On entering a piece of woods, three roads so diverged they were doubtful which to take, lest they should miss the right way. The day was declining, and a rising mist obscured the distant view. Major J. advised his companions to halt, while he went forward to seek refreshment and shelter for the party; at length he obtained a glimpse of a habitation, and hastened his steps.

As he approached he was met by the owner, who addressed him in a kind and courteous manner, thinking some accident had befallen the lonely stranger. A brief statement of their condition was sufficient to excite the sympathy of one so kindly disposed, and a short time only elapsed ere the whole party were safely housed in his hospitable mansion; with unaffected politeness the members of the family gave them a cordial reception.

The whole vicinity bore marks of the desolating scourge of war. This dwelling presented the aspect of ancient grandeur, and the little band now felt that an angel of mercy had guided them to this good Samaritan to bind up their wounds, and pour in oil and wine. The sick were nourished and medical aid afforded them. They were thus fed and clothed, and even the crippled beasts seemed to partake of the general rejoicing at their unwonted plenty. At times they felt as if all this was visionary, and they were with superior beings, for it was to them a heavenly asylum.

Their wounds were partially healed. The sick pronounced convalescent, and the animals in good condition, and the day of departure drew nigh. Their kind host most feelingly regretted his inability to furnish them with funds for defraying their expenses home. "Why shouldst thou be as a stranger in the land, that turned aside to tarry for a night?" As thou art in the midst of us leave us not.

A worthy lady who had been an attentive listener to the Major's narration of dangers, toils, and privations, borne for seven years in defence of his country, and had evinced a deep interest in the soldiers while they were under the fostering care of this excellent family, solicited a private interview. She had a secret to communicate which he must promise not to reveal. He gave the assurance, and she handed him a purse containing several gold pieces, saying she had retained it unknown to the family, through many trying scenes, fearing a greater emergency, as she saw paper money so depreciated. This was the cause of secrecy.

The Major politely declined to receive her extreme liberality, as he had no prospect of an ability to repay it. But she urged him to accept her mite towards relieving the necessities of his way-worn soldiers, returning from the perils of war, with impaired health and shattered constitutions, too often the only inheritance of the brave defenders of our common country, and she said, "Be assured it rejoices my heart to have this boon to offer, which has so long been kept as a sacred deposit," which the Major could no longer refuse, being so generously bestowed. Thus the wants of these weary pilgrims were amply supplied, until they reached the desired haven of rest.

The Major on his return home found his farm in a dilapidated state, and destitute of the means to repair and improve it. Besides this, the support of an aged mother and infirm sister devolved upon him. Under these adverse circumstances, his physician announced that a voyage to the West Indies was the only chance for the restoration of his health. This visit his poverty forbade, and his spirits were sinking under the pressure of his misfortunes; so many of his fellow officers had been cut off in the field of battle, and it seemed as if he was only permitted to come home to die.

Deeply impressed by his adversity, he met Joseph Tatnall, Esq., who most cordially welcomed him home, and regretted to hear of his feeble health, and inquired if he had consulted a physician. He told him the advice, and his inability to comply. There was a pause, and this kind friend replied—

"Peter, thou must go! Seven years spent in the defence of thy country, with no renumeration, and a broken constitution without an effort to repair it, will not do; money is very scarce at this time, or I would give it thee without hesitation. However, I can manage the business, by letting thee have flour to cover thy expenses." So the generous sympathy of this friend was not defeated. He gave him the amount of twelve hundred dollars in flour, the proceeds of which paid all the expenses of his journey. He went on his way, rejoicing to have met such a friend in this last extremity. In ten days he departed for a more genial clime, and in a few months returned with renewed health.

Not many years before his death, he paid this debt, though the money had never been demanded. The noble patriotic lady, as he used to style her, who gave him the purse of gold, was dead; but he paid her friends in after years principal and interest, amounting to over five hundred dollars. He mislaid the statement of this account. A year before his death, Mrs. Jaquett found it among old muster-rolls. Feeling it was justly his due, he presented it to Congress for payment. As that honorable body always move slowly in matters where they have no personal interest, the Major died before it was acted upon.

Here we have given two noble instances of patriotism, one from the ancient dominion, the other from little Delaware, and record them with pleasure.

Mrs. Jaquett died May 5, 1834; she was a worthy woman, and deeply interested in her church and religious institutions. Her afflictions were a grief to the Major, who proved his affection by unremitting attentions. He was never seen to smile after her death. His closing scene on September 13, 1834, was serene and tranquil. "I am old, stricken in age, and behold this day I am going the way of all the earth, and you know in all your hearts the Lord your God is he that hath fought for you, hath driven out from before you great nations and strong; no man hath been able to stand before you unto this day; take heed therefore unto yourselves, that you love the Lord your God, lest you perish off this good land which your God hath given you."

This reminiscence is not added to repair an omission in the preceding narrative, but is elicited for its remarkable tendency.

During the Major's sojourn here, in impaired health, continued chills enervated his system, so that when discouraging news came from the army it overshadowed his mind with gloom, and he imagined his path clearly pointed to the gallows. In this despondency he felt his services could be no longer useful to his country, even should his health improve, and that it was expedient for him to resign his commission, and await his doom.

An elderly female friend of his, who lived near, had often given him good counsel, and was of a cheerful disposition, and never despaired of the success of her country. Besides, he was in love with her daughter. Thither he concluded to bend his steps, and while away an hour. On entering the domicil, he was struck with her sad countenance, so unusual. Time passed away in conversing on the adverse circumstances of his country, and other topics of national interest, until too late for him to return that night.

In the morning, as he entered the breakfast-room, the good lady addressed him, "Peter, how did you rest? and what is this dream that thou hast dreamed?" His answer was, "As usual, I passed a wretched night, very little sleep, with distressing dreams." "Well, tell us what they were." "O, I never tell the confused nonsense that disturbs my sleep." "You must tell me, Peter, what you recollect." "If it will gratify you, I can remember my morning vision, and will relate it."

"I thought I was returning home and had to pass that old oak tree yonder; under its shade a lion was couched, looking me in the face most ferociously. There seemed no other path by which I could escape; my only hope was to return to the house, and even this was uncertain. Trembling and gazing at the fierce beast, I half turned with extreme anxiety, to elude its claws, when I saw an eagle pounce from a bough of the tree upon the lion, entangling its talons so in his mane as to draw his head back with such force that he roared aloud, and I awoke."

This patriotic lady sprang from her chair, and with the most enthusiastic ardor, said, "Peter, you were not born to be hung. Our army will yet be victorious. Arouse, shake off your ague; join your regiment without delay. Mark my words, you will return home crowned with honor." "Thou shalt not die by the sword, but thou shalt die in peace."

Her enthusiasm was like an electric shock, and so excited him that he set off in two days for the South; and, strange to say, his ague was checked from that hour. This incident he seldom related. The old lady was Mrs. Stidham.

Governor Bennet being alluded to, it seems the place for a passing tribute to his memory, as a patriot of '76. He was a lieutenant in

Captain Kirkwood's company. Major Jaquett and he were most affectionate friends during life. They passed through many harassing scenes, and many escapes from danger, though neither of them ever were badly wounded. Lieutenant Bennet was not in as many battles as Captain Jaquett, being often sent home to recruit men. In this service he was very successful, but was so fortunate as to be present at the capture of Lord Cornwallis. Captain Jaquett always lamented being absent on that important event.

They both entered the army in '76, and continued to the end of the arduous struggle for their country's independence. Lieutenant Bennet, as stated by their captain, was a very moral young officer, addicted to none of the vices common in camp at that day. He never knew him to be intoxicated but once, and that was by accident. Neither did he use profane language; two remarkable traits, which will be remembered with commendation.

His services in battle were sufficient to prove his bravery, which was never doubted. His hospitality, fondness for dining parties, and the dance, remained with him to old age, and made it more extraordinary that he should escape the vices of the day. He was brought up a Friend, and professed a great regard for their principles, and never liked to hear of the affair at Guilford Court House—the taking the Friends' shoes, as he was present at that scene. Major Jaquett would often remind him of it, merely to tease him, when he would express his partiality for their principles, and say, "You call yourself a Friend, and will both fight and dance."

He was elected governor at an advanced age, for his revolutionary services. His friend, the Major, disapproved of giving offices of state to military chieftains as a reward, and thought they seldom made good statesmen, and that the country was bound to pay well those who fought its battles, leaving those offices to men whose habits of reflection were better adapted for the management of state affairs. They were of different politics, the Major a Whig, the Governor a Democrat.

The latter was deeply afflicted at his friend's death, and felt that his time was near at hand. His death took place soon after, while he was in office, and living in the house where Dr. McKinley died. He left a widow and children, men and women, to mourn the loss of an affectionate father and husband, while others remembered him as a kind neighbor. "Man abideth not in honor."

The next place in our way was in days of old called Monckton Park. About the commencement of the Revolution, it was owned by an English gentleman, who had spent some time in the West Indies, and visited Philadelphia. But taking a deep interest in the American cause, was obliged to remain in this country until the close of that event, and engaged in the shipping business there. This was his country-seat, which he frequently visited on horseback, for exercise. Being a public-spirited man, he made great improvements, and was an acquisition to the neighborhood. He was the first person who proposed mile stones in this county, called a meeting for that purpose, and presented the stones, which extend to the Red Lion; others interested paid for their being set.

Mr. Haines was the friend of Robert Morris, Esq., and those gentlemen originated the Bank of North America; others may have been connected with them. Mr. H. was remarkably neat in his person, and systematic in his business. While his daughters were at boarding-school in Philadelphia, he regularly called to take them to church on prayer days, Wednesday and Friday morning. Neither inclement weather nor pressing business interfered with this duty.

Once he made out an invoice for the cargo of a vessel to sail next day, and was obliged to complete it at a very late hour. At the finishing moment, a small dash of ink fell on it, and he spent the night in copying it over. He wore large metal buttons, fashionable at that day; no hurry or weariness prevented his covering every one with tissue paper, before he hung up his coat at night. With all this neatness, he had to pass through a process in traveling from Philadelphia to Boston that must have been intolerable, even for a slovenly person. It being the custom of the day, I will relate the anecdote.

The small-pox was viewed as the most terrific pestilence, and dreaded everywhere. At this time it was prevailing in New York, as he passed through. No stranger could be admitted into a house until he was thoroughly smoked in a place provided in every town for that purpose. So again and again he went through this ordeal, and when he returned and related his journey, he said he had not escaped one smoke-house from New York to Boston, and thought he had made a most miraculous escape in not being suffocated.

I have seen letters written by him after he passed fourscore years, in the most elegant hand and extreme neatness.

At the close of the war, he returned to England, and sold this place to his friend Robert Morris, Esq., who owned it for years. Henry Physick married his youngest daughter, near London, who, late in life purchased the house owned by Governor Dickinson, where he resided more than ten years, and died, leaving a large family behind him, and a reputation for integrity which few men have equally sustained through a long life.

Near the close of the last century, M. was the owner of Monckton Park, whose noble appearance, gentlemanly manners, and respectable talents made him an acceptable companion to the higher orders of society. Mrs. M. was plain and retiring in her habits. Their family was large, and the second child was an only daughter, for years the pride of her father's heart. She was now about sixteen, and though little known, was spoken of as a promising belle. She was a handsome brunette, with expressive black eyes, glossy raven hair, a fine figure, and graceful manners. Her talents were of high order, with a very imaginative turn of mind.

The time of which we speak was an eventful era. The appalling scenes of the French revolution, though just passed away, were fresh in memory, and infidel writings were circulated, freely patronized by some of the great men and mighty of the earth, who fearlessly avowed those principles; while to profess deism was viewed as a proof of superior sagacity or mental energy.

Alas! it was this young lady's sad fate to have a fond father of this class, who most assiduously imbued the minds of his household with his precepts, especially his beloved daughter. The only book prohibited from the family library was the Bible. No wonder this young disciple should be led by such teaching, unblessed by any counteracting religious influence. Yet, after all this care on his part, she evinced a deceptive restlessness of mind, harassed by a desire to investigate the subject, and elicit the opinion of others in regard to the immortality of the soul.

Three sisters, respectable women, who earned their livelihood by sewing, were there at work this year. To those she communicated her views freely, and requested theirs on a future state and suicide, and which they thought was the easiest death to die. Conscious of her superior powers in argument, they evaded discussion by entreating her to change a subject so revolting and painful to their feelings, that they shrunk from it with horror. At times an unnatural calmness was visible, at others a solemn sadness would cloud her brow with deep and anxious thought.

About six weeks previous to the thrilling part of this narrative, we were companions on board a packet going to Philadelphia, under her father's care. On entering the Delaware, a sudden flaw of wind blew like a mighty tempest. Every part of this small vessel seemed as if it would rend in pieces. To the terror of all the passengers, a frail sloop was so near that the danger increased, lest the two should run into each other.

In this state of excitement, the mast of the sloop snapped off close to the deck. The awful crash made us all tremble, except this interesting young girl.

At this crisis, her father seeing the confusion, haughtily exclaimed, "Patty, certainly you are not alarmed?" "No, sir, not in the least!" "I thought not, my daughter." This to me was strange. The danger soon subsided, and we had a very pleasant trip (so called). Her father was prevailed upon to leave her in the city, and here she was caressed and admired. As the fashion then prevailed of wearing the hair short round the head, leaving it longer on the top, with a few thin curls over the forehead, hers was thus arranged.

During her visit, an officer became pleased with her, and escorted her to the old ferry, on her way home. She declined his further attention, feeling assured it would not meet her father's approbation. On the following day her father observed her hair had been cut. As he had always viewed it as an ornament, and spoken of it with pride, now in a moment of passion he seized a pair of scissors and cut it all off. This first instance of his displeasure made her very unhappy for a time. She then had it shaved, and wrote to a friend in town, requesting a correspondence kept up until she could again appear in society.

Miss Hays, a young lady of more than ordinary talents, and religiously educated, readily complied. Miss M. feelingly related what had passed at home, then gave an account of her visit to Philadelphia, and concluded with a request to give her views of a future state. This was promptly answered, in accordance with the doctrines of the Bible, as the foundation of her belief. To this Miss M. wrote a reply, with great care, fully developing her sentiments, and soliciting an answer, wishing her opinion on suicide and of future rewards and punishments, with all the arguments she could advance to sustain either.

This letter caused sorrowful tears and deep reflection and solicitude to answer it wisely. R. H. knew the father was an infidel by report. Her duty was an arduous task. For what argument could she advance to penetrate a heart so guarded and entwined by parental influence? No reasoning would seem to avail, unless guided by the Holy Spirit, to rend the veil of darkness, and shed rays of light divine on a mind so prejudiced in error.

However fruitless the attempt, she resolved to be faithful to one whom she loved and pitied. With gentleness and sympathy, and in the most touching manner, all her questions were answered with scriptural reasons.

As a dutiful daughter, she felt her father ought to be informed of the contents of a correspondence carried on by one under his roof. However correct this feeling of honoring her parent, to comply with it was sufficient in its effect to render powerless this noble effort of her friend.

On a memorable day an epistle was written in a bolder strain, advocating the right to shorten a miserable existence.

The same afternoon, Judge Bedford and lady made a visit to Monckton Park, by her invitation. Calling on a friend, on their return that evening, they spoke of their pleasant visit, and of the charming Miss M. Mrs. B., an old accomplished lady of elegant manners and accustomed to the very best society, observed that Miss M. was an astonishing girl, brought up in retirement as she had been. No lady educated in the most polished court in Europe could have behaved with more dignity and grace, nor entertained with more ease than she had that evening.

In taking a view of the grounds, they walked to the inlet near the garden that emptied into the Christiana. In this she observed the tide ebbed and flowed, and named the hour of high water that night, and showed its usual height.

As they drove away from the gate, and she turned to walk up to the house, S. came down the lawn to meet her. The night was calm. A cloudless sky was studded with stars, and the moon soaring upwards in all its brilliancy, reflected through the trees on the green grass a soft light, and a beautiful view of the distant hills, while its silvery beams were glistening on the water without a ripple. The whole firmament presented a most glorious brightness, inspiring the heart with rapturous joy, on contemplating the majesty of the great Creator, who framed this wondrous world and sustained it by his Omnipotent hand, while a desire to remain in it a little longer would seem the natural bent of a youthful mind.

But ah! how thrilling to reflect, one so sensitive to all the beauties of nature should be so insensible to an accountability to the source from whence they flowed—shrink from all those delightful scenes, and plunge into an unknown eternity. Surely this is strange and inconsistent, not to have strength of mind to bear some imaginary sorrow that might pass away as the early dew, yet arouse their energies with such power as to rush heedlessly into an unknown eternity. This is an insanity that can only be accounted for by Him who seeth not as man seeth; therefore, to his wisdom we submit.

On entering the room where an infant sister lay asleep, she kissed her several times. Then in the kitchen she spoke kindly to the cook, and gave her a small piece of gold as a remembrance, retired to a chamber, washed and dressed. On entering the room with a note in her hand where S. S. slept, she said, "You would be glad to read this," and pinned it in her bosom. She then sat down by a window that overlooked the old church yard, and exclaimed, "What a lovely spot, Sally; remember I wish to be buried there." Reclining on her elbow, in deep reflection, she said, "How I wish I was laid there now. Oh, how lovely!"

With a book in her hand, she commenced to read. S. entreated her not to bring in the musquitoes with the light. She then went into another room. The conversation seemed so to bewilder the imagination of S. that for a time it chased away sleep. At length, overcome and weary, she slept till morning, when she saw M. was not in bed. She ran down stairs alarmed. Her father inquired if his daughter was not up. Finding she was not in the house, he was very indignant, concluding she had gone with the officer (named). He gave himself no further trouble. S. S. ventured to tell him her fears that she was drowned. He would not listen to any suggestion of the kind, while it was evident that was her fate.

The creek was dragged, and in this inlet it was supposed the dreadful deed had been effected. The father could not be aroused from his stupor, but sat in sullen silence. While the neighborhood was overshadowed with gloom, the most energetic efforts were made to trace this solemn event. "Oh, my daughter, they who lead thee cause thee to err, and destroy the way of thy paths, because they have cast away the law of the Lord of Hosts, and despised the words of the Holy one of Israel" In this agitating state of suspense, six weeks had elapsed.

A farmer on the Delaware, two miles above the Christiana, was mowing his meadows, and there the remains of a female were found in a mutilated condition. As the families had once lived near each other, his daughter recognized the disfigured form, and discovered the letters on her clothes (three M's), and the note pinned in her bosom, now illegible.

The distracted father was sent for, and oh! what a thrilling moment. Is it possible this can be the remains of his beloved daughter, so lately the admiration of her friends, now terrifying to look upon? "I was bowed down at the hearing of it, I was dismayed at the seeing of it. My heart panted: the days of visitation are come. All ye that pass by, behold and see if there be any sorrow like unto my sorrow; I will weep bitterly. Labor not to comfort me, for my grief is desperate." The bones were deposited in a box, and privately interred in the burying-ground on the farm.

"Ah! how misled that bosom mild,
By treacherous magic was beguiled,
  To strike the deathful blow:
And filled her soft ingenuous mind
With many a feeling too refined,
And roused to livelier pangs her wakeful sense of woe.

"Vain man! 'tis Heaven's prerogative
To take what first it deigned to give,
  Thy tributary breath.
In awful expectation placed,
Await thy doom, nor impious haste
To pluck from God's right hand his instruments of death."

The mother was overwhelmed with sorrow, and from that time was a regular attendant with her small children at Friends' meeting, where they had been brought up. The father became such a skeleton that no one would have known him in a few weeks. He shunned society, and some time after he removed to the West, and was no longer known here.

Years have now glided over this spot for half a century, and the moon shines brightly, the trees renew their verdure and the grass its freshness; the ploughman whistles as he tills the land, and the earth produces grain, and the water flows in its wonted channel; yet this mournful tragedy of an interesting young soul rushing to her doom, from that hour remains enshrouded in mystery.

As we have referred to Miss Hays, we will here pay a small tribute to her memory as the friend of her youth. But we will first mention her excellent parents. John Hays was the first cashier of the Bank of Delaware, the oldest bank in the State, and always sustaining its credit, under every pressure, equal to any in the United States. As a proof of the importance of a right beginning, during the prevalence of the yellow fever in Philadelphia, dry goods merchants were here conducting their business, and had transactions at that bank. I have heard them speak of Mr. Hays with the highest commendation of his promptness in business, readiness to oblige, and said they had known men as ready to accommodate a friend, but never had met with any man so willing to extend his favor. Yet he was most fortunate in not losing by this generous kindness. It might be said he was more ready to give than receive.

His daughter was very young when he engaged in the bank, and attending school for several years after. From thirteen years of age she generally managed his private concerns, as his health was delicate. A relative of ours wished to purchase a farm near this town, and called on Mr. Hays, who referred him to his daughter, observing, "Any contract she made would be confirmed on his part." This was done, and he became owner of the farm. He afterwards spoke of her business powers, and on settling up her father's estate, as executrix, Chancellor Ridgely, a very exact man, spoke of the admirable manner in which all had been arranged.

Mrs. Hays was eminently pious. Meekness and humility were her prominent traits of character. She was a very delicate woman, and for the last thirty years of her life was afflicted with a most distressing cough. A few years before her death, the eldest son, then father of a family, died very suddenly. The first time I saw her after his death, she observed, there was a time when such a calamity would have overwhelmed her frail frame, she feared. Now she felt herself no longer an inhabitant of this earth, had given up all her concern for worldly affairs, and committed herself and family into the hands of her Maker, who doeth all things well. For years she had retired at night, expecting to awake in eternity.

Mr. Hays died suddenly. The old lady was from home, and on her arrival found her husband a corpse, walked up and looking in his face, exclaimed, "Bless the Lord, O my soul, and praise his holy name, in his judgments as well as his mercies." She died some time after. "Well done, good and faithful servant, enter thou into the joy of thy Lord."

We have noticed Miss Hays' business powers, and shall briefly delineate her social qualities. We consider the female character of far greater importance in society than many are willing to admit: the first bias of the infant mind is received from maternal instruction, and if this teaching be void of religious principle, there will be little disposition to have them inculcated in the minds of her children; and though she may permit it for sake of form, this faint outline will soon pass away as they grow older, unless her practice comport with those rudiments of Christianity thus taught.

It was the happy lot of this exemplary female to be under the constant influence of religious example and precept, and to make religion her rule of faith and practice; and though she was not instructed in any of the ornamental branches of an education to finish an accomplished lady, she had been well taught in all that could adorn the mind. These her own labors continued to cultivate with gentleness and refinement. She was considered to possess more than ordinary mind, and to be an acquisition in any company in which she chanced to be placed.

Our acquaintance commenced in early life, and on an eventful day, that Gen. Washington passed through Wilmington, as President of the United States; and it must have been soon after his elevation to that office, for I well remember the crowds of people rushing on to the "Baltimore road" to catch a glimpse as he passed.

There was a point of what was called Quaker Hill jutted out very high, and overlooked every high place around, so that nothing here could obstruct your view, and descending so abruptly as to make the side impassable towards this road. No more favorable spot could have been selected, and here was an old apple tree, the last fragment of an orchard; under this same tree the ground was carpeted with grass of the richest green.

Here our venerated General had spent many hours in admiring the surrounding scenery, especially the beautiful windings of the Christiana, and as the setting sun was emitting its last rays, and twilight commenced, the softness of their light reflected the shadows of the trees on the silvery water, delightful for an admirer of nature to behold; and on a limb of this very tree we were perched together, with as lofty feelings as any ladies in the land, looking down on our companions with the greatest complacency.

It was a day of great enjoyment; all was on tiptoe of expectation, when his chariot appeared, driving slowly through the crowd, he bowing, hat in hand, and white handkerchiefs waving, and every face flushed, and eyes sparkling with joy. Then a reverberating shout, "Did you see Gen. Washington?" "Yes! he bowed to me!" was again echoed through this immense multitude, all of one mind, paying their respects in this rustic way, to the father of their country.

On the Monday following we became schoolmates, and continued so for years. There a true friendship was cultivated, only ending in death. "A friend loveth at all times."

> Thus passes o'er, through varied life's career,
> Man's fleeting age—the seasons as they fly
> Snatch from us in their course, year after year,
> Some sweet connection, some endearing tie.

"Train up a child in the way he should go, and when he is old he will not depart from it." "Have not I written to thee excellent things in counsel and knowledge, that thy trust may be in the Lord."

This worthy family were members of the Society of Friends. The condition of these two families, united in worldly friendship, widely differing in principles, both possessing superior mental attractions, fully illustrate the errors of false teaching and the excellencies of religious example. "Halt ye between two opinions? As for me and my house, we will serve the Lord."

This once lovely spot we can now only trace from memory. Such a feeling to bring all things to a level pervades the community at this day, that it produces astonishing faith, followed by works; for only say to the hill, "Be thou removed," and it vanishes. It may be an advantage to make the rugged places smooth, and the crooked paths straight, in some instances; yet we all see it is carried out so extensively as to destroy the beauty of the town, connected with a reverse feeling in building narrow houses, soaring up like the "Tower of Babel."

Nearly forty years have passed since Peter Bauduy, Esq., purchased Monckton Park; he had emigrated to this town soon after the French revolution of '90. Mr. B. was an enterprising man, of affable manners, and possessing great taste in the fine arts. A relic of his skill in painting, once much admired, is yet to be seen, though much defaced by time, and retouched by a less skilful hand. It represents the fabled story of Phaeton, son of Phœbus, driving the chariot of the sun so furiously as to threaten universal conflagration. It has been removed from Market street near Seventh to the corner of King and Sixth streets.

On removing to this farm, Mr. B. made great improvements, and altered its name to Eden Park. Formerly, this district was very unhealthy, but draining the marshes has changed its character. Mr. B. speculated largely in merino sheep, and imported a shepherd and his dogs from the Pyrenees to guard them. This project seemed unsuccessful, and caused his removal to the island of Cuba, where he and his wife died. During his residence here, Mr. B. was esteemed a useful citizen and a kind neighbor.

Mrs. B. was a handsome and an accomplished lady, and there are many survivors of her who remember her with great affection.

Mr. B. established powder-works at Eden Park, which are owned by his son-in-law, J. P. Gareshe, Esq., who resides there, and pursues the powder business. It being so near town, when explosions have occurred they have caused much excitement, and with great anxiety till their extent has become known.

CHAPTER VIII.

English Fleet—Panic—Hessians—Deserter—Battle of Brandywine—Tranhook—Fairfield—Old Ferry—Swedish Colonists—Rocks—Cave—Indian Mounds—1812 War—Mud Bulwark—Hon J. A. Bayard—Peace—Note—Major Cass.

About the period of the battle of Brandywine, part of the English fleet, the Roebuck and Liverpool, with their tenders, were lying opposite the town, with the design of bombarding it. Providentially, the distance marred the attempt. Many farmers and their families who lived in the neck stood on the shore to view the fleet, when the orders were given to fire. Such unexpected inhumanity threw the whole community into a panic.

Boats manned with Hessians landed, to whom orders were given to take the men prisoners; and great efforts were made to entrap a militia captain, who fled to the house of a relative, desiring to be secreted. The host was a widower, with four daughters, and he, their only protector, was sick. His house was too near the river to afford the captain security, and if found there, might be the occasion of insult to the family. He was advised to let a man at work in the yard show him a hollow log, in which he might be secure. The hint was good; he crawled in, the man covered it over with leaves, and the enemy scrutinized every nook about the premises in vain. Joseph Stidham was the captain, and Jonas Stidham the farmer.

The latter, the day before the battle, took his daughters to the very spot, placing them at a farm house for safety; so contrary to the expected rout; and during the engagement, the balls were whistling over the house where they were compelled to remain. It was deemed a place of security, and many persons sent valuables there. A looking-glass, now valued as a relic, and in good preservation, was sent by my mother, with all her best furniture, to be placed there. But the house was injured by the balls, and everything destroyed, except this glass and a cradle. These were brought home on a loaded wagon, and are now valued as a memento of that eventful day.

Several of these Hessians deserted. One of them, Peter Davis, was well known as "Dutch Peter." He sought an asylum with Mr. Girelius, the Swedish minister, with whom he resided, taking charge of his horse and cow, and faithfully performing his duty until Mr. Girelius left the country.

He was long sexton of Trinity Church, and guarded well its premises. His love for the spot was proverbial, and on Christmas week, Peter was sure to visit the congregation, seeming to feel that they were his parishioners, having learned to speak English his own way.

On entering your dwelling with the salutation of the season, when his health was inquired after, his answer, "Very well, God be tankful and tings." On these annual visits, it was the custom to present him with a piece of silver. If my mother was tardy in presenting her offering, Peter would exclaim, "Oh, Mrs., how well I dosh remember your daddy and tings!" This had the desired effect to draw out a silver piece, and a drink too; for those days were before the temperance reformation.

Peter was an uncouth man, and had his infirmities, but was an attentive and accommodating sexton. Besides his escape while a soldier from bullets, he was blown many feet into the air by the blasting of rocks, and his face so disfigured by the powder being thrown into the skin, that the boys used to call him "Old powder proof."

He for a long time had charge of the Old Academy, and lived in the basement; and the boys and girls who went there to school long remembered how well Peter guarded his castle, and what a high-toned commander he was when the young urchins attempted to invade his rights, not forgetting Jenny's molasses candy. The poor fellow, after miraculous escapes, was drowned near the church; and strange to say his successor was drowned by falling with his head into the spring within the cemetery two years after.

On the decease of Frederick Vertz, he resided with Dolly, who left him her house and valuable lot for his attention.

On the road to the ferry, the Swedes built their first church of logs. The place was called Tranhook, and was in a dilapidated state, when Trinity Church was erected; and near the creek was Fairfield, many years the residence of Dr. Alexander, a surgeon of the Revolution. He was a Democrat of the old school, famed for his hospitality, and as a valuable member of this community he died lamented.

Here was the New Castle road, and the old ferry was the only crossing place; it was often dangerous in high winds or drifts of ice. Many accidents and even loss of life occurred, when the boats or flats were driven down the creek, and it was occasionally impassable.

An incident fresh in my memory may suffice to show the danger, though more than thirty years have passed since it occurred. The ice had floated and partly dissolved into its watery element. Mrs. M. and her daughter had arrived here at dark in the stage from Dover. The ice was drifting, the day had been unpleasant; melting snow covered the ground, rendering it inconvenient to get in and out of the carriage, especially to this lady, who was large and not active; and the driver and boatmen advised her to keep her seat, as there was no danger. They said it was usual for ladies to sit still; thus her own judgment was overruled.

As the horses were stepping into the boat, the feet of the leaders slipped, causing confusion with the others. In the struggle, the flat dashed off into the floating ice ere the men could extricate the horses. In this alarming situation, their screams reached the cars of some sportsmen who were drying themselves by a fire in the opposite house.

They rushed out and put off in a boat, just in time to save these females from their impending fate. The stage was half filled with water, and receding from the shore, when the ladies were rescued by the most energetic efforts. In this state of insensibility, they were conveyed to the old ferry-house on the west side. Preparations had been made at that place for their reception, and an express sent for Dr. M., the husband and father, who lived two miles from town. On his arrival they had revived, and their hearts were glowing with gratitude towards the Almighty Disposer of events, who had guided these men to their deliverance. "This is the Lord's doings, and marvellous in our eyes."

We pause as we stand now on a renowned site in ruins, hallowed to our mind from association. Here the Swedes made their first settlement. On one of the fanciful windings of the Christiana is a reef of rocks, so steep that it forms a quay where vessels lie securely. There is a gradual ascent carpeted with rich grass, and ships sail to and fro almost within your reach; fields and meadows, luxuriant in pasture; the old church in sight, with its solemn and ancient burial-place, partly screened by lofty sycamores which throw their shadows over the graves of many worthies whose dust is now mingled with the soil; and hills on hills crowned with verdure. On this spot the Swedes built a fort, and within it a chapel for worship, they being religiously educated.

In some traits of their character, they resembled the patriarchs in simplicity and honesty, for example, saying, "I am a stranger and sojourner with you; give me a place that I may bury my dead out of my sight;" and as Abraham weighed Ephron the silver which he had named in the audience of the sons of Heth, so these just men paid the aborigines of the land, as the patriarch paid the Hittite: "They did justly, loved mercy, and walked humbly with their God."

Thus they secured this old grave-yard, the depository of the ashes of many from foreign climes, whether from the remote regions of the north, or from "India's coral strand." They inculcated peace in their intercourse with the savage tribes, desirous to teach the importance of Christianity by example—"doing to others as we would have them do to us." "For they got not the land in possession by their own sword, neither did their own arm save them, but thy right hand and thine arm, and the light of thy countenance, because thou hadst favor unto them."

This spot, once so delightful and admired, has been shorn of its greatest attraction, torn up by the blasting of rocks, as if the destroying angel had passed over it, and swept away every fragment of antiquity, leaving no vestige for the admiration of man. It was the home of my maternal ancestors, the birthplace of my mother, and her inheritance from her mother, Rebecca Hoffman. At the commencement of troublesome times, mother disposed of it, to her great regret afterwards. Here, and to the church, she made an annual lonely visit, even to the last year of her life.

In describing this place as it was in days of old, she said that when the first colonists came, they found a cave, of which the interior was impressive, the size of the room, and so high that the tallest man could stand erect. Over the bottom was a smooth rock, and in the corner a spring of delicious water, with an opening to convey it off, and her mother used it for a milk-house, having a door made to close the entrance. It was viewed as a curiosity, and preserved with great care by the early owners. The fort was in ruins from my mother's childhood, but there was a mound marked as an Indian burial-place, which was also preserved from injury. Here the children of the family found many implements, as tomahawks, hatchets, and wampums.

In the days of my childhood, I knew an old man who lived solitary in a cave, and employed himself in digging tussocks out of the marshes. Though it was a voluntary act on his part, the owners remunerated him for the valuable services rendered them.

Trivial incidents, especially if connected with great men or noble deeds, increase in interest as years roll on. Therefore, as we are on the spot, it may be appropriate to relate some events of the war of 1812. Previous to that responsible declaration, our quiet little town was not ambitious of military display, even to show off a military company, or to listen to the roll of the drum. But when the trumpet of war resounded through the land, the town being in a defenceless state, the emergency roused our townsmen to action, and it was deemed important to make some preparation.

The "Rocks" were selected as a place fitted to throw up a mud bulwark, where cannon could be mounted to check the approach of an enemy by boats. Among the most energetic of our citizens was the statesman, whom Delaware claimed as her own, second to none either in the courts of justice or legislative halls, the Hon. James A. Bayard, so lately distinguished in the United States Senate by his speech on the subject of war, laid aside his robe of state for a season, put on the garb of a laborer, with ditcher's boots, and a shovel on his shoulder, marched with the mass to achieve their muddy work, and with spirited men labored from the rising to the setting sun.

An artillery company was also to be raised as a defence. Here again Mr. Bayard was seen in rear of the drum beating up for recruits. His noble figure has passed before us in both positions. This company was soon complete, and one of our respected statesmen, Hon. C. A. Rodney, was elected captain. To patronize such energetic measures, the ladies presented a flag, made of lasting, as bunting was scarce, with an elegant staff; the cost being one hundred and thirty dollars.

Years have glided away, and many of those patriots descended to the tomb, with a number of the donors, who, if their voices could be heard, would be unanimous in wishing that flag to be preserved in commemoration of that eventful day. Yet to the great chagrin of some who were interested in presenting it, they saw it flying at the door of an engine house, in Hanover Street, for which purpose it was never designed.

In conclusion, we shall briefly remark that that eminent statesman, J. A. Bayard, was soon appointed by the executive to embark for Europe on an embassy of peace, and this proceeding is recorded in our national annals. But it is sad to think that one so robust in constitution, vigorous in mind, whose heart was glowing with patriotism, should be cut off in the flower of his age, amid the joyous hopes of his relatives and his country.

At the close of a successful mission, he reached his native land, and was brought up the Christiana, and landed at "The Rocks," amid the gloom of midnight, to avoid excitement. Yet hundreds of his countrymen went there to welcome his return. The aspect of the hour was melancholy, and the mysterious awe of death threw around the assemblage a sad and solemn silence. No voices were heard, nor the tread of footsteps to disturb the repose of him whom the people delighted to honor. It seemed as if they were breathing a requiem over the grave of the statesman, whose last service was to hail his country with the olive branch of peace.

And in a few days, he bid a sorrowful adieu to the youthful family of his affection. Those bereaved were left to weep and mourn, and the nation to deplore the loss of a great statesman in the prime of life. "And the ambassadors of peace wept bitterly."

James A. Bayard and Cæsar A. Rodney were political opponents, and often took adverse sides at the bar and polls; yet to their honor be it remembered, this opposition never marred their friendship.

Many little events gather consequence by rolling years—for example: such a small affair as a black cockade has been the topic of conversation among men of high order, and discussed in the newspapers. So it would be appropriate here to sketch the history of one.

In the winter of '99 and 1800, a detachment of the United States army was stationed in Wilmington, under Major Cass, who with his family were very popular, and highly esteemed by the best society.

The black cockade was worn by the officers generally, and a lieutenant of this regiment was desirous of having a new one, and his taste was not easily suited. Simple as this was, there was some difficulty in procuring it. The paymaster purchased a handsome one in New York, and having this pattern he solicited Miss D. C. to form it, by whom he was referred to a friend, who promised to try, though it would be her first attempt. The effort succeeded so well that Major Cass requested to wear it.

The young officer apologized for disposing of it, and was presented with a second. The donor, feeling a high regard for the heroes of the Revolution, felt a pride even in doing a trifle for one who had been in his country's service from the battle of Lexington. On the first fire on that occasion—and they heard him repeat this story of his youth —at seventeen years of age, he ran without a coat, with musket in his hand, and took part in the engagement to the end. Then he entered the regular army, where he was continued to the present time ; besides suffering many privations during an Indian warfare.

In 1812, when Mr. Bayard was ready to sail for Europe, the sister of his private secretary, at the request of her brother, from the same individual obtained a similar favor. As it was the custom of those attached to the legation to wear a black cockade, it was made like the former, and when it was sent home, Mr. Bayard saw it, and remarking "it was what he wanted," placed it in his hat, and sent his respects to the manufacturer, "that it would be exhibited in St. Petersburgh, and held in remembrance." Another was made for Mr. Milligan—and thus ends my sketch of the black cockade.

In agitating the best means for the defence of the town during the last war, Mr. Bauduy proposed to overflow the meadows to the Delaware, as a safeguard from an invading enemy by water. But the expense of the plan prevented its adoption, though it was approved. Incessant alarms of an advancing army were prevalent, and caused useless expense by removing valuables, though they originated in fruitful imagination, and many amusing anecdotes might be told.

We close our tour round the environs at a very appropriate spot. On every side, life's checkered scenes have been reviewed. As we have encompassed the city, crossing creeks and rivulets, ascending hills and descending into glens, our path has been strewed with roses and thorns. Here imagination has been cheered by some pleasing reminiscence; there touched with sorrow; on tracing the valued life or noble deeds of a loved or respected one, who through fleeting years had almost passed into oblivion.

CHAPTER IX.

Cemetery—Swede's Church—Ancient Customs—Rev. Erick Biorck—Rev. Petrus Tranberg—Rev. Israel Acrelius, Historian—Mr Benzell—Rev. Lawrence Girelius—His Successors—Chapel—Old Church Dilapidated—Renovated.

MANY, after their tumultuous journey through life, traversing the stormy ocean, climbing icy mountains, or enduring India or Afric's burning sun, have made this noiseless abode their earthly resting-place.

A venerable relic of antiquity, in the midst of a "valley of dry bones," arrests our attention. The loneliness of the sleeping dust, and crumbling stones of the old walls, softened by the gray tint of age and decay, make every sound within the gate reverberate "time's parting knell." If no other inducement than curiosity is felt, one is amply repaid for the trouble of a visit, defaced though it is by time and rude hands.

You can enter this gate, or to the left turn down a lane, overhung by lofty trees of luxuriant growth, where "the fowls of the air have their habitation, and the birds make their nests and sing among the branches," shading the beasts of the field, which are standing harnessed for the service of men. Here let down the bars and pass over. Or you may turn to the right, down the thorn hedge, midst its ocean of foliage, where the mocking-birds build their nest, greeting you with their mimic notes.

Here you cross an old stile—but be cautious in descending its time-worn steps; they seem to remind one to tread lightly over the ashes of the dead. Majestic walnut and oak trees are interspersed through the yard. The wind whispering through the leaves seems to breathe an air of piety, so mournful that it sounds to the listening ear like the sighing of a dirge over the grave of one beloved.

The mouldering wood, and even the iron letters, form sentences on the decayed wall, though partly removed by being torn away or fallen off. From all these relics a thrilling voice is sounded, for it repeats the story of the past, and makes one feel that some ancient sanctity rests here. Wherever our footsteps linger within, on the old brick aisles, or amid the grassy graves, to the mind "all is hallowed." "Memory, like the ark's lone bird, sweeps o'er the past, with a few bright leaves that have not perished," and recalls forms long since glided down the shoreless sea of death, and the final resolving of all things into dust.

Even yon broken spot in the ceiling, which affords a resting-place for the twittering swallow to form a sheltered nest, and perch himself on the old cornice above your head, darting down to provide for his young, is an emblem of decay. And the legends of its remote history seem to whisper, as we narrate its annals, of all those who have here bowed the knee in prayer, or sat under the hearing of the Gospel, or been brought here to moulder into dust. What is now known? Their story may have grown so dim that it is not worth repeating. "So the places that now know us will soon know us no more."

As we view these memorials of death, whose stern decree causes floods of tears in the hearts of the bereaved, we are taught that earthly affection is soon quenched, and that we too are mortal and destined soon to give place to others. This mouldering dust was once as cherished as ours now. While the valued outer robe is mingling with the soil, the immortal soul has winged its flight to an eternal home, and in reality to appear before an omniscient God to receive the plaudit of "Well done, good and faithful servant, enter thou into the joy of thy Lord!" or "Depart from me, I know you not."

These are solemn reflections. The rich man and Lazarus mingle in the same earth. Here are doctors of divinity, law, and physic, the man of science, the honored merchant, farmer, mechanic, and laborer, the lamented matron, the fair lady, the statesman, and brave warrior, who rushed into battle and escaped unscathed with the laurel on his brow, all lie mingling together, and their story ends in—Here they lie, too powerless to crush the worm invading the cell.

In the midst of this ancient cemetery stands the church of our fathers, in sweet seclusion, situated below high hills on the north, and more elevated on the west, sloping to fine meadows embanked on the south and east, and bounded by a graceful bend of the Christiana flowing around, with the Delaware river in full view, giving the whole scene an imposing and picturesque effect.

> "Half screened by the trees, in the Sabbath's calm smile,
>   The church of our fathers, how meekly it stands;
> Oh! villagers, gaze on the old hallowed pile:
>   It was dear to their hearts, it was raised by their hands.
>
> "Who loves not the place where they worshipped their God?
>   Who loves not the dust where their ashes repose?

> Dear even the daisy that grows on the sod,
>   And still dearer the dust is from whence it arose.
>
> " Then say, shall the church which our forefathers built,
>   That the tempests of ages have battered in vain,
>   Be abandoned by us, from supineness or guilt,
>   Oh say! shall it fall by the rash or profane?"

Many recollections of my childhood, in reference to this spot, crowd upon my mind, but they might weary you. A brief statement of the mode of conveyance in those primitive days may not be uninteresting.

Many crossed the Delaware from Jersey in boats; others, from the Christiana and the neck, landed at the rocks; canoes and batteaux were used, although very unsafe. In winter, rough sleighs, sleds on runners, and jumpers, were common, as the snows were deep and lasting. Some went on horseback, with one behind, plunging through the snow. There was no fire in the church, even while they were listening to a long sermon; and there was but one service each week. These religiously disposed people highly valued the privilege of hearing the Gospel preached, and they never allowed the weather to be a hinderance.

In summer, an old-fashioned chair with one horse was in use, and once upon a time there was but one of these. A rough wagon would be geared up on Sunday morning for the use of the family; but riders on horseback were most numerous, and many walked. Even in my day, the very air was clouded with dust, and each one had to beware of accidents from the number of equestrians. Family wagons were the next improvement; and in later years, phætons and chariots. Dr. Wharton rode in the former, and Dr. Girelius in the latter; and after a time, numbers of handsome coaches and carriages were seen in the lane.

On Sunday, the congregation was large; aged people often preferred going on foot. Several of the Stille family are remembered among the pedestrians. A female told me she had been baptized by Mr. Tranberg, had been a regular attendant, walking three miles, and then in her eighty-fourth year. She knew me as the youngest child to attend regular service, and also recollected my ancestors.

An aged female, in conversation to-day, said, "Thirty years ago she often walked from Dupont's Banks. In passing the toll-gate, the keeper would sometimes say, 'Old Aunty is before on her way to church. She is nearly a hundred years old, and can walk miles.'" George Cartmel, from the foot of Shell-pot Hill, walked in every Sunday. He was an aged man, with a staff and three-cornered hat and cue, and is still in remembrance.

On Sunday morning, my venerated grand-sire took me under his fostering wing, and impressed upon my mind that we were going to church to worship God, and that I must sit still, and only rise and kneel when he did so. I was placed upon my seat not to turn my back upon the minister, which in those days was considered disrespectful. If this golden rule for children to sit still during divine service was followed by the present generation, we should have much better order during divine service.

On the road to the Old Ferry we crossed a run, turned through a field to the lane, now Seventh street. Here we were sure to meet a large number of the neighbors' cows hastening towards the church on the ringing of the bell. This practice had been kept up from time immemorial, while the service there was regular. The attraction was good pasture on opening the gate. Once our cow left her companions and followed grandfather to his pew-door.

A gentleman in Germantown told me that his grandfather remembered when most persons in Philadelphia kept cows, and employed a man to drive them to the Commons in the morning and return in the evening. His stand was at the drawbridge; he blew a horn, and the owners opened their gates and the cows assembled, stood until the company had collected; when he blew the signal they all filed off in order.

Some seasons the walking here was very bad, and the good deeds of one poor man deserve our notice. John Canouse, a day laborer, desirous to improve the pathway, prevailed on two or three men to assist him in drawing gravel down to the Ferry Lane from the gate; part of the way he placed posts, laying on the top a piece of scantling, and digging a gutter on the outside. All this was done at his own expense, hoping his example would be followed.

When the Rev. Richard D. Hall was Rector, he had tan laid from town on the path, which was a great improvement. The country members brought in their carts and drew the tan, while the town members displayed their hospitality in providing refreshment for the laborers.

From my earliest recollections, the swallows built their nests in a broken place in the ceiling. In damp weather they were flying over your heads, and were a great annoyance. The pulpit stood between the north porches, on the east side. It was removed somewhere about

1793; the wood is black walnut. The present trimming was in use before the Revolution, and the chancel was in its present position. A small round stand, with a glass basin, was in use as a baptismal font, where thousands in infancy were dedicated to the Lord, and hundreds presented themselves in riper years, who have long since paid the debt of nature and rendered up their account.

The venerable Bible, in use for more than a century, and in occasional use for the last twenty years, is in good order. It was presented by Queen Anne in 1712. In 1820, on rebinding it, the notice of the donor was lost. The silver chalice and plate, presented by the miners of Sweden to Rev. Mr. Biorck, is still in use.

Near the chancel stood the primitive stove, an old cannon, in which the first fire was made, for such comforts were unknown in its early days. I remember well seeing people hover around it before they entered their pews, and the coals raked out on the brick floor to warm the feet. The pipe went through the south window, and high winds blew back the smoke in thick volumes. At other times people were shivering with cold, but these inconveniences were borne with Christian patience. As it was their duty to go to church on Sunday, they did not let a passing cloud or too little fire be an apology for absence.

Long after, a large square stove supplied the west end, greatly increasing comfort, except when the west wind blew. Then we had a thorough smoking, as this pipe passed over the gallery. At length, the old cannon, so often fired, was discharged; and a huge square stove filled its place; it is yet used in the Sunday School, not retained for ornament, but for its uncommon power in dispensing heat.

On Christmas, Peter Davis dressed the church, and there was always green enough and to spare. To adorn this spot was his peculiar pleasure, so he felt the gathering of green no labor.

> "Welcome bright evergreens! the heart doth leap to see you there,
> Year after year, to watch your verdure creep
> Silently eloquent! God's house of prayer;
> Welcome on each return of holy morn,
> When shepherds hailed the Saviour newly born."

At the intersection of the aisles, he sometimes planted a cedar, over which he once dusted flour. If asked why, he said, "Dish make it semble de shnow and tings, and give it de vintry look." Branches like young trees darkened every window. A superabundance of laurel ornamented the pews, where holes were bored to secure it, almost obstructing one's entrance.

The rector ascended the pulpit cautiously, lest his gown should mar some of Peter's tasty fixtures. Entering the south porch, Peter was sure to salute you, wishing you "a happy *Chrismos*," and say, "*Vell! vot dosh my folk tink of my tressing and tings dish Chrismos?*" "Oh, it is very handsome, Peter, and we are pleased with the trouble you have taken." Then Peter, drawing a long breath, would exclaim, "*God be tankful for all dish plessings and tings.*"

That stone in front covers the remains of Petrus Tranberg, rector from 1742 to '48. It is said that all the materials were carried in hand-barrows, and that the women filled their aprons with sand, handing it to the workmen, so anxious were they to have the building completed. It was dedicated on Trinity Sunday, 1799.* The minister wore a white surplice. The collection was over two hundred dollars, and the congregation dined with the rector. Such ample provisions were made that the fragments were carried away. In 1698, William Penn, being so much pleased with their energy, presented them a bill for fifty pounds sterling to aid in the good work.

The belfry was over the northeast porch, the minister's pew on the north side of the chancel. At first the pews were sold; men who had families bought two. The men sat on the left side, the women on the right, advancing to the chancel. The congregation so soon increased that one was given up and the family sat together.

In early days, Sunday collections were made, though discontinued before my day, and only collected for special occasions. During the ministry of the Rev. William Wickes, the amount from a charity sermon was sixty dollars for the Dorcas Society, not attached to this or that church. In the following winter, a collection for the same by Rev. Levi Bull, forty dollars.

Rev. Petrus Tranberg left a widow who long survived to mourn her bereavement. His only son, an officer in the army, was buried here with the honors of war, Andreas Tranberg, and two daughters. At the corner of French Street and Spring Alley stands a relic of more than a hundred years. When built by Mr. T. it was a noble mansion. The workmanship was so superior that people came from New York and Philadelphia to see it, and his descendants occupied it the fifth generation.

Digging down the street has made the only change in the exterior by raising it one story. The interior is much the same. Carved fix-

---

*Said to be on the 4th of July.

tures over the mantle are gone, on which stood fine porcelain jars for ornaments. The walls were decorated with family portraits of Mr. and Mrs. T., &c. Mahogany chairs with high backs, seeming to reach half way up the wall, tables with innumerable legs closely carved, the large silver tankards with lids, &c., and the tiny but rich China cups, all brought from Sweden, are still had in remembrance. A beautiful garden joined one belonging to the parsonage.

The eldest daughter married Col. Benzel, stationed at Crown Point, long before the Revolution. Events which occurred during Mrs. Benzel's residence there were related in my presence to my mother, and though I was a little child, they impressed me with intense interest for the Indian character, and are still fresh in my memory. Those people made frequent visits to the fort, and though they were friendly at times, they were furious when intoxicated, and much dreaded in the absence of the principal officers.

Being fond of exhibiting war scenes for the amusement of the white people, they would propose the war-dance and the war-whoop, and show their manner of using the scalping-knife and tomahawk, and form a ring, place one within as the object of their vengeance. Then they would dance around and sing, and give the war-whoop, with horrid yells, until they became so excited as to be terrific. Yet none dare object, or appear dissatisfied with these exhibitions. One of their chiefs, named Johnson, was a noble fellow, with superior tact to govern them, and if he was present to control them there was no fear.

On his annual visit to Mrs. Benzel, he was accompanied by his wife, a well-behaved, handsome squaw, his two daughters and their governess, who was an accomplished English lady. His family remained at the fort, while he went to New York to make purchases; and he would return, bringing the most costly apparel—and they were agreeable companions. He placed his daughters in a convent, at Montreal, where Col. Benzel's only child was educated.

During their term, a sad catastrophe happened. The soldiers and their wives lived in the fort, and one of the women was boiling fat to make soap; it turned over and set the wood-work on fire. The buildings were constructed of logs, founded on piles, and the magazine, containing a quantity of powder, blew up. The principal officers, and many soldiers were absent on duty, and it continued burning for a month, until the whole was consumed. Numerous women and children were inmates, most of whom made a miraculous escape, having orders to run to the lake and throw themselves on the shore, letting

the fiery logs pass over their heads. The spectacle was awfully magnificent; some were injured, and a few were killed.

Mr. Tranberg's youngest daughter married the Rev. Orloff Parlin, pastor of Wicaco from July 1750 to '67, the year of his decease. His remains lie beneath the chancel, there covered by a stone, which bears a latin inscription, expressive of his learning and piety, and that he was held in great estimation by the community. His widow, with her two young children, returned to her mother, at this family mansion, where they ended life's pilgrimage.

Rev. Israel Acrelius, the historian of the Swedish churches here, came in 1749. He, it is said, recorded more marriages than any other. He baptized my mother according to the Swedish usage, dipping her head partly in a basin of water, at eight days old. In 1756, he returned to Sweden. His portrait was left in the parsonage, now in the lecture room of the chapel, with one of his successors.

Rev. Andreas Boreal, pastor in 1762, was provost over all the Swedish churches. He died, unmarried, in 1767. As there is no memorial of him, some suppose he was not interred here, but my impression is that his remains lie a little space from Mr. Tranberg's; for there was a spot, the size of a tomb, where the bricks were laid across as if to designate the spot for a stone. Besides, my mother would have referred to this removal had it ever taken place. She spoke of all the Swedish clergymen being present at his funeral, that he died on Sunday morning, and that her father was sent for to the church. His disease was jaundice. Many other little incidents were often repeated. He was remarkably handsome, and his manner very attractive.

Most of the missionaries brought their portraits, leaving them as a remembrance. Mr. Heselius, and Lidenius, each left one.

The last Swedish minister here, Rev. Lawrence Girelius, some of us can remember as an accomplished gentleman and scholar of a high order. He was Rector of Trinity Church twenty-three and a half years. In 1791, he left here with the kindest feelings. He was advanced in life, with a young family, for whom ample provision would be made if he died in his native land, but if left here they would be destitute. Thus he was prompted by duty to depart for Sweden. The text of his farewell sermon was, "Oh, Jerusalem, how oft would I have gathered thy children together, as a hen gathereth her chickens under her wings, but ye would not; behold, your house is left unto you desolate."

It was a solemn and touching separation. He had visited in affliction, and hovered around many a dying couch; to the living was a steadfast friend through the woes of life; "now sorrowing most of all for the words he spake, that they should see his face no more." If one of his flock was missing on Sunday, like a faithful shepherd, he made a pastoral visit the following week, and expressed his regret at their absence. This had an effect to secure a regular attendance. There was no weekly service except on some of the holidays.

It is much to be regretted that his last letter to the congregation is lost. It was almost like an epistle from the dead. It was dictated in his last moments, and written by his son as he was about entering the valley of the shadow of death.

It was read by the Rector on the following Sunday after its reception. The most impressive solemnity prevailed during the reading of the good man's parting blessing. With his dying breath a prayer was offered up for the spiritual welfare of his beloved flock at Christiana. They were his early charge, as a missionary in a strange land, then he was their chosen pastor, and had passed with them the most important part of his ministry, leaving them with the kindest feelings to all.

The children of his departed friends, and those with whom he was associated, were remembered in this letter. The ardent affection for this portion of his beloved Zion, and the pious ejaculations, touched the hearts of those who received it as refreshing dew, mingling with their tears grateful recollections of his kind attention and christian sympathy in sorrow's dark hour. And yet this affecting event has passed away "as the early dew," which none seem to remember. "Brethren, my heart's desire and prayer to God for Israel is that they might be saved." "Finally, brethren, farewell; be of good comfort, be of one mind, live in peace, and the God of peace shall be with you." The following is an extract from Mr. Girelius' resignation:—

"Lawrence Girelius, D. D., the last Rector of the Swedish Church in Wilmington, commissary of the Swedish congregations in America, with whom the Swedish mission to America ceaseth—after having continued for near one hundred years, namely, from 1697 to May 8, 1791, when he meaneth to preach his farewell sermon." After having been in America twenty-three and a half years, and lived in this world fifty-two, taking with him to Sweden his wife, Christiana, whose maiden name was Lidenius, thirty-two years old, and children, John Adolphus, going on eleven, Brita Catharina, going on eight, Lawrence Gustavus, going on four, Carl Jacob, ten months old.

For its singularity, I will describe the dress of his eldest son, a boy of nine or ten years of age. John Adolphus Girelius, if living, is a minister in Sweden, and I have heard he was a bishop. His long flaxen hair was powdered, cued, and tied with a black ribbon. A ruffled shirt and cambric stock plaited fine, fastened behind with a buckle set with stone; buff vest and breeches; knee and shoe-buckles set, white silk stockings and black slippers, the buckles of which covered the whole instep; a long-tailed coat, of either scarlet or blue broadcloth, and a three-cornered cocked hat; a gold headed cane. This, his full dress, worn on such occasions, was a miniature of the Swedish court-dress.

During Mr. G.'s pastoral charge here, and during the Revolution, the Rev. Mr. Patterson went to England, leaving his wife under the care of Mr. G., and his business concerns to Joseph Shallcross. He died there, and Mrs. Patterson died here soon after the peace. The tombstone is in good preservation, being well done, and under the inspection of Mr. Shallcross.

A clergyman's widow from Virginia, Mrs. Hamilton, came to reside under his fostering care, and called her abode the "Widow's Retreat," where, with a faithful servant, Belinda, she enjoyed the comforts of life in a small way. Mrs. Hamilton's dignified manner, erect person, low curtsey almost touching the ground, towering head-dress, green calash and rattling silk, with high French heels clicking down the aisle, are not easily forgotten. This worthy lady was removed by death in old age. "All the days of my appointed time will I wait until my change come." Doctor Wharton, of whom we have given a sketch, was successor to Mr. Girelius for a short period.

The next pastor of the Swedish Church was the Rev. Joseph Clarkson. In 1793, the broken place in the ceiling was annoying to the whole congregation, looked at, and talked about often, but was still suffered to remain. But at length two goodly matrons resolved it should be repaired, collected funds, employed workmen, and labored with their own hands. No painting had been done inside before this, and it was a laborious task. The broken places in the ceiling were plastered, the church painted and whitewashed. This was the first improvement of its interior, done through the energy of Mrs. Isabella Crow and Mrs. Margaret Cartmel, who were respectable members of Swedish descent.

In 1812 the Vestry had it thoroughly cleansed and painted. Then the pulpit was spoiled by painting the black walnut. Next the Rev. William Wickes was pastor. A lecture-room in Hanover street was purchased, and a few young men on Sunday afternoons gave religious instructions to larger children, and this was the first attempt at Sunday School teaching in this town. Some of these instructors are at present ministers of the Gospel, viz., Rev. Samuel Brinckle, Rev. S. Stratton, &c.

On the sixth day of June, 1818, a Sunday School, with fifty scholars, was regularly organized under the care of Rev. Levi Bull, Rector of this parish, and very soon it enrolled three hundred scholars, when it was removed to the Academy, by invitation of the worthy Latin teacher, Joseph Downing, who assisted every Sunday. Many scattered sheep were brought back to the fold, and numbers added.

In 1820, by female energy, the church was cleaned, the walls stained, and the brick aisles mended and painted. Besides, the window-curtains, new carpets and cushions, made a great improvement. E. M. made the collections one hundred and thirty-four dollars. The bills were sent receipted to the Vestry, and their vote of thanks to the ladies received.

One cheerful giver, who is "no more," deserves our notice. Isaac Stidham, when asked to contribute, handed a purse filled with silver, and said, "Take what you please, for it rejoices my heart to hear the women have engaged in this good work, and let them call freely on me for assistance to promote any improvement for the interest of my church. I was nine years a member of the Vestry, and did no good thing, nor witnessed any effort in my colleagues. The breach in the ceiling was viewed and talked over every Sunday, until the women aroused, went to work, and had it repaired. My only hope for preventing that ancient edifice from crumbling to ruins rests on the energy and zeal of women."

At a subsequent day this hope was realized. At twelve o'clock on Saturday night it was completed, and Sunday morning one hundred and twenty-eight were confirmed by our venerable Bishop White, and six months after, fifty-seven more. Rev. Richard D. Hall, as a faithful pastor, was rewarded by a harvest of ingathering.

In 1830, a chapel was built in town, while Rev. Isaac Pardee was pastor. At Christmas the Old Church was left for the winter, intending to resume service there on Easter Sunday. The windows being without shutters, were opened and broken, despoiled of curtains, &c. They were so shattered that no attempt was made to repair what reckless mortals had done to aid time in this devastation.

The Old Church had long been mouldering into ruin, and its forlorn state lamented. Much was said and written without effect, until a second proposition was made to remove the bell to the chapel.

This aroused a few, who most strenuously opposed it. Two or three females talked over the disgraceful condition of the church of their ancestors, and resolved on making an effort to resuscitate the venerable pile. Aware of the difficulty, " the lion in their path was met," and one obstacle after another overcome.

" Then contended I with the rulers, and said, Why is the house of God forsaken? and I gathered them together and said, See the distress we are in." " Why should not my countenance be sad, when the place of my father's sepulchre lieth waste!" And they said, "For what dost thou make request?" when I replied, " Come, let us build up the walls, that we be no more a reproach;" and they said, " Let us build." Now an arrangement was made with the vestry, and the women assembled in numbers, much interested, though all declined but six, as money was scarce, on the first suspension of the United States Bank, and they feared a failure.

This little band engaged in it under the guidance of a special Providence, with the whole heart, and soon had the inexpressible pleasure of seeing the work prosper in their hands.

Free-will offerings were sent. Twenty dollars from Mrs. Hammond in France, and one hundred dollars from the Misses McCall of Philadelphia, and many others. Our collections exceeded nine hundred dollars. One-half was roofed anew, new windows with stone sills, which cost twenty dollars were presented by Nelson Clealand. One window shutter, which cost ten dollars, by Mrs. Francis, of Philadelphia; another shutter costing the same by W. H. Keating, of the same place. The east shutter, which was the largest, twenty dollars, by Charles Bush, deducted from the price of the iron gate which he erected, and twenty dollars in work by Elisha Huxley. The bell was secured, a stone wall built on one side of the grave-yard toward which Major Peter Jaquett left the handsome amount of four hundred dollars—and coping was laid around the whole, with an iron gate. So the wall was finished in the year 1837. " It gives us a reviving to set up the house of our God and repair the desolation thereof."

Mrs. A. G., Mrs. A. B., Mrs. E. C., Miss E. M., Misses A. and S. A. H. accomplished this work, intending to place a hipt-roof stone fabric near the gateway, in keeping with the ancient edifice, to be occupied by the person who had charge of the cemetery.

The church was then under the pastoral charge of Rev. Hiram

Adams. That this intention was not completed is now to be regretted, as the present structure is so unsuited, and spoils the antique appearance, besides concealing the view on one side.

The exterior being respectable, induced Miss Henrietta Almond to leave by will seven hundred dollars to repair the interior. The ceiling was renewed, and the gallery with the same pews as of old. Down stairs the pews were so destroyed by rude hands it seemed expedient to place benches, and lay a floor over the bricks. It was painted, and when reopened for occasional worship, such crowds assembled that hundreds could not gain an entrance. They came even from Philadelphia.

The stairs were formerly in the south porch that led to a balcony, the entrance into the gallery. The rise and progress of this church is so well known as a matter of history that it needs no comment. This being the only detail of its fall and restoration, is our apology for minuteness. As we may have wearied you with repairs, we will conclude with a new subject more entertaining to the youthful mind.

CHAPTER X.

A Ghost Story—Esquimaux—Cemetery—Solemn Funeral—A Sad Accident—Dr. Capelle—Adventures of a French Soldier—Dr. Bayard.

ONCE upon a time a story was afloat that a ghost was seen in the old churchyard. However, the present generation are too enlightened to give credence to such legends, which, without patronage, must die, and this was almost gone.

A spot better fitted up for a ghost story could hardly be imagined. Here was an old church, isolated in the midst of an ancient cemetery, surrounded by the remains of departed ages; an old bell which had tolled at each funeral rite for upwards of a hundred years. There, too, were lofty old sycamores, which had shaded many an animal from the burning rays of the sun in this lane, and while the master was listening to the sound of the Gospel within, they enjoyed this outside shade, for the merciful man has mercy for his beast. Trees and thornhedges, inhabited by feathered songsters tuning their varied notes, made this a rural spot.

To add to this fitness, the Christiana, with its inimitable bend, was flowing at the foot of the yard, and this was a stream traversed in bygone days by the notorious buccaneer Blackbeard, by whom it was said much booty had been buried on the banks. And tales were in remembrance of men digging for the treasure, and seeing hobgoblins and Jack O'Lanterns who led them astray at the moment of success. The rocks within sight were his landing-place, and even in my day silly men went there to dig for money.

Well, a wonderful incident revived the extinguishing embers of this story. On a clear hot night in summer no one is disposed to retire early. About twelve o'clock the old bell rung. It was very strange. There could be no mistake in the sound, for it was a first-rate bell for its size. What could it mean? Every one was aroused. At daydawn the sexton went down to examine, and found all right, and it was impossible to ring it without entering the gallery, as the stairs were on the outside. A massive door opened in a balcony within the south porch, and it was fastened with a huge lock brought from Sweden, which few, even with the right key, could unlock.

The same hour on the succeeding night it rang again. Now it was minutely investigated, but no clue appeared to unravel the mystery, and it became the chit-chat of the whole vicinity. A third was watch-night till long past the time. But no sooner had the watch left than ding dong went the old bell. Three successive nights! How ominous! One thought it portended war, another famine, a third concluded pestilence was the most probable. Well, this was as superstitious as the belief in ghosts, which did not bear the light of the age. So conjecture was at its wit's end.

On the following day some Esquimaux Indians, who had been here a few days, having their canoes of skin about three yards long, with a hole in the middle to get in with their feet, and a paddle in each hand, proposed to exhibit their skill on the Christiana this afternoon, if some expert boatmen would race with them. Thousands assembled at the bridge and wharves to witness this novel exercise, and it was really amusing to see how swift these canoes could glide over the water round the boats, splashing the men with their paddles, wetting them all over. At sunset the sport ended.

Two young girls, previous to going to the bridge, had been to the old church, where one left her bag in the balcony. Now, here was a sad dilemma. What could she do? Not go home without her bag. At last her friend agreed to accompany her, and wait outside the fence. So with fear and trembling she started into the yard, and found the lost treasure in the balcony, but in descending the steps screamed aloud, fainted, and fell! The other ran, called men to her assistance from the brick-yard, who carried her home insensible.

A physician was sent for, who found her ill. Days elapsed before she revived a little to give an account of the cause of her alarm as follows: She was not much afraid, as it was yet daylight, but in coming down the steps, the rays of the setting sun glittered so beautifully on the creek, her attention was for the moment arrested. As she moved her eyes from this object, the bushes in a thicket at the lower part of the yard were in motion. This alarmed her, and her strength failed.

Instantly she saw the skeleton of a man arise; his head was distinct above the bushes; then her heart went pit a pat; she felt the hair rise on her head; now powerless she saw a human hand uplifted, and with a large bright knife sever the head with one blow. She screamed and fell insensible, and remained so for days.

This girl was of an age to discern aright, had the character of telling the truth; besides, her condition made it evident that something more than ordinary must have happened.

This, added to the unaccountable tolling of the bell, fanned the embers of the dying story until it flew on the wings of the wind, gathering as it went. One would say, "What do you think?" A sage one, famed in legendary lore, could relate the adventures of her grandfather in pursuing ghosts; another the nurse story of haunted houses; each one well authenticated, while a third one had read a very long mysterious affair, related by a clergyman on his own veracity. These added to the budget. Yet no one was in the least superstitious; no, indeed! This generation was too enlightened to give credence to ghost stories.

Notwithstanding their assertions, and the wisdom of the age, all were on the tip-toe of curiosity to unravel the mysterious affair, and we know not the extent to which imagination would have led many had not the story been unraveled by the honest avowal of two boys, in search of fishing-rods, who went to the thicket at the time mentioned. One found the skeleton of a horse's head, and held it up just as the other struck his knife to cut a rod. The stroke caused it to fall from his hand. So ends this ghost story; and it is supposed that some one placed a ladder against the belfry window, and ascended in that way to ring the bell. The quietness and rural scenery of this sequestered spot has passed away; no longer to be admired for the green fields, lofty oak trees, thorn hedges, or melodious songsters. Even the frogs seem to have sought more retirement. Within a few years all have vanished, and their places filled by whole streets of houses occupied by the human family.

While we are in this old grave-yard, we will sketch some reminiscences of the departed. It may be proper, in rescuing this relic from the ravages of desolation, to notice one of our associates, Mrs. Eliza Cox, who speedily left her earthly labors, and her soul winged its flight beyond the grave, while her mortal part lies beneath these sods.

Years have rolled down the stream of time, since at yon old chancel she knelt and vowed to serve the Lord. The love enkindled in her bosom for the spot, it ever burned brightly, prompting her to aid in its prosperity; and few were more efficient, though without wealth or much influence. She did a good part because her heart was warm, and her purse and hands never closed to charity.

In this town, most benevolent societies sustained a loss in her death; while her private acts deserve especial notice, for they were of rare character. Many are as ready to relieve an afflicted friend, and even make sacrifices to oblige; but I have never known one so ready to leave her domestic concerns, set aside prejudice, selfish feeling, &c., and enter the most loathesome abode of poverty, unawed by disease, regardless of unworthiness, and strive with all her powers to alleviate suffering. "The blessing of him that was ready to perish came upon me, because I delivered the poor that cried, and him that had none to help him."

That gray stone, some distance south of the porch, cut like a heart at the top, is I believe the most ancient in the yard. The inscription written in capital letters, with no pointing, it is hard to decipher. It commemorates William Vandever, who lived about 1700, and is quite a curiosity in the present day.

On the east is the tomb of Hon. Samuel White, U. S. Senator. He was extremely handsome, and of noble appearance, and died in the prime of life unmarried. His country lost a worthy citizen, and his friends an acceptable companion. By his side lies his worthy friend Dr. Horsey. To the eastward lies Dr. Dale, who once felt a deep interest in the prosperity of this church, who was suddenly called from his youthful family to rest in yon tomb, and when his useful labors ceased, many mourned his loss.

On the south side, without a stone to mark the spot, lie the remains of Peter Caverly, Esq., a worthy son of Delaware, who resided some years in Wilmington, and was cashier of the Farmers' Bank. He was suddenly called from his labors to leave an interesting family to mourn. Mrs. Matilda Caverly was an estimable lady, long a valued member of Trinity Church.

Here also lie the remains of a surgeon in the Revolution, Dr. George Stevenson. Though advanced in age, his appearance was as in the prime of life, fine looking, his faculties unimpaired, and his manner polished. A large family and many friends lamented his loss. "But man dieth and wasteth away. Yea, a man giveth up the ghost, and where is he?"

Rev. W. Price and two wives are interred near the south porch. Rev. Ralph Williston, when Rector, lost an estimable and beautiful wife. In the twinkling of an eye, she was summoned to leave nine children, the oldest sixteen, the youngest an infant not even of days. This mournful event awakened general sympathy, and as the solemn interment was unusual, a sketch may not be inappropriate. An immense procession waited the arrival of expected friends, until day had nearly closed—then in solemn stillness they proceeded to the gate.

> The evening clock had tolled, and hark! the bell
>   Of death beats slow. Heard ye the note profound?
> It pauses now: and now, with rising knell,
>   Flings to the hollow wind its mournful sound.
> Yes; a mother's corpse is on yon sable bier,
>   Where cold and wan the slumberer rests her head;
> In still small whispers to reflection's ear,
>   She breathes the solemn dictates of the dead.

The late lamented Rev. Wilson Prestman, in a deep and touching voice, pronounced, "*I am the resurrection and the life; whosoever believeth in me, though he were dead, yet shall he live.*"

The evening was clear and calm; the sun had retired beyond the western hills; but its faint beams glistened on the water. The long shadows of evening were thrown over the noble trees, as the mantle of sorrow enwrapt the multitude who had assembled to behold the mournful sight of eight young children following to the grave a devoted mother, taken in the flower of life.

As the words "*earth to earth, ashes to ashes, dust to dust,*" were heard, and the sad sound on the coffin, aided by twilight and the soft reflection of the moon, an awful silence pervaded the company. No confusion marred the solemn order. Naught was heard but infant sobs, though it was supposed three thousand persons were present. The inhabitants said, "This is a grievous mourning, indeed."

A sad disaster befell a sister of the deceased on her return to New York. Mr. Williston resigned her, on board of the boat at Philadelphia, to the care of a gentleman who promised to escort her home. They were strangers to each other. It was the gray dawn of morning, and he only saw a tall lady dressed in black.

Two opposition boats started at the same hour, and resolved upon a race. Rounding from the wharf occasioned a slight accident, which caused alarm. The captain imprudently expressed his fears that this boat would sink, which threw the passengers into confusion. They all ran to one side except Miss R.; she sprang into the small boat at the stern. It turned, and she fell into the river. Some one cried "There is a person overboard;" but it was unheeded.

The captain of the other boat, now ahead, saw the plunge, lessened his steam, jumped into the boat, and caught her by the hair at the moment she was sinking exhausted by her long struggle. She was rolled in blankets, and laid in the berth.

In the meantime, as they were sitting down to breakfast, Dr. McLane inquired of Miss R's escort "where she was?" He replied, "In the ladies' cabin," as she declined taking breakfast. The Dr. rose to insist upon her taking some refreshment, but could not find her. A general alarm ensued, and now it was announced that some one had fallen overboard, and the captain was freely censured for his indifference. They hoped she had been rescued by the persons in the other boat, as they had observed them letting off steam.

The moment it was possible, the doctor went to her assistance, and found her almost lifeless, and they were making an effort to take her on deck; but the draught of air would have caused instant death. By the greatest care she revived; was taken to Philadelphia. Dr. McLane watched over her until morning. By skill and kindness, she partially revived. Weeks elapsed ere she could take one step; and her hands and feet remained black, though in time she recovered. "All thy billows and waves passed over me."

A sorrowful incident of more recent date will end the record of the rectors of this parish. When a stranger, the Rev. J. W. McCullough lost an estimable and interesting wife, who left four children, one an infant of days, to weep over the loss of a mother. Sympathizing strangers poured in oil and wine to heal this wound of an afflicted family, and a monument is here erected to her memory.

In our reminiscences, we have not observed chronological order, because we relate from memory facts as they are revived, either passed under our own observation or collected in past days, from well authenticated sources. An extraordinary funeral procession, in the Masonic order, is next related.

Dr. Capelle, a surgeon in the French army, who came with General Lafayette, and served through the Revolutionary war, after peace was declared, made this town his residence, and married a young lady from Maryland. He was much respected as a practitioner and a gentleman, but died, after a short illness, in 1796, leaving his widow and children to mourn an affectionate husband and father.

Respect for his memory, and the display of a procession, gathered a large company at his funeral. He was to be interred with Masonic honors. The coffin was deposited, and the funeral services of the church performed; musicians were engaged to sing, and while concluding the hymn, "Vital spark of heavenly flame," &c., suddenly it grew dark, and a high wind which had prevailed increased almost to a hurricane; some crows which had perched on the old sycamores, in the lane, were routed, and the gale being so strong that they could not soar, descended among the people, flapping their wings over the grave.

This strange incident terrified the ignorant, who were prepossessed with the idea that the Free Masons had dealings with evil spirits, and now this was confirmed to their own senses, for they saw the little black demons flitting around, while darkness and thunder, and wind, awfully terrific, seemed their appropriate element. Attributing the whole to Masonic mystery, they sprang over the wall and ran for life, and the event led to great speculative argument on the science of Masonry. "And his servants said to him, Behold, there is a woman that hath a familiar spirit at Endor; and Saul disguised himself, and put on other raiment, and he went, and two men with him, and they came to the woman by night."

Another French physician claims our notice. Dr. Bayard emigrated here during the troublesome times in France; he purchased the house corner of French and Kent streets; he did not practice, but, as a benevolent man, gratuitously gave advice in cancerous and scrofulous diseases, in which he was eminently successful. His patients were kept under strict diet, often provided in his own house, at his expense, if they were poor. Those are living to testify to his benevolence.

In 1797, many distinguished persons followed him to the grave. "The steps of a good man are ordered by the Lord."

Mrs. Ann Armor, a worthy member of this church, and whose family in those days were among our most respectable farmers, in whose mansion so many friends were hospitably entertained, followed him to the grave with the deepest expressions of grief. As his patient, she now felt her own case hopeless. "I am bowed down greatly, I go mourning all the day." She, too, was soon after borne to this ancient cemetery.

Here, too, lies a French soldier, of whose interesting adventures we will give a brief sketch. This man entered the army with Bonaparte, and accompanied him in his campaign in Egypt, through all his hardships, privations, and dangers; and, as a war-worn soldier, ended life's career in this quiet town.

In 1812, he lived near us, and as a machinist toiled hard. He was employed by E. J. Dupont, and his industrious habits and cheerful disposition attracted notice, especially as most of his life had been spent in the field of battle or in a camp. He rose at daydawn, and sung at the anvil, while his wife often blew the bellows; none seemed more happy. Their only child was an interesting little girl four years old, and the admiration of all who saw her. The parents, though coarse in appearance, inherited the national civility and pleasing manner.

One stormy day a most respectable French colored woman, Lorette Noels, came in tears to ask counsel of my mother, what could be done for this lovely little one, alarmingly ill. The parents were in deep distress. The mother could not speak English, and the father but imperfectly. In this dilemma it was concluded my services would be acceptable, as I had a smattering of French. On entering the room I perceived her disease to be croup in the highest state.

An old French doctor was present, giving barley water, &c., and no one dare to interfere, though it was evident such powerless remedies could not be efficient. I remained to do what I could, and was amazed to hear, when she could speak, expressions from this sensitive little sufferer, entreating her mother not to cry, for soon she would be in paradise, where suffering would be no more. This parent's grief was excessive, and the father's violent, who could not restrain his feelings. In a few hours this lovely little one fell asleep to awake in heaven.

As soon as the mother was convinced that the spirit of her darling had fled to a calmer rest, she laid her on the couch, and knelt by the side in perfect composure, offered up her prayer, in thanks to her Heavenly Father, for all his mercies in preserving her through life; then for the release of her darling child from suffering, and for her removal from a world of sin and sorrow in the days of her innocency, to be conveyed to Abraham's bosom; most ardently imploring his grace to strengthen her resignation to his will under the sad bereavement.

Never had I witnessed such apparent Christian submission as exhibited in this woman, who, like David, said, "While the child was alive I fasted and wept; but now he is dead, can I bring him back again? I shall go to him, but he will not return to me."

The father was absent at the moment of dissolution; when he entered and saw she was gone, for a moment he was powerless. Then starting back flung himself on the couch, choking with sobs, in a paroxysm of wild grief; seized the corpse, ran up stairs with it in his arms. Then rushed into the yard, frantically exclaiming, "Who shall I work for now?" and in incoherent sentences, screamed, "My beloved Mary Anne, will you leave me? leave your doting father? No more cheer me with your sweet voice! To lighten my labor and soothe my cares! I cannot, no, I cannot live without my sweet baby."

The scene was thrilling to witness; a rough old soldier so agonized with grief, as David, on another afflicting event, "went up to the chamber over the gate and wept. O! my son Absalom, would to God I had died for thee, O Absalom, my son, my son!"

No Catholic cemetery was within six miles, and the snow was unusually deep. J. I—— was aware of this, and I proffered to secure a spot in this yard near the part appropriated to foreigners. My offer was gratefully received, and the Rector performed the service for the dead. Through the kindness of neighbors, all was done decently and in order. One good neighbor, Cyrus Newlin, employed two men to clear a path. Their gratitude to me was unceasing. The mother, past eighty, now living alone, assured me last week, that from the hour of her child's death she had daily offered thanks to God for removing her darling from a world of temptation and sin.

This afflictive dispensation led to the relation of their romantic story, as follows:

J. Isambrie was a soldier in the army of Bonaparte, from his rise and progress, in all his victories until his return from Egypt. Then he was sent to St. Domingo, where he was taken prisoner by the British, and brought to Canada. His wife was a native of St. Domingo, but married at Paris, where she lived at the time of his capture, and heard that he was in North America. She despaired of meeting him again, and came with a family to reside in Philadelphia, unacquainted with the English language.

After six months' residence there, as she was washing the front door steps, with her dress pinned up, two Frenchmen passed, who were conversing about J. Isambrie. On the sound of his name, she dropped her bucket and brushes, entreating those men to tell her of whom they spoke. They replied—"He was a blacksmith, living in Southwark, and had been a soldier in Egypt with Bonaparte." She told her story in few words.

They were on their way to see him. And her own description of the scene was, "Den de mans did run; and vid no bonne, no put down dress, Mam Bassee, I did fly tru de stree, and all de peop did call vot de mat, vot ail de uman, is he craze? Den me cum to de plas; an vid de own eye, see me mon vurk! O, Mam Bassee, me most die; for why! me feel so much de joie to see me Josef once more, me own Josef." "Then Joseph made himself known, and he wept aloud." Some time after their re-union they came to Wilmington.

The gentlemen visited his shop, and listened to details of the campaign in Egypt, endeavoring to elicit his views of stories circulated respecting the cruelties inflicted by order of Bonaparte. He was intelligent, but positively denied the whole, though he denounced war, and said he had aided in the slaughter of thousands, that he now shrunk with horror from the reflection of such scenes of carnage. Yet such was his infatuation, Bonaparte was an idol, and he could not endure to hear him censured; would say, "the other potentates of Europe were worse, Bonaparte could not fight alone;" always concluding his remarks by saying, "Bonaparte loved his soldiers, and they loved him, who submitted to the same toils and privations."

Joseph Isambrie was a great sportsman. Distinguished French gentlemen often called on him to gun; General Moreau and Marshal Grouchy, and others. On an unlucky day, his gun burst and shot off three of his fingers. Doctor Didie would not permit his hand to be amputated, consequently the lock-jaw ensued, of which he died. Much feeling was expressed. His industrious habits and correct morals had won the good will of his neighbors, and this was more strange, as he had so long led the reckless life of a soldier. Though the conclusion may seem strange, it is no less true, that this same Doctor Didie was the physician who attended his wife's family in St. Domingo, and the first who knew her who nursed him in his last illness in Wilmington, and shrouded him for the grave.

Another grave, without a stone to commemorate the spot, attracts our notice, where lies the mortal part of an interesting young lawyer of great promise, Joshua Gordon Brinckle. He was endowed with high intellectual powers and correct principles, for he was piously disposed; his exterior was prepossessing and manly. Being engaged in an important suit at New Castle Court, where he spoke some hours with a sore throat, on his return he retired to his chamber, from which, in thirty-six hours, his noble spirit winged its flight to the other world, leaving the inanimate clay to mingle with the dust, and like a dead leaf in autumn, he lies buried out of sight.

But we trust the spirit has renewed its verdure in immortal spring. "As for man, his days are as grass; as the flower of the field, so he flourisheth, for the wind passeth over it and it is gone, and the place thereof shall know it no more."

On the east lie the remains of a revolutionary officer, Major D. J. Adams. He married in this town. After the peace he was brigadier-general of the militia, then sheriff of this county, and was engaged in commerce, when death summoned him to his abode in the tomb. A widow with eight children were left to mourn their sad bereavement.

CHAPTER XI.

Sketch of Miss Vining—Ex-President Jefferson—Gen. Lafayette—Duke de Liancourt—Duke d'Orleans—Gov. Dickinson—John Vining, Esq.—Mrs. V.—Miss V.—Visits Philadelphia—Wm. Henry Vining—Decease of three brothers—Miss V.—Closing Scene—Jane Mauthrell—Mrs. Curtz—Alice Hough.

From the following brief biography, a few facts may be gleaned of a distinguished individual, who flourished amid renowned men of an eventful day, and of whom it may be said—"A woman is of few days, and full of trouble, cometh forth like a flower and is cut down, fleeth as a shadow and continueth not." What though the brightest hues of the bow of promise arch her morning dawn, and the meridian sun in glorious splendor crown her with unrivaled celebrity, the clouds of adversity and disappointed hopes may overcast her evening with sorrow.

In tracing this fair lady through the vicissitudes of her life, first in the fashionable circle in which she moved, and adorned as a brilliant star, glittering and dazzling the centre, encircled by nobles of the land; her rare beauty and graceful form commanded admiration; intellectual endowments, a mind stored with historical knowledge, and sparkling effusions of wit, entertained the literati, and amused the joyous. Her fluency in speaking the French language attracted distinguished men of every nation, giving her a notoriety in foreign climes.

On the authority of Ex-President Jefferson, when he was introduced at the Court of France, Queen Marie Antoinette spoke with enthusiastic ardor of Miss Vining, and her desire to see one of whom she had heard such flattering encomiums. Mr. Jefferson observed his reply did not tend to lessen this feeling, as he felt a pride on hearing an American lady so extolled at one of the most polished courts in Europe. Again, her name was mentioned with admiration at the English Court, in the reign of George III., and likewise at the Court of Germany.

The era of this belle commenced in the revolution. Her associates were the officers of the different armies, and leading characters of those momentous times, giving her a celebrity rarely attained. A correspondence with some of these eminent men continued, and with General Lafayette until her death. She was then engaged in writing a history of the American Revolution.

With all her mental endowments, there was a peculiarity of habit, leaving no doubt that yielding to admiration was a leading foible. Caressed and admired without, and adored within her own domicil, she gained an ascendency over most persons. One peculiarity was to conceal part of a beautiful face. If you ask how could this be done, or why, it is not easily answered. A veil thrown over her face, or a fan, &c.; in later years, a cap. Another peculiarity was never, or rarely, to be seen in the street except in riding. Therefore, we suppose, her motto was, "Beauty rarely seen is most admired." Another query may arise, why one so much admired was never married? Many engagements were reported, and death dissolved the first and last, in youth and age.

If distinguished foreigners visited the vicinity of her abode, an introduction to Miss Vining was solicited. Among her guests was the Duke de Liancourt, and the Duke d'Orleans, late King of the French, Louis Phillippe, and the remembrance of his arrival is impressed on memory. The notorious General Miranda once passed through here in the mail at night, and left his card in the post-office for Miss Vining.

Distinguished men were frequent guests of Governor Dickinson, and when invited to dine, Miss V. was often the only lady present not of his family.

Having sketched the brilliant career of her early days, we pause ere we enter upon another era of her eventful life.

A brother of great promise was elected to represent this State in Congress, at as early an age as the U. S. Constitution would admit members. In by-gone days it was not usual to advance young men to such high honors. His intellectual powers acquired him fame, and he was styled the pet of Delaware, as he was the pride of his household. An ample fortune, a widowed mother's fondness, and a sister's celebrity, flattered his ambition. Even in the legislative halls, amidst great men, he had a name and a fair prospect of promotion.

Mr. Vining married Miss Seaton, of New York. It was said when her father inquired what were his prospects, his reply was, "*Sir, my prospects are unbounded!*" So little did he reflect on the evanescent nature of earthly greatness. High in rank, encircled by rich and influential friends, he trusted in his own powers as a shield and buckler. His brilliant talents, not nourished by application, withered in the bud. Indolence and generosity engendered extravagance that wasted his substance.

His interesting and lovely wife, in deep affliction, as gloom overshadowed her once cheerful abode, bemoaned her blighted hopes, and as a child of sorrow was consigned to an early grave.

Mrs. Vining ofttimes wrote poetry, and we have before us some verses composed by her on the birth of her last infant; wherein she speaks of the deep affliction of losing both her parents, and we give an extract of the first and the last two verses.

> Ah! tender infant of my hopes and fears,
>   With trembling joy I fold thee in my arms;
> Thou com'st in happy time to check my tears,
>   And sooth my sorrows with thy opening charms.
>
> *   *   *   *   *   *
>
> Sure, lovely little infant, but for thee,
>   I soon had sunk beneath this weight of grief;
> For thee I strove to bear the sad decree,
>   And forced my tortured soul to seek relief.
>
> May wisdom, virtue, prudence gild thy days,
>   Make heaven thy stay, the only and the first;
> Live happy, when thy mother and her lays
>   Are buried in obscurity and dust.

Hon. John Vining had fallen, then drooped and died in the flower of his age. "How are the mighty fallen." "Tell it not in Gath." His mourning sister was now guardian to four small orphan boys, her income reduced to a scanty pittance by his mismanagement. "I am distressed for thee, my brother! Very pleasant hast thou been to me."

Those adverse circumstances forced this gifted lady to live in seclusion in her retreat at the Willows (a small house adjoining W. Rogers, Esq.,) and was but once tempted to stray from her solitude. An intense interest for those beloved nephews, on the dawn of the second to manhood, induced her to visit Philadelphia to intercede in person for his welfare.

Then, as a twinkling star bursting through a dark cloud for a moment, soon retired again to obscurity. But neither the seclusion for a lapse of years, nor the twilight of her day, withered her powers of attraction. A multitude, among whom were eminent men, crowded around this faded belle, who was evidently the central star, even amid youthful beauty, but a few years before her closing scene!

Our notice of her has been limited by personal appearance and and worldly estimation. No allusion has been made to the refined feelings of the heart. Nursed in the lap of indulgence, educated in luxury, flattered by the great, sustained by beauty, talents, and wit, it would be singular if she had been free from vanity and ambition. But in life's checkered way, her character was displayed anew.

In declining years, in comparative poverty, and loss of friends, an infant family was thrown upon her care to be fostered by her scanty means, which demanded great self-denial and sacrifice of personal enjoyment. In this new sphere we see her rise above every selfish feeling; her heart, talents, and resources were devoted to the orphans. No mother could have done more to guard them in infancy, and guide them in youth.

Beholding her adopted sons rising to men of promise, and realizing her fondest hopes, it seemed the veil of gloom that so long had overhung her dwelling was now dispersed, and the setting sun was gilding her evening hours with peace and hope. Three of those youths were no longer dependent on their kind aunt.

One, of superior talents, the pride of her heart, with a manly form and an intellectual face, was patronized by his uncle, Mr. Ogden, of New York, and was reading law. This was a most painful separation; but the unyielding doom of stern necessity demanded the sacrifice for his future prosperity. On the morning of his departure from home, excited feeling forbade his bidding adieu; as a gifted poet, he left a farewell address "*to my beloved aunt at the Willows,*" "*the guardian of my infant days and friend of my youth.*" It was well written and highly prized. Henry Vining, like the night-blooming cereus, that opens for a few hours, sheds its fragrance and dies, was prepared to practice law with the brightest prospects, when he was attacked by that withering disease consumption, and only survived his aunt a few months. Thus was she spared the anguish by her previous passage to the grave. He was the second son. On a voyage to the West Indies in pursuit of health, he wrote a few verses, which were found in his pocket after death—"Lines by William Henry Vining, of Wilmington, written at sea." We have taken an extract of two verses:—

> "Yet not from thirst of fame or wealth,
>   I left the lovely haunts of home;
> For thee, for thee, inconstant health,
>   O'er ocean's dreary waste I roam.

*   *   *   *   *   *

> "With intellectual thoughts that shake
> My struggling spirit's steadfast aim,
> With all the ills that bend, that break
> This trembling heart, this feverish frame."

The two elder were providing for themselves, and looked forward to the future with confidence and hope; fully appreciating their honored aunt's solicitude in their infancy, promised consolation and support in her declining years. But, alas! these cherished buds of hope, ere they bloomed, withered at her feet. The eldest, in the navy, came home indisposed, soon sickened; "behold at eventide trouble, and before morning he is not."

The youngest, on the eve of his departure to make his way through life, was hastened to his youthful grave. The second son died young amid strangers. Again the mantle of sorrow was thrown over this desolate home; with weeping and mourning, "for the hay is withered, the grass faileth, there is no green thing left at the Willows."

As Miss Vining's evening shadow lengthened and earthly hopes faded, she viewed the past as "vanity and vexation of spirit," and sought happiness in religion's ways, the only path to peace. This lofty spirit, which had never bowed, was made willing in meekness and deep humility to bow at the foot of the cross. Christmas day was determined for her union with the church. A stormy morning and heavy rain were a barrier to its fulfillment. With intense anxiety this failure was lamented to the Rev. R. D. Hall. On Easter Sunday she determined to surmount every obstacle she could in the path of duty.

As the morning of Good Friday dawned, her soul winged its flight to mansions in the skies, and on Easter Sunday afternoon, the rector from whom she had anticipated to receive the bread and wine as spiritual food to nourish the soul, saw the perishing body deposited in the earth, and performed the solemn service "dust to dust." Her funeral was imposing; six ladies, with about three yards of white linen drawn over the bonnet tied under the chin, hung loose. Not a stone marks the spot of this once celebrated belle. "Thy nobles dwell in the dust." "They flee away, and the place is not known where they are."

In 1821, about sixty-three years of age, death closed the scene; not a gray hair mingled with the soft glossy brown, nor a wrinkle on the brow marred the beauty of an incomparable forehead. Few females are less personally known at home, and none more celebrated abroad than was Miss Vining. Even amid neighbors who were most desirous to see her, many were never favored with a passing glance. But a few fleeting years have rolled over us, and one the theme of admiration is forgotten. Some may ask who was Miss Vining? Or did you ever see her? While many others never heard of this belle.

The following lines, which for some time remained in her chamber, are consistent with the kindness of her heart, and her sympathy for the members of her own family as well as of her feeling for her friends in affliction.

> "By angels caught, all hallowed as they flow,
> Are tears we shed for sorrows not our own;
> The bosom beating for another's woe
> Wafts its own incense to the heavenly throne."

A small tribute is likewise due to a worthy woman of her household, Jane Mauthrell, who, with warm Irish affection, managed her domestic concerns. She had been brought up by Mrs. Vining, and was instructed as a good housekeeper, and waited on this lady in the noon of life, midst gayety and pleasure. In the evening of adversity, she was a companion and friend. By her economy and attention, Miss V. was aided in providing for the orphans, over whose tender years J. M. watched with a mother's fondness, and guided their childhood in virtue's ways; in sickness she was their nurse, and in death closed the eyes of three—one died among strangers—and none more deeply mourned their fate.

In searching the memory for reminiscences connected with this ancient church, we turn over things new and old. Legends and every musty relic of its early days are so graciously received, that we sketch a few of recent date, to which succeeding years may add a deeper interest. As small causes often effect great consequences—from an acorn springs the majestic oak—so the following sketch of a tiny slip from a withered branch, planted in a cold soil and struggling for years, has put forth a hopeful bud, which if nourished with care may yet blossom as the rose, and shed a sweet fragrance over this part of the Lord's vineyard. If watered freely by streams of liberality, a noble institution may arise; flourishing like the green bay-tree and shadowing forth rich verdure, as a goodly heritage, where the aged and infirm may cease from labor and be at rest.

When time has fleeted away, some one may inquire how it originated. Then the King of Terrors may have chilled each warm heart, deadened every active hand, and silenced the only voice that can recount the story.

Yon headstone near the gate commemorates a lonely widow. How affecting to look upon one friendless and bowed down by age, her lowly cabin darkened by the cloud of adversity, no longer able to toil for her scanty meal, a dependent on the cold hand of charity! Such was the condition of Mrs. Elizabeth Curtz.

> "Turn not away, ye happier, from her door,
> Nor shun the widow helpless now and poor,"

for "blessed is the man that provideth for the sick and needy; the Lord shall deliver him in time of trouble."

Three neighbors, compassionating her condition, provided her with sustenance; aided by her pastor, Rev. R. D. Hall, to systemize, their charity served on alternate days. As the years glided by, Mrs. C. E. united with them. This widow had passed four-score, and living alone caused much anxiety to her benefactresses, as the shades of autumn were closing, to make arrangements for the inclement winter.

At this time an event awakened their sympathy for another destitute female. Death had borne away the elder of two aged spinsters, who had passed a long life together in harmony. Hester and Alice Hough were celebrated spinners of every variety of stocking yarn. In olden times, stockings were manufactured at home, and every female taught to knit, however it may seem incredible. A daughter of Rev. J. Clarkson knit her own stockings from four years of age. So these women were important persons, and well known to the community.

As their cottage and implements of labor would be a curiosity now, a sketch would not be amiss. Wintry storms and frosts were excluded by a fixture at the front door, like a box. The interior, by its simple furniture, indicated poverty, and when the labors had ceased, two large and two small spinning-wheels were set aside. A reel, fine and coarse cards, and a hackle occupied half of the room.

In looking around this humble apartment where the absence of comfort and apparent means of happiness were displayed, you were agreeably surprised at the cleanly appearance of the rustic inmates, and their countenances beaming with cheerfulness and content. A holiday dress was a light blue calimanco skirt, shining like satin, without spot or wrinkle, and a clean calico short gown, white apron, and thin handkerchief neatly pinned, with a long-eared and high-crowned cap and roller. So ancient looking were they you might supposa they had dressed in Noah's Ark.

On the mantel, an hour-glass, with its wooden frame and portion of sand, kept true time. A library, consisting of two volumes of almanacs preserved from time immemorial, yearly adding a new number, were hung on either side of the fire-place, and became thoroughly smoked. These scientific reminiscences were studied with care; and it would surprise you to hear them tell to a minute, exactly, when the sun rose and set, the length of the day, changes of the moon, its influence on the mind and on vegetables; when to sow seed and plant roots, cure meat and make soap; point you to the morning and the evening star, and tell when it was flood or ebb tide,

"Till your wonder grew
That two small heads could carry all they knew."

Yet their knowledge pursued a higher theme. On the top of a rude press lay a large Bible, and on Sunday it was perused with diligence, and few were more familiar with the lives of the patriarchs, the bondage and wandering of the Hebrews, travels and doings of the apostles. But soaring higher they studied it as a spiritual guide to instruct them in the precepts of the golden rule of "doing to others as we would have others do to us," and this precept was obeyed, and it was a lamp to enlighten their pathway to the grave.

Hetty, being robust and active, did the errands; while poor Alice was a stranger to the world in which she had passed four-score years, and rarely ventured beyond the precincts of her habitation, or gazed on other objects than her walls embraced. Her condition aroused sympathy, and the almshouse seemed to offer her the only asylum.

On Sunday morning, Hetty was interred at the old Swedes cemetery. On the close of the afternoon school, two of the teachers resolved to procure Alice a home. Mrs. R., ever prompt to engage in a good work, proposed to prevail on Mrs. Curtz to receive Alice as an inmate. And if E. M. could make an arrangement with Alice, and secure wood, little advance of means would be needed. The Lord's day was no hinderance to this work of mercy. Their negotiations succeeded with both parties.

Alice was overpowered with gratitude for the unexpected favor. In meekness she requested that Miss Jane Wilson, their friend, be consulted, who rejoiced at the plan, promising to remove her next morning, and send a cord of best wood. Edward Gilpin, a charitable friend, called on E. M. to say he would aid in their support, and he also sent a cord. And on Monday evening they were comfortably settled.

Mrs. Curtz's temper was austere, and she was a church-going woman. Poor Alice was delicate and timid. All her long life she had never ventured out at night, and rarely by day, shrinking with horror from darkness or street rambles. But our old heroine, past eighty, with her staff and lantern, was used to attend night lectures, and urged Alice to go; that having neglected her duty thus far was the stronger reason for being zealously engaged now. To talk of taking cold was nonsense; neither was there danger, if she leaned on her arm for support. So the timid one became a regular attendant on night lectures at eighty-four, a wonder to all who knew her former habits. They passed a happier winter than was anticipated.

Several ladies of the Friends Society sent them supplies; they really lived on the fat of the land. Mrs. Morton and Mrs. Adams were kind friends. They had been affectionately advised to bear and forbear with each other's infirmities, and as time elapsed, it was hoped it would be a permanent home. But as spring renewed its verdure, our old hostess revived in vigor. "Alice's wheel was a torment," she said, "it was whizzing in her ears from morning till night." It was as dear to Alice as the apple of her eye. She could not live without it.

However, all difficulty might have been overcome had not an interested woman, who wanted Alice's services for a season, interfered; and when weary of old age sent her to the poor-house, without consulting any one, there to end her days with the unknown dead. The Hough family were reputable spinners of stocking yarn for more than a century.

"Let not ambition mock their useful toil,
Their homely joys and destiny obscure,
Nor grandeur hear with a disdainful smile
The short and simple annals of the poor."

Mrs. Curtz, once more dependent on her former friends, and alone, regretted her conduct to Alice, and solicited Mr. Hall to take her old fabric and support her. As this did not meet his views, though he knew she must be cared for, and felt it right to secure it for charity, he consulted E. M., who made a proposal to a few ladies of the church; and on due consideration they agreed to provide for her, she signing an article that they should claim the house on her decease for a charitable institution. The deed was conveyed in trust to the Vestry of Trinity Church, February 16th, 1821, and their duty faithfully performed. In November, 1823, she died in an epileptic fit, and was followed to the grave by those who had supported her, and by whom this stone was erected.

CHAPTER XII.

Banks of the Christiana—Melancholy Catastrophe—Irish Trade—King's Ships—Primitive Customs—Packets—Capt. J. Foudray—Capt. Samuel Bush—Mode of Traveling—Steamboat—Wharves—Jonathan Rumford, Esq.—Eleazar McComb, Esq.—James Brian—Ship Building—Thomas Willing—Barney Harris—William Woodcock.

Many incidents in the lives of those who slumber here are faintly impressed on memory, and are to be easier imagined than described. Time and reflection may aid us to develop a few touching facts. So we leave the hallowed spot, anticipating a renewal of our visit to gather the gleanings, and pass on to the banks of the Christiana, to converse of seasons long past.

When this was a beautiful walk, in neat order, partly shaded by trees and large bushes, flags, lilies, &c., ornamented the borders, and reeds and rushes edged the fanciful stream, enlivened by the numerous winged and finny tribes. Even the little migratory reed birds, so long the prey of sportsmen, have become nearly extinct; the fishes, forced by the power of steam, have sought a more quiet channel.

Gunning on these banks once afforded great amusement; also fishing at the Rocks. We are now opposite the spot which presents to memory a melancholy catastrophe, and, though of more recent date, we will relate it as a warning to heedless youth.

Two lads, who were playmates in infancy and passed the days of boyhood together, when childish plays and adventures were giving place to other views, they were sometimes perplexed at separation in their sports. One was fond of gunning, and skilled in the art; the other was the only child of a timid widow, and was prohibited from joining in this exercise till the father of his companion induced his mother to yield to his entreaties. Then fully equipped and joyous, they crossed the bridge, anticipating many such excursive pleasures on yon bank, which was swarming with game.

Here they made a stand, and proposed to shoot. The novice, under the guidance of his tutor, was to fire at the word of command, while his companion stooped to watch the birds. "Fire!" was the order, and, alas! promptly obeyed, and, shocking to relate, stilled that voice in death! In a sport so anxiously desired, his first essay did such terrific execution as to sever the head of a beloved friend.

His wild agonizing screams brought assistance, but surgical skill was of no avail to his dear mangled companion. How swiftly did death steal upon his youthful victim! What an awe was flung around this resemblance of breathing life, that in a moment annihilated all joy from the heart and left the canker-worm of despair!

The maternal grief of the widow was deep and poignant; but the still small voice of religion soothed the hours of affliction. The scene of distress in the family of the slaughtered youth, and the anguish of a fond mother, we leave for imagination to conceive.

A timid parent's fears were fatally realized, and her cautious admonition deeply impressed on her distracted son. How unavailing when the dread deed was done! The unfortunate survivor, too, died young. "Behold, there was a young man carried out, the only son of his mother, and she was a widow.

The dwelling of Mrs. Mary Bingham, the afflicted mother of one of the lads, has gone. Her obliging manners, patient kindness, and just dealing, secured her the best customers in the dry-goods business. By these she will be long remembered, and although death rushed in suddenly to call her hence, her house was in order, and with faith she did exclaim—"Lord Jesus, receive my spirit."

The other was the son of a very respectable man, John Sellars, whose ancestors were here in olden days.

Scenes of by-gone days are now presented to our memory, when ships and brigs, in the Irish trade, arrived in midsummer, crowded with passengers, and were towed up the creek with small boats ahead; and ropes were thrown to the multitude assembled on these banks, who would pull with all their strength to get them to the wharf.

No steam-power then lightened labor. Things were done more by scriptural rule: "By the sweat of thy face shalt thou eat bread." It was amusing to see the people land in the hot sun, without bonnets, and often wrapped in a red or blue cloth cloak. All well dressed, and, in a few days, went off to the west with means to provide a home. The lowest order were called redemptioners, and sold for three years to defray their passage. Many of those became respectable members of the community, and were never thrown upon its charity. Their training taught them the usages of the country, and they imbibed a spirit of independence to live by honest industry. We never heard of their going to the almshouse.

Good health and cheerful faces were pretty general. In a few instances, long passages and short allowance engendered disease. Small-pox was most common. There were occasionally ship-fevers. An alarming sickness, termed the Welsh fever, brought by passengers from Wales, in the ship Liberty, prevailed to some extent, continued long, and was communicated to the inhabitants. Tents were pitched in the outskirts of the town, and barns were used for hospitals.

In those days, there was an odd custom in practice, called *chairing the captain*, if his treatment on the voyage had gained their good feelings, and the captain would submit to the lofty honor. Two long poles were fastened under an arm-chair, where he was seated; four stout men each took an end of the pole on his shoulder, bearing the chair, paraded the street, men, women, and children following in a long procession, cheering and shouting, " *Hurrah, hurrah for captain B.*" Captain Thomas Fort once made a very short passage, wanting a few days of six weeks. As he had told the passengers that was the shortest time possible, one family positively refused to go on shore till the time expired.

In olden times, the wharves were places of business, and commerce flourished. Many instances of their former glory are recalled, when the king's ships sought a safe harbor for winter quarters in the Christiana. A sloop of war, commanded by Captain Hawker, who was a very accomplished gentleman, passed more than one winter here. This officer was very popular; and with those under his command frequently visited the villagers, and must have been amused at their rustic simplicity.

To give an idea of these primitive times, an anecdote of my grandfather may suffice; he was a widower, with two daughters and a step-son. He owned a store-house on the lower wharf, and rented it for the use of those ships. The officers were in the habit of visiting him, and sometimes came to spend an evening.

A clock stood in the corner; as it ticked to strike, grandfather laid the fire in order. Then the girls felt their faces glow, and were so confused when he said, " Gentlemen, my hour for family prayer is nine o'clock; it will be quite agreeable to me if you will remain, but after service we retire."

The hint was sufficient; they withdrew with a bow. Then the youngsters would declaim against such rustic habits, and say, "Father, these officers must think you are very rude." But father coolly replied, " My children, God divided the times and seasons; the light of day to labor and visit, the darkness of night for rest; so I shall observe them, and not permit man's notions to obtrude and alter the law of nature."

An aged gentleman said "he recollected, when he was young, being near the lower wharf, and seeing a vessel of two masts anchored in the Christiana creek, with the deck full of negro slaves from Africa."

They were sent among us by their British owners from the West Indies, probably about the year 1760. In 1761, a gang or drove of slaves, numbering twenty or thirty, was passing my father's door, driven by their owners for sale; as Friends at that period held slaves, my mother purchased a boy of nine years of age, who remained long in the family; finally he was manumitted.

More than a century ago this was Harvey's wharf; about sixty years since Capt. T. Mendenhall became the owner, and entered into the flour trade, and kept packets to convey it to Philadelphia. The first bell to notify their departure was hung on his store house. Numerous teams from Lancaster brought the flour, and often thirty of these remained over night in his wagon-yard, just above Front street, reaching from Walnut to French street, where there was a house to accommodate teamsters and sheds for horses.

The next wharf was John Foudray's, who long sailed a packet to Philadelphia. His dwelling is a relic of that day, corner of French and Water streets. The latter street only extended thus far. The entrance was a porch with three steps, yet in high tides, the family had to enter the house and leave it in boats.

Captain Samuel Bush purchased this wharf, and it is now owned by his son, who improved the old fabric and added a new one. Captain Bush sailed a packet to Philadelphia previously to the Revolution. In carrying forage for the army about the time of the battle of the Brandywine, his sloop was in the Delaware; and to escape the enemy who was pursuing it, he scuttled and sunk her, but afterwards was enabled to raise her.

It may be appropriate here to notice the mode of traveling in the days of our fathers. From this wharf many have entered the packet, carrying their little basket of provision, providing for day and night, which was often spent on board. The passage was a half-dollar. These primitive people adhered to the course of nature, dropped anchor to wait for flood or ebb; and never attempted to sail against wind or tide. When meals were provided on board, it was a great accommodation. Many inconveniences occurred in winter from bad roads.

When the dawn of a new century had burst upon us, numerous persons were waiting in Philadelphia to return. The packets were laid up, and stages breaking down from bad roads, made traveling dangerous. Among those detained were Cæsar A. Rodney, Esq., his wife and two daughters. Mr. R. knew Captain Milner was venturesome; the weather was mild, and the ice floating. He wrote to solicit him to bring his packet.

Milner came, and his packet left Philadelphia at one o'clock, crowded with passengers. The captain promised to lay at Marcus Hook from dark to daylight. The moment before sailing, Mr. Rodney hired a barge with men to row his family down to this place, on the 17th day of January. In an open boat, they left Chestnut street wharf at one o'clock, landed safe at the old ferry, and the boat returned to Marcus Hook that night at eight o'clock, just as the passengers were stepping on shore to await the return of day. This was spoken of as a novelty.

Captain Milner was famous for carrying sail, and sometimes performed exploits. In 1802, near the old ferry, with all his canvas flying under a stiff breeze, and crowded with passengers in a state of great excitement, some in full glee, others imploring him not to drown them. Capt. Hunn was on board, and saw the danger, pulled off his coat, saying, "Milner do you mean to drown us?" At the moment the shallop upset, many boats went to rescue them from a watery grave. Even in sober times, with far less traveling, there were disasters.

The land conveyance was a four-horse stage, which left here at 8 A. M., and arrived in Philadelphia at lamp-light in winter. The fare was two dollars, and at Chester fifty cents for dinner. And if the road was bad, you had the privilege to walk half-way, and this was unavoidable.

True, this short journey did afford variety. Here was an alarm; there was a break-down or an overset. The drivers loved to race with other stages passing through, so the adventures of a day's ride might result in sad bruises, black eyes, or broken bones. With all these disasters, there was less murmuring than in a short detention now in the cars or steamboats.

Hacks superseded stages, with very careful obliging drivers; among these was Joseph Todd, a very respectable man, who continues to keep hacks at this day.

Steamboats next supplanted all other public conveyances. Capt. Milner plied the first regular boat to Philadelphia. The Vesta was soon unfitted for service, and when out of use was accidentally burnt at the wharf. The Etna was thought unsafe, and disposed of. The Wilmington was long in service, first commanded by Captain Milner, then by Captain Read, both very popular in consequence of their accommodating manners.

Dreamy recollections seem floating in memory of a boat, plying this creek in 1790 or '92, with paddles at the stern, going up and down; such a thing I saw, and believe the owner was John Fitch. Great predictions of its future usefulness were then in circulation.

The third wharf was Shallcross's; he was long in the shipping business. The next owner of it was William Hemphill, who was also largely engaged in commerce, and died here in a good old age.

Below Robinson's, a jut of land where boats could unload freight, but not sufficient depth of water for vessels, belonged to Henry Whitsal, cedar cooper, who was an innocent good man, one of the early Methodists in this region. His dwelling adjoined the present dilapidated custom-house.

Though it is changing our subject, and to some may not seem our direct way, we would rejoice to hear that our citizens had aroused from their slumber, to ask a pittance from the treasury, and rear an edifice fitted for Government business in Wilmington. Surely, the powers that be could not hesitate to grant the claims of a little sister State, whose treasures were exhausted, and much of her precious blood spilt, to achieve independence.

Besides, to the wise men who guided the Ship of State through the ocean of conflicts, to found the Constitution, Delaware was a leading star, which in rolling years has not been eclipsed by the mist of disunion.

The fourth wharf was Robinson's, who before the Revolution commanded vessels from this port, then declined a seafaring life, and became a shipping merchant of some note. Mr. R. was a very worthy man; he built a house in Front street near Market, where he died in the prime of life, leaving a widow and two children to bemoan their loss, and many friends to sympathize in their sorrows.

His widow married Samuel Carswell, who removed hence to Philadelphia, and was many years successfully engaged in the mercantile business, when he died and left much wealth and a fair name. The next owner was Warner; it is below the bridge.

On Rumford's wharf above, George Taylor lived, who sailed a packet; he was from Holland, and his time was purchased by my grandfather, and for many years he sailed grandfather's packet to New York, till his health was impaired. Then Taylor entered into the business with Archibald Little, one of the first in this line, who was a very respectable man, and his daughter, a worthy woman, married Robert Hamilton, Esquire.

George Taylor was an industrious, useful man, and acquired a handsome independence. These persons sailed packets before the Revolution. Taylor died about the year 1787.

The wharf above the bridge was Rumford's. The owner was a respectable shipping merchant long before the Revolution, and an enterprising and useful member of this community; many vessels and houses were built through the means of Jonathan Rumford. That large mansion, corner of Front and Thorn streets, and parallel with his wharf, was erected and occupied by him till death released him from earthly cares.

In troublous times he leaned to royalty, but never meddled with the affairs of State. It was a crisis when he who declared himself neutral was deemed to be guilty, and the innocent often suffered for opinion's sake, while the criminal escaped.

In those days, his dwelling was in Fourth street below Market, and was entered by a few fanatics, who professed zeal for the cause they disgraced, threatening destruction to all his property and death to him. Snatching firebrands from the oven, they scattered them through the rooms, and abused his person in the most brutal manner, fracturing his skull with a blacksmith's hammer, an implement of the leader's trade.

Mr. Rumford lay apparently lifeless on the floor, when Captain Hugh Montgomery, my father, was called to his relief; who on his way was joined by two militia captains, Kean and Stidham. Everything was in the greatest confusion, and his family panic stricken; no one dared to go to his relief. His wife was in deep affliction, having an infant, her only daughter, ill with the small-pox. She knew not where to fly for safety.

Captain Montgomery advised the distressed mother to hand the child over the fence to her kind neighbor Miss Peggy Allison, who was willing to take charge of it. This infant was then in a dying state, and from exposure soon sunk into a happy rest.

My father was the first to ascend the stairs, amid showers of firebrands, which singed his hair and ruined his coat. The others followed, who fared but little better. Those gentlemen saved him from a violent death, and his house from destruction.

Though he recovered from the wounds, his faculties were impaired, and his capability for business so injured that in a few years from a very rich man he died poor, and his ignominious persecutors were branded as cowards, and their ruin soon ensued.

About 1791 or '92, this mansion and wharf were sold to liquidate his debts. Doctor Nicholas Way was empowered by E. McComb, Esq., to purchase the whole property at a limited price. It was sold for much less than he offered, and the balance generously presented to Mrs. Rumford by Dr. Way.

Mr. McComb fitted up the house in handsome style, and removed from Dover; and we remember the beautiful hot-press paper imported by him from France to ornament the parlor walls. It was so great an affair in this region that it was noised abroad, and well preserved for nearly half a century. It was in good order when renewed a few years since.

Mr. McComb entered into the flour business, and kept packets in connection with Col. Tilton, and was a public-spirited man, who did much to improve his neighborhood and benefit others.

In 1793, when the yellow fever first prevailed in Philadelphia, he accommodated Mr. Wilcox, an eminent merchant there, with part of his house for his family, and the wharf for his ships. Mr. and Mrs. McComb were worthy persons and highly esteemed, very prepossessing in their personal appearance and manners. They had four children, who lived to be men and women, all very attractive.

But the eldest son, Thomas McComb, and the eldest daughter, Mrs. Clayton, were remarkably handsome. To her, the beloved companion of our school days, we must pay the tribute of affection to say she was as lovely as she was beautiful. Both those valued members of the best society here, Mr. and Mrs. M., fell victims to the yellow fever in 1798, and none were more deeply lamented.

They were professors in the Presbyterian Church, and suddenly called away. "Yet I will rejoice in the Lord; I will joy in the God of my salvation."

After the death of Mr. McComb, this estate was purchased by James Brian, a Friend, who continued the same business, and in 1802 his wife died here with yellow fever, and left one daughter, a very estimable woman, whose husband, John Stapler, continued the business. Mr. Brian was largely engaged in the Nova Scotia trade, and made extensive contracts with Captain Cuffe, whom we shall notice hereafter.

Ship building was carried on to a considerable extent, and it was the custom for the owner of the vessel, while on the stocks, to furnish spirits for the workmen, sending it twice a day to the yard; and they usually bought it by the hogshead, for it was drunk pretty freely. They also had to give the dinner at the launch.

Thomas Willing, from whom this town was first named, built a sloop for grandfather, who often spoke of him as his friend, and an enterprising man, and pointed out his dwelling; it is yet standing as a relic of antiquity, and one of the first brick houses built in the village; it is in Second near French street, and built one-story and hip-roofed. He married Catharine Stedham, a Swede.

In colonial times, a relative of Mr. Willing lived here, who was married to Mr. Relf. A very handsome lady was often their guest, Mrs. Dolly Willing, wife of Captain Willing; occasionally she wore a diamond ring, so rare in these primitive days as to attract much notice. The Swedes of higher order brought much valuable plate from Sweden, which they had in use, but they had very little jewelry.

Near this wharf was a ship-yard of note for years. There Barney Harris built the famed "Nancy," whose adventurous story will be narrated. William Woodcock also occupied the same spot, and built many vessels. These persons were masters of their business, and were highly respected to old age. Near here were built in my days the ships Washington, Wilmington, and Liberty, with numerous brigs. In later times, Enoch Moore built vessels here.

In this neighborhood was an old pottery carried on for a time by Samuel Preston Moore, but for many years by John Jones, a very worthy man, and a member of Friends' Society.

The wharves were owned by men in the shipping trade; and we have heard of others engaged in it, Dawes, Giles Bennet, Gilpin, Tatnall, Montgomery, &c., before the Revolution; and we know so many in our day which confirms the opinion and reminiscenses, it proves the fact that this was early a commercial town. When we remember the name of a person in any business connected with it, we have noticed it.

The old house at the corner of the bridge, now a tavern, was long occupied by Jonas Matson, blockmaker. Mrs. Matson was famed for her kind attention to the sick and afflicted. Her purse was small, but her heart was expansive, and her hands never wearied in good acts. "Silver and gold have I none, but such as I have give I thee."

Near the corner of King street was an old brick building, and in days of yore the upper story was the sail-maker's loft of Alexander Davis, whom we have noticed. This is now the steamboat wharf.

CHAPTER XIII.

A Singular Incident—Brig Friday—Capt. J. M.—Prizes—Robert Morris, Esq.—Brig Nancy—Capt. H. Montgomery—Sails under British Colors—News of Independence—Arms the Brig—Invited Guests—St. Thomas's hauls down the Flag—Hoists the first American Flag in a Foreign Port—Lands Ammunition and Arms—Explosion—Lieut. Weeks Killed—Scuttling a Brig—Raising Her—Cargo arrives Safe—Capt. H. M. fell in 1780.

In narrating scenes on the ocean, memory will throw its hues of sorrow and of joy over those who "go down to the sea in ships, for they have heard evil tidings; there is sorrow on the sea, for those whom the raging billows have buried in the ocean's depths, and no man knoweth his sepulchre unto this day."

> "When the dread trumpet sounds to wake the dead,
> Not a single spot of burial earth,
> Whether on land or in the spacious sea,
> But must give back its long committed dust
> Inviolate. Ask not how this can be;
> Almighty God has done much more."

Of those who cry unto the Lord in their trouble, and he saveth them out of their distresses, "maketh the storm a calm, so that the waves are still, he bringeth them to their desired haven," to end life's voyage in peace, and to lie beneath the clods of yon valley, slumbering in the earth which embosoms their dearest friends.

> "'Tis but a night, a long and moonless night;
> We make the grave our bed and then are gone.
> Thus at the shut of even the weary bird
> Leaves the wide air, and in some lonely break
> Cowers down and dozes till the dawn of day,
> Then claps his well-fledged wings and bears away."

My mother was witness to a remarkable incident at the closing scene of her half brother. He enjoyed excellent health and great energy, until the age of twenty-five; then a neglected cold affected his lungs, and as medical skill proved ineffectual, emigration to a warmer climate was recommended. Conscious of his hopeless case, he desired to die at home, and this caused him to procrastinate until the most favorable moment for his departure had glided by ere he reluctantly sailed from this port in 1767, bound to a West India isle.

A prosperous voyage and mild climate had no effect, and he made haste to return; and it was arranged that, should death bear away the immortal spirit on the deep ocean, the remains should be brought home and deposited by his mother's side in the Swedes' cemetery.

At the time of his embarking he was so enfeebled that it was deemed highly improbable that he should reach home alive. His anxiety was intense, daily inquiring of the captain how they progressed, and expressing his ardent desire to die at home. After a few days on the sea, life seemed drawing to a close. The captain and even the crew were much excited.

In sight of Cape Henlopen, a violent storm arose with contrary winds, and the brig was blown off to sea, and amidst the gale his pulse had ceased to beat. As soon as the captain was relieved from duty, he performed the sad task of attending to the corpse, and he was buoyed up with the hope that the wind would soon change and be permitted to convey the remains home in a state of preservation.

But days passed with little variation in the weather. There was a daily examination made of the body, which exhibited no change, and this seemed mysterious, for the captain and sailors affirmed that on that day a week, at sea, they witnessed the sad event of his soul departing, when they bore the clay tenement of this beloved one to the abode of his step-father, where his relatives had assembled.

Contrary to medical advice, this parent gave orders to lay him in his bed as a sick person. Very soon he opened his eyes, and in an audible voice thanked his Heavenly Father for his mercy in bringing him home to die among his relatives. Then taking his father's hand, he said it had been long since he had taken any nourishment, and that he needed something to strengthen him, for he had much to communicate that was important, and but a very little time allotted him to remain here.

Wine was offered, which he refused, saying he preferred chocolate, and thought it was the only thing he could take. The process of preparing it was slow in those days. He inquired for the Rev. Mr. Boreal, and when informed that he was dead, he replied that he knew it. A similar question was asked relative to another individual who had also died during his absence, to which he made the same response. When my mother brought him the chocolate, he reached forth his hand, and in a moment was gone.

"And he that was dead sat up and began to speak, and there came a fear on all." This rumor of him went throughout all the region. This young man was John Hendrickson.

A singular fact next comes under our notice. Isaac Harvey was in the shipping business, and intended to build a brig. In those days, prejudice was very strong against commencing any transaction on Friday, which he resolved to make a strong effort to do away by entering into all his contracts on that day.

The timber was engaged, the carpenters employed, the vessel put on the stocks and launched, and she was named "Friday." And they began to load her on that day; but he had much difficulty with the sailors, and was obliged to bribe them to loose from the mooring and make sail.

On that unlucky day week, in the midst of a most awful gale, the crew of a homeward bound vessel saw this brig, and the men with axes cutting away the masts. From that hour neither brig nor crew were ever heard of, and as there was no insurance his loss was great.

Mrs. Harvey strenuously opposed the design at first, and predicted that it would end disastrously. When the loss of the brig was certain, she walked the floor, wringing her hands in despondency, and exclaiming, "Isaac, this is all thy sixth day's doing. I warned thee of the consequences."

In the Revolution, a Scotchman, Captain James Montgomery, commanded a small armed vessel in the Continental service. One morning, while seated at breakfast at a hotel, news was brought that several store-ships of the enemy were coming up the river. He quickly rose from the table, saying, "Gentlemen, now is my harvest time." His vessel was soon under full sail, and, before the sunset, he brought up this creek three valuable prizes.

Another store-ship, with valuable goods and much booty, run on shore above the creek. A few daring spirits boarded her in boats, and landed her whole cargo. A choice prize.

In all ages the mind of man has been alive to the narration of thrilling events; but none of the vicissitudes that humanity is heir to so readily awakens the sympathies of youth as the diversified adventures of life on the ocean. It is listened to with intense interest, and read with an avidity which overlooks any defects or lack of skill in the narrator. In imagination they rise with its raging billows mountains high, descend into its deep abyss to behold its wonders, or are wafted over the rolling waves by balmy breezes, to view the novelties of foreign realms.

The fancy of another may be suited by the simplicity of the story, if it is truth unadorned. Such is the following, and no doubt its value will be enhanced by being an interesting fact of the Revolution, though unhonored by a place in the national annals. It is glanced over in the Journal of the Secret Committee for Public Safety, and at the dawn of that eventful day the issue was hailed as an important item in forwarding the cause of independence, and those who achieved it were lauded throughout the colonies for heroic patriotism.

In the winter of 1775, Robert Morris, Esq., Financier for the Continental Congress, chartered the brig Nancy, of Wilmington, Del., owned by Joseph Shallcross, Joseph Tatnall, and others, and by Capt. Hugh Montgomery, who was the commander. The ensuing March she sailed for Porto Rico, under English colors, and landed Don Antonio Seronia to procure arms and ammunition by a contract previously made with the Spanish government.

Thence the brig sailed to different islands to elude suspicion. At St. Croix and St. Thomas she took in produce by day and munitions of war by night; these were sent in small vessels from St. Eustatia, being neutral islands.

When the cargo was nearly complete, information was received that independence was declared, and a description of the colors adopted. This was cheering intelligence to the captain, as it would divest him of acting clandestinely. Now they could show true colors. The material was at once procured, and a young man on board set to work privately to make them.

He was well known here in after years as Capt. Thomas Mendenhall. The number of men was increased, and the brig armed for defence, and all things put in order. The day they sailed the captain and Mr. A. S. had invited the Governor and suit, with twenty other gentlemen, on board to dine. A sumptuous dinner was cooked, and a sea-turtle being prepared gave it the usual name of a turtle feast.

As the Custom-house barges approached with the company, they were ordered to lay on their oars while a salute of thirteen guns was fired. Amid the firing, this young man was ordered to haul down the English flag, and hoist the first American stars ever seen in a foreign port. "Cheers for the National Congress;" cries of "Down with the lion; up with the stars and stripes," were shouted.

This novelty caused great excitement to the numberless vessels then lying in the harbor, and to the distinguished guests it was a most animating scene. After the entertainment was hurried over, they returned in their boats, and the brig was soon under full sail. On her homeward voyage she was often chased, but being a superior sailer, escaped.

Near the capes of Delaware, enveloped in a dense fog, they saw a fleet, but could not discern the colors. They had been informed that Congress was fitting out a fleet from the Delaware Bay, and perhaps this might be the one. However, it was soon known that the enemy was pursuing, and that there was no hope of escape, their entrance into the bay being cut off by two frigates and their tenders.

In this dilemma, the only feasible plan appeared to run the brig on shore and make an effort to save some part of the arms and ammunition near Cape Island. The place where this important landing was effected was called Turtle Gut Inlet. At this crisis, Lieutenant Weeks came with a barge filled with men, sent by his brother, Captain Weeks, commander of the Continental fleet in Delaware Bay, to look out for the "Nancy," and warn her of the danger, as the enemy were on the alert to capture her.

This was a momentous period. The country was engaged in war with a powerful foe, with very little powder or arms for defence. Captain Montgomery was aware of this, and though not one who had sounded the first trumpet for war, but united with those who were willing to forbear longer, was a faithful patriot still. The evil had come, and must be met.

He assembled the crew, and stated his determination to defend the munitions of war at all hazards; he did not wish to conceal the imminent danger of contending with such a superior force. The officer said, "If there is a man fearful and faint-hearted, let him go. The boat is ready to take him on shore. These public stores must be protected to aid our destitute country in the dark hour of need, in the noble cause of liberty." There was a momentary and solemn silence when the young man who had made the flag stepped forward and said, "Captain, I will stand by you." Then three cheers were given, and not a man flinched from duty. Lieutenant Weeks and men were placed on shore to protect the stores, when landed, for the Tories infested these places. "Ye approach this day unto battle against your enemies; let not your hearts faint; fear not."

The frigates with their long guns commenced firing, but did little execution. The tenders nearer kept up a constant fire, while small boats manned made three desperate attempts to board. For nearly twelve hours, those brave men made their defence against such formidable odds under heavy firing of cannon and small arms, and succeeded in saving the greater portion of the powder and arms, landing them safe and untouched, while the sugar and rum hogsheads alongside were fired into and some entirely destroyed.

The brig was so shattered that not a sail or a spar was spared, the caboose was shot away, and the hulk so perfect a wreck that it could be no longer safe. One tottering mast, with the national flag flying, seemed only left to guess her fate.

Still a quantity of powder and valuable merchandise was below, and it was resolved ere she was abandoned to prevent these stores from falling into the hands of an enemy by blowing her up.

The plan was arranged so that the men could have time to leave, and the captain and four hands were the last to quit. As the boat distanced the wreck, one man, John Hancock, jumped overboard, as he said, "to save the beloved banner or perish in the effort." His movements were so sudden that no chance was afforded to prevent his boldness, and they looked on with terror to see him ascend the shivering mast and deliberately unfasten the flag, then plunge into the sea and bear it on shore.

But oh! what a terrific catastrophe this exploit caused! The enemy supposing it a signal of surrender, hastened in boats to take possession of their prize. They drew near, rending the air with shouts and hurrahs. There was an explosion, and the brig and nearest boats were blown to atoms. Not a soul of the unfortunate crew of the boats was left to tell the awful story.

No such disastrous event was anticipated, and sorrow and sadness clouded every brow while engaged in the decent interment of the remains floating on shore. Men who had barely escaped from battle looked on the scene of carnage with horror.

Such are the inconsistencies of war that we are lost in wonder how men in this enlightened age, when the Sun of Righteousness has arisen in glorious splendor, displaying in vivid colors all the immoralities and evils connected with such a cause, can aid or espouse it. Yet

more, how can they who are appointed as overseers use their signatures to involve a Christian nation in such miseries?

If it be for honor and glory, then the inheritance lawfully belongs to those who encounter the perils and gain the victories. But too often they descend to the grave in obscurity, while their hard-earned laurels adorn the brows of the powers that be.

For a season prosperity may cherish the verdure in freshness, and imagined glory possess a joyous heart, but when prostrated on the couch of death, the world and its honors receding, how valueless is the withered laurel! Imagination may be tortured by the thought of the desolate widow and orphans, of mangled martyrs, and of the sad policy of strewing with thorns one's pathway to the grave.

The explosion of the brig was heard forty miles above Philadelphia. A hogshead of rum floated on shore, where the men, who had suffered hunger and thirst for twenty-four hours, knocked in the head and turned the liquor into a well to assuage their burning thirst.

Though the engagement was over, the frigates kept up firing, and might renew the attack by landing men. The captain, much fatigued, was seated on a chest, and as he drew away his leg, a ball entered the spot, which Lieut. Weeks handed to him, and the captain expressed his gratitude for the hair-breadth escape.

"The young man replied, "My brave officer, these balls were not made to kill you nor me." In the moment, a ball severed his head! A brave, noble youth, and the only man killed during the battle. He was the youngest of seven brothers, who were in their country's service, and five were killed during the revolution.

A lad was badly wounded in the thigh, and when brought home, they found a piece of his check shirt had been shot into it. Joshua Giffin was the lad's name, a native of this town. He proved himself a brave youth, and was one of the many who sailed from this port, and in succeeding years found a grave in the ocean. His father was an old and worthy townsman, whose descendants are still here, and remember the circumstances of this narrative.

Every vehicle on the island was put in requisition to convey the stores over to the bay side, where they were placed in the Wasp, Capt. Weeks. They were joyfully received by the authorities in Philadelphia. "We will bring it to thee in floats to Joppa, and thou shalt carry it up to Jerusalem."

During the action, the sailors had landed many valuables owned by the captain, which were stolen, and no remuneration was ever made

20*

by government for these important services, though the transaction was deemed of great consequence at that momentous crisis. A letter from one of the signers of the Declaration of Independence, now in the archives at Washington, naming the captain and brig, will testify the approval of that honorable body at the time they received news of the explosion.

Eventually it cost Captain Montgomery his life, in 1780, when returning from New Providence, where he had been a prisoner. The vessel was attacked by one of superior force, and he fell a victim to the horrors of war. His fate was deeply deplored, for he was a brave and worthy man.

There are a few yet living who recollect it, and it has been stated that on the arrival of the sad news, the town was overshadowed with gloom; every window was bowed, expressive of sorrow. A widow and infant daughter were left to mourn. "Weep sore for him that goeth away, for he shall no more return to his native country."

Years rolled on, and business was neglected. The widow was enshrouded by a deep and abiding sadness, which blighted much of the joys of life, and she ordered her papers to be burned. Though death had dissolved the tie which bound her to the husband of her youth, the spoiler had no power to remove his image from her heart. Though his mortal part had faded in a watery grave, she cherished his image until the close of a long life.

In the fall of 1801, through the advice of Gov. Dickinson, an application was made to Congress for remuneration for services and losses, by our representative, James A. Bayard, Esq., (a limitation act was in force.) Proper papers could not be procured, yet those gentlemen foresaw no difficulty to substantiate the fact while so many witnesses of the highest respectability were living.

When a petition was required, Mr. Robert Morris was applied to, who kindly offered to take the whole affair upon himself, although he was just released from prison. He thought it his duty to go to Washington, and search for the papers there, by himself deposited, relating to the transaction, because his influence had induced Capt. Montgomery to undertake this hazardous voyage.

But the office had lately been burned, and the papers lost, and there was no money in the treasury. To acknowledge this claim would be to invite others, and it was thought best to defer it to a more propitious season. But it was marked for a future day.

In 1831, the daughter was urged by an officer of the Revolution, who knew the justice of the claim, to renew it. Most of those interested were now dead. Application was made once more, and he who in youth who had hoisted and completed the flag, now a hoary-headed sire, went to Washington, and stated to the committee on claims the facts.

No doubt existed of the merits of the case, and that a debt was due the heirs of Capt. M., but as the amount of the claim could not not be ascertained at that late day, justice was withheld.

That honorable body were too conscientious to squander public money, and feared to pay one dollar more than was due. We venture to say, had it been their own interests to be served, conscience would have been less exacting, and justice been done to the claimant. The thorough knowledge Robert Morris, Esq., possessed of revolutionary affairs, was sufficient to satisfy the most incredulous. However, such injustice is no new thing, for we read in ancient times that "there was a little city, and few men within it, and there came a great king against it and besieged it. Now, there was found in it a poor wise man, and he by his wisdom delivered the city. Yet no man remembered that same poor man."

Another eventful story of the Revolution, previously occurred about the year 1777, involving a few of the same individuals, is next presented. A brig owned by Joseph Shallcross & Co., and commanded by Capt. Montgomery, homeward bound with a valuable cargo, and in order to escape the enemy he ran into an inlet near Egg Harbor, unloaded and secreted the cargo, and scuttled the brig.

An express was sent for Mr. S. to bring down ship carpenters and others, and while preparations were going on to reload, the enemy was informed that the rebels were at Tucker's on the beach, and sent a file of men to capture them.

At night the Captain felt insecure, and went to provide a boat in case of danger. Mr. Shallcross was in bed in a shed-room on the ground floor, easy of egress, and the Captain returned at midnight and saw that all was not right. But he soon heard much noise and merriment, for the loyalists were rejoicing at their project, being, as they thought, sure of capturing two notorious rebels.

Captain Montgomery cautiously opened the window, and dragging his friend out of bed, with his clothes on his arm, both ran, and jumping into the boat pushed off.

It was soon known that the rebels had fled. Just as the boat was loosed from the moorings, the soldiers pursued and kept up a constant firing of musketry from the beach. With the balls whistling around them they rowed for life, expecting every moment to be shot. Although they escaped unhurt, it was an alarming adventure.

Their pursuers, not being aware so much valuable property was within their grasp, returned to their camp. The rebels resumed their work, and soon refilled the vessel, with the assistance of two experienced carpenters from Wilmington, Barney Harris and William Woodcock, who united to hasten the work, and had the satisfaction of seeing her land her cargo in good order at the wharf.

This enterprise was thought an extraordinary feat. W. Woodcock lived to old age, much respected, and at eighty years of age, in full possession of his faculties, and without glasses, gave his testimony in writing relative to the explosion of the Nancy.

Few of the present generation know how conspicuous a part Wilmington bore in the Revolution, therefore it affords me pleasure to give all the information the chamber of my memory retains.

Near the time of this event, Mrs. Phillips, a married daughter of Mr. Tucker, fled to her father's for safety. She arrived late in the evening fatigued, and was put into this shed-room with her infant to lodge. Everything was in disorder, and the furniture had been sent away. No candlestick was at hand, and she looked around for a place to fix her light. She saw some kegs in a corner, one with a hole in the top. Here she secured her candle, and being overcome with fatigue, forgot to extinguish her light.

Next morning she found to her great horror that these kegs were full of powder, left here from the brig, because they dared not return for them. Providentially the light soon went out.

Mrs. Phillips was our neighbor for years, and often spoke feelingly of this merciful preservation. Her husband, Capt. Phillips, was a respectable pilot, and sailed many vessels out of this harbor. He and his son, a youth, were lost at the same time during a violent storm near the Capes in March, 1794. They were on board different vessels. I believe four brigs from this port went to sea the same day, and not a plank was ever seen by which to guess their fate, nor was there a soul spared to tell the sad story.

CHAPTER XIV.

A Swedish Minister—Catastrophe—Capt. H. Geddes—Shipwreck—A Singular Incident—Solemn Reflections—Capt. S. Lovering—Mr. A , a British Agent—Adventures of a Lady—Anecdote of a Sailor—Algerines—Captures—Cruelties—Bondage—Prisoners Ransomed—Arrival—Capt. Penrose—His Story—Remarks on their Character.

As we narrate ocean scenes, glimpses of olden times revive in our memory many disastrous events, which were listened to in childhood and made an impression never to be forgotten, no, never; and one is now presented, the story of a Swedish family, which, though not belonging properly to our reminiscences, we will relate.

A minister, who often officiated at the Swedish Church, and some of his wife's relatives, were the early colonists here. In troublous times, the Rev. Andreas Georgeson was Rector of Wicaco Church, and after a long illness became insane. Every means of restoration failed. By the advice of friends, a way was provided for his return to Sweden.

So soon after the war, many obstacles were to be met in this long voyage, and his wife's relatives and friends prevailed on her to wait here until she heard how crossing the ocean affected his mind. Having two young children, she acquiesced, and in due time the joyful news came that he was landed safe in his native country with a sound mind, and became permanently settled.

His dread of the tempestuous sea separated him from his family for some time. A relative of his wife accompanied her to London, where she was resigned to a friend, who was to convey her to Stockholm with her children, a daughter twelve years of age, and a son younger.

Her sister in Philadelphia received a letter from her dated London, in which she expressed her ardent gratitude to her Heavenly Father for her safe guidance across the ocean, and for her kind reception by the friends of her husband, and a second also dated on her embarkation for Sweden. In this the anticipation of a family meeting seemed to cast away all fear of the stormy sea. A strange land and distance from affectionate relatives claimed not a passing sigh; all was absorbed in this one desired event.

Pleasant weather and a prosperous voyage had brought them within a few hours' sail of their destined haven. The day was fine, and all hearts were sanguine with hope. The lady had been brought on deck to view the promised land of her future abiding place. The ship under full sail struck on a rock, and beat so violently they feared it would rend in pieces.

Amidst the alarm and frantic terror, Mrs. G. most imploringly entreated the captain to put her and her family in the long boat. He at length reluctantly yielded, and her protector, with the mate and two sailors, went into the boat. When a few yards from the ship, those on board witnessed the mournful catastrophe. The boat struck a rock, turned and sank. In an instant every soul perished, but the ship arrived safe at Stockholm.

Mr. G., amidst the state of excitement, went on board to meet his beloved family. When the sad news was communicated of the fate of those dearest to him on earth, whose absence was so long lamented, and but a little time ago almost within his embrace glowing with life and joyous hope, he swooned away, and his reason fled it was feared forever.

> "Farewell, my best beloved, whose heavenly mind,
> Affection, virtue, strength with softness joined,
> And I—but, ah! can words my loss declare,
> Or paint the extremes of transport and despair?
> Oh, thou, beyond what verse or speech can tell,
> My guide, my friend, my best beloved, farewell!"

All our sketches of ocean scenes, with the exception of the preceding, relate to persons sailing from this port, or living here at some period.

Capt. Henry Geddes, a native of Dublin, and for some years a midshipman in the British navy, landed in Wilmington in 1775, joined Col. Duff's regiment, and served for some time. His preference for the sea induced him again to brave its perils.

In after years he commanded the sloop-of-war Patapsco, and died in his eighty-fourth year, near his adopted home. It might be said of him as of Moses, "his eye was not dim nor his natural force abated." His last earthly resting-place is the old Presbyterian cemetery.

Through many perilous scenes he barely escaped, and a cheerful temperament buoyed him up amid danger. In 1778 his vessel was overset at sea, and twelve people were saved in a boat. For seventeen days they were without provisions or water, except twenty pounds of damaged flour and a dog. Five souls perished with hunger and thirst, for the inhuman act of drawing lots to take life was not conceived, when a brig bound to Alexandria, Va., relieved them.

In 1779 again his ship was wrecked, and himself and crew made a hair-breadth escape.

Years after, when in a new ship bound for Dublin, he was driven by a violent storm into the Irish channel, and wrecked near White Haven, where relief and all necessary assistance were rendered. Among the most active in saving valuables was a young man with a wheelbarrow. In time the ship was refitted, and performed her voyage.

A young girl was sent for by her brother, who lived in Alexandria, and was placed as a passenger under the captain's care in Dublin, and while waiting for a safe conveyance was entertained at his house; this kindness was gratefully acknowledged.

Years glided on, when she was traveling north with her husband, and called to pay her respects to the captain, and introduced her companion, who immediately made himself known as the young man so busy with his barrow at White Haven, now a respectable merchant in Alexandria. "Thrice I suffered shipwreck, a day and a night have I been in the deep, in perils on the sea, in weariness and painfulness, in watching often, in hunger and thirst, in fastings often, and in cold."

The following is an extract from his thoughts arising from his great preservation:—

"Oh, thou most merciful and all powerful God, suffer me to approach thee with reverential awe and perfect thankfulness for thy singular favor showed in that most extraordinary deliverance, experienced after seventeen days' exposure to the raging of the sea, with eleven unhappy companions, five of whom perished in a boat of fourteen feet, where there was no eye to see, no hand to help, no heart to pity. Every moment we expected to perish in the enraged element, suffering the most excruciating pains of hunger and thirst.

"Thou Omnipotent Being, thou saw, thou relieved us. Oh, may my spared life be devoted to thy service. Let it not be my condemnation that those days were given only to fill up the measure of my iniquity. But may I, through the assistance of thy Holy Spirit, spend the remainder of my life as one who has received an accession of years through the infinite goodness and compassionate love of the most Holy God. In this great and and arduous work, I pray for thy help; of myself I am insufficient, being naturally prone to sin as sparks fly upwards. Therefore of myself I have no merit, but thou who knowest the weakness and impurities of my heart, assist me, as thou didst once from the dangers of the sea, to escape the infinitely greater danger of eternal destruction.

"Suffer me, oh Lord, to lay my trust on one almighty to save, even on thy only Son, our Saviour Jesus Christ. On his mediation I depend; on the merits of his death and suffering I place all my hopes of eternal happiness. Oh, Heavenly Father, guard me from all temptations that may interrupt this design, and to thy name be honor, glory, and praise, through the endless ages of eternity.

"*July* 17, '78.   HENRY GEDDES."

Near the close of the last century, Captain Samuel Lovering, who was a native of Boston, sailed from this port at the age of seventeen; he entered the army at Boston, and being taken prisoner by the English was confined six months in the old Jersey prison ship, where so many of the youths of our country fell victims to disease and cruel treatment. He was graciously spared to reach his birthplace, Boston, where from his skeleton form and tattered outer garments he was not recognized by his fond mother.

When he recovered strength, he preferred a life on the ocean, and Wilmington became his abiding place. Here he married a most estimable young lady, daughter of Joseph Shallcross, Esq., in whose employ he sailed. During the troublous times of the subsequent European war in San Domingo, he and his crew were pressed by the French commander to aid in quelling the insurrection there. He was detained six months in actual service, enduring perils and hardships.

After returning home safe in the prime of life, disease by slow steps warned him—"Set thine house in order, for thou shalt die." With resignation he bowed to the afflictive decree, leaving a heart-stricken widow and three children of too tender an age to estimate their loss, and their numerous friends sympathized in his premature departure.

In 1793, when the yellow fever first visited Philadelphia, many of their vessels entered this port, and others landed passengers from ships anchored in the Delaware opposite the town. From the ship William Penn, Captain Josiah, was landed an English agent, his wife and two children.

At sea this ship, in the midst of a terrific storm, was struck by lightning, and having also aquafortis on board, she was found to be on fire, which continued for five hours. In this scene of terror the passengers were brought on deck, where they were fastened to prevent the raging billows from sweeping them into the deep. The flashes of lightning and flames were so dazzling as almost to cause blindness, and they were in momentary fear of being enveloped in flames or engulfed in the fathomless ocean.

By their severe labor the officers had been disabled from performing their duty. One of them had a spike run through his hand. Through the efforts of four energetic and faithful seamen guided by an overruling Providence, this awful fire was extinguished and their lives spared through the storm.

A lady passenger in frantic despair made a rash vow that if the Almighty Disposer of events in mercy would spare her life to land even on a desolate island, there should the remnant of her days be spent. Nothing would tempt her again to cross the water.

This lady had embarked from England with her husband and two children under very peculiar circumstances, so as to form quite an event in our narrative.

Her husband was an agent for houses abroad, and was a man remarkably handsome and courteous in his manner; he was esteemed by his new acquaintances as a worthy man: but when in England an ample fortune had been wrecked by him in the destructive vice of gambling.

At last, gathering up the broken fragments, a new home was sought in a strange land, and he, too, in remorse and despair at beholding his wife's fortune dwindled to a mere pittance and his means of living gone, made a vow to forsake the errors of his way, and every companion who could entice him to pursue such practices; if the wife of his choice would consent to leave her native land and beloved relatives and follow him to seek a place where he could engage in lawful business, his leisure hours should be devoted to his family.

Contrary to the advice of her best friends, with perfect confidence in his sincerity, however painful the trial, she deemed it her duty, and promptly acceded to his wishes.

When the pestilence disappeared and business revived, Philadelphia was their adopted home, and they suited their style of living to their income. Once more happiness smiled upon her. A husband's devoted attention, added to his reformed views and exemplary conduct, was ample reward for the sacrifices she had made. To attain domestic felicity she had abandoned rich and noble relatives; poverty and its attendant privation were borne without a murmur.

The change was equally grateful to his own feelings, and he often expressed his gratitude at his escape from the verge of ruin. In a few months a prosperous business, with health and happiness to enjoy it, seemed his future portion.

Anxious relatives were impatient to hear of Mrs. A.'s fate, and she wrote to them, portraying her bright prospects; that she was indeed living in a new world, and did not dare even to lament her separation from the friends so much beloved. But, ah! how uncertain are earthly expectations! Ere this letter filled with so joyous a theme, reached its destination, that rejoicing heart was again clouded in sorrow, and she felt how evanescent were her felicitous moments.

This apparently strong-minded man, possessing such talents for business, with deep conviction of the evil, when assailed by temptation, had again fallen.

A few of those sharpers had attacked his weak point, invading him in an unguarded hour, and filched him of his last dollar. His wife's timely remittances alone saved them from absolute poverty, or dependence on newly-made friends.

In tears and sighs this unfortunate lady bemoaned the sad and sudden reverse. She felt that no country was free from this bane. No sooner was access gained to his house, than it was assailed night and day by men whom she compared to the monsters of the deep, following the wake of a ship ready to pounce upon any victim which might fall as their prey. Without resources to sustain his family, conscience doomed him to sleepless nights.

It soon became evident that neither her devotion to him nor remonstrances availed anything. An Omnipotent hand alone could check this propensity. In this sad dilemma her only course seemed to be to forego this rash vow, and once more to cross the tempestuous ocean to her native land, and leave him to pursue his own course— neither her persuasions nor reproaches should molest him thereafter.

They embarked at New Castle, in the ship Wilmington. The four old sailors we noticed in the storm were there, and reminded her of the rash vow by expressing surprise to see her on shipboard after forming such resolutions. It was a touching rebuke, and she candidly owned her error with such feelings as to cause the tears to flow freely from those rugged tars.

A speedy voyage brought her safely to her affectionate friends

The unhappy husband returned a second and third time, and the last sad remembrance of him was related in our presence by a distinguished gentleman from Philadelphia, Joseph Taggart, Esq., President of the Farmers' and Mechanics' Bank.

On the eve of embarking for England, with a large sum in his possession, he was beset by a gang of gamblers, whom it seemed he had not the power to resist, although he was sure to be the loser. His loss that night at the billiard table was seventeen hundred dollars, and he was left distracted by remorse. This affecting story is no imaginary picture; it is too true—the life of an interesting man a slave to one vice which proved his ruin.

The same painful epidemic of 1793 induced another English gentleman to sojourn here, where he made the acquaintance of many of our respectable townsmen. In after years he resided in Batavia as British consul. There he married an accomplished lady, and secured a handsome fortune.

After making the tour of Europe, he settled in London, when untoward events reduced his means to a slender income, and memory brought to his recollection this little spot, where he had passed so many pleasant hours, and now concluded it would be a desirable place for him and his wife to reside on his limited income.

They came, and were soon settled, as they thought, in a permanent home. This lady possessed numerous curiosities collected in foreign climes, and many of her own sketches from scenery and views of castles, all executed with taste.

Her life was filled with adventures, and especially diversified scenes on the ocean were very interesting, she having crossed the Atlantic six times, and the equator four, and was once on board a ship burned to the water's edge. In their greatest extremity a frigate relieved them, but bore them far from their destination.

On another occasion, the ship was wrecked in a terrific storm, and lay eight days on her beam-ends. Several persons were dashed into the angry ocean, and some perished by hunger and fatigue, while the survivors, conscious that a few hours must terminate their earthly existence and consign their mortal part to a watery grave, they awaited their doom in despair. In this state, an English East Indiaman came to their rescue, and found only ten living.

By humane and judicious treatment they were soon restored. Instead of Havre they landed at Calcutta, and her determination was never again to venture on the ocean.

Yet after being settled here for a short time, news from London assured Mr. Emsley of a large sum of money, which could be recovered were he on the spot to attend to it, and this once more allured them to cross the billows, and see the works of the Lord. "He commandeth and raiseth the stormy wind."

An anecdote of a sailor, though it sounds like romance, is from a well authenticated source, and may add variety to our narrative.

After the peace of 1783, the sailor left this port bound for the West Indies. Time passed, and the brig was not heard from. The owners feared she was lost, and withheld the usual pittance allowed to sailors' wives. The wife of this one gave up her house, and rented a room in French street near Sixth. Hope of her husband's return had nearly vanished, when on a stormy night, about nine o'clock, this brig arrived at the wharf, and our sailor had leave to go on shore.

At his late dwelling he was informed where his wife lived; his acquaintance with the town led him to the spot. As he ascended an abrupt hill on the way, which was made slippery by rain, he fell, rolled down, and was covered with mud.

Having dressed himself neatly to meet his wife, he was sorry to be in such a plight, and recollecting the draw-well in front of the house, he aimed for it. Lifting a heavy lid which covered it, some part broke, and in he went, with a piece of the windlass, and the lid came down closing him in the well.

In this sad predicament, at his wit's end for a way to escape, but being nimble in the heels, he scrambled up the wall, and when at the top was so exhausted that he was unable to lift the heavy cover, and called aloud for help.

The old lady below was awakened by the noise, and knew the sound came from the well. His wife up stairs had just extinguished her light, and ran down alarmed; her hostess, placing a candle in her lantern, assured her some one was in the well, and would perish without instant relief.

These women were very superstitious. As the wife approached, the sailor by a mighty effort had raised the cover, and dripping wet was ascending, when she recognized him; in terror she dashed away her lantern, ran in screaming, and most positively asserted that the ghost of her husband had appeared.

The old lady firmly believed it, for she had seen strange things herself; besides, the fact of his coming out of the water proved he had been drowned in the deep, and thus it was manifest to her senses.

Their fears were awfully aroused by the darkness, and they screamed aloud.

The neighbors were alarmed, but were unwilling to meet the ghost, though they heard the noise. However, the poor wet sailor groped his way through the dark passage, and affirmed that he was no ghost but her long absent husband, French Kellum. This was hard to believe.

Succeeding the Revolution, our commerce was for years intercepted by the Algerines. No American vessel would near the Straits of Gibraltar without a Mediterranean pass, otherwise they were captured and the crew enslaved. Many of our countrymen were there in cruel bondage for years. This pass was a ship painted on parchment and cut in two parts; the Algerines held one-half, the purchaser the other. When boarded by them it was brought forward and must fit exactly.

A tribute was annually paid by our Government to the Algerines for permission to navigate the Mediterranean, which was an expensive security, and Government at length aroused from their apathy and ransomed their subjects. Ships loaded with valuables were sent as presents to the Dey. Captain Geddes was one of those to whom this trust was consigned; and after performing his duty, he arrived at the wharves with a few of the prisoners, among whom was Capt. Penrose, who had been commander of the ship President, of Philadelphia, and who had been kept in captivity for years.

Although half a century has glided over us, memory renews its freshness as we wander back to the time when we listened to the narration of Captain Penrose, and recollect with what intense feeling he spoke of their hardships, and how excited we were to hear about their capture—arrival in Algiers—presentation to the Dey—being chained —sold in the market—treatment—news of their ransom and final release.

My description will make but a faint impression on your minds compared with that made on mine. In my case, the narrator was a sufferer just returned to his native land and to the society of an affectionate wife—a happiness he had long despaired of enjoying, and she felt as if one had risen from the dead.

His sad, haggard countenance, tall, slender, and emaciated form, bowed down by grief, made all feel that he was scarcely an earthly being. His deep sympathy for his companions, whose hardships had been still more severe than his own, and his great effort to suppress feeling while relating those scenes, cannot be accurately detailed.

Death soon released many captives. There was one reason why we were more susceptible on this point; it was the daily theme of conversation familiar to our youthful ear. Example taught us to think, talk, and weep over their hard fate; every heart warmed with the love of our country had become interested in their cause; amidst this excitement, they returned here to relate their mournful adventures, and bid us rejoice at their escape.

On being boarded by the crew of the Corsair, an intense feeling pierced each heart as though a death warrant was presented in its most dreaded form; their doom was irretrievable. At Algiers they were handcuffed, chained by the leg, two together, driven to the Dey's stable, and placed with horses to await his mightiness' orders, for above two hours.

After separating their chains and conducting them through a dark passage, up many steps to an opening, where they were obliged to take off their shoes and crawl on their knees through an aperture, and remained in this position until the Dey, who was seated on a magnificent couch, was pleased to address them when on their knees.

He reproached the Government harshly for allowing its subjects to remain in bondage. He said it was disgraceful. "Who is your king or president, or the man you call great, who rules your country, and leaves you my slaves? Away with them to the market-place, and sell them to the highest bidder; tell him I do not need your services."

They were then driven from the place as they came. Happily for Capt. Penrose, he was sold to a ship-builder, and they were fitting out a fleet. He embraced the earliest chance to disclose his aptness in sail-making, a business so important to them that he had constant employ, where he was shielded from the scorching sun.

Capt. O'Brien had been sold on his arrival to a high officer, and he had charge of a huge mastiff, to feed him well and keep his house clean. He was most peremptorily ordered not to let him bark at visitors, an offence in his keeper which would insure severe chastisement.

For a time things went on so easily that the Captain consoled himself that if his post was not the most honorable, his duty was not hard. Besides, he was well fed, for the dog's food was excellent and abundant, and he partook with him, otherwise, as the rest of the slaves, he was on short allowance.

However, the memorable day came. This pampered animal chose to amuse himself by barking at one of the Dey's life-guards. His keeper was reprimanded, and sentenced to hard labor for one month, to carry stones down a steep hill and throw them into the sea.

This was a regular employment for the slaves; it was done to prevent the earth from being washed away at the shore, from the low part of the city. They never thought of building a permanent wall, but kept the slaves engaged in the laborious work which was never finished, though it had caused death to so many.

If one flinched on lifting these heavy stones, an overseer was ready to give him so many lashes, and this cruel labor was performed under a scorching sun. The month passed, and Capt. O'Brien was reinstated. He was in captivity nine years.

Sometimes their labor was like beasts of burden, yoked to carts, and though a little varied, it was also grievous, and the shortest intermission was a valued favor. Twilight closed the business of the day. Early in the morning their fare was coarse bread and water; this sustained them during their working hours, and in the evening they were driven back to their hovel.

Near this place, a scanty supper of some kind of slops was provided, and when eaten, they were penned in for the night to lie on an earthen floor or stones covered with straw.

Exhausted by fatigue, at times almost famished with hunger and infested by all sorts of vermin, weariness alone could induce momentary repose. Their physical strength gave way and their minds were weakened. They would weep for food and want of sleep like children. Country and friends had long been given up in despair, and death was hailed as a welcome messenger by these poor oppressed Americans.

At this most distressing crisis, a humane gentleman, the Swedish consul, came to their relief as if raised up by an Almighty arm, and ordered each one a bed of straw placed on a frame to avoid vermin, and gave a monthly sum to provide a plentiful supper. His kindness induced the cruel masters to be more lenient.

Feeling they were cared for, hope once more cheered their spirits, and a few months brought the joyful tidings that the country had aroused in their behalf, and arrangements were in progress for their ransom.

The joy was too overpowering for some enfeebled frames. One fell dead on hearing the news; another so enraptured threw himself into Captain Penrose's arms and expired. The sick were soon convalescent, though many were too emaciated to cross the ocean, and never reached their homes.

Excessive feelings of mingled joy and sorrow caused some to fear lest this news was a delusive dream; they thought no such happiness awaited as their deliverance. "Grace hath been showed us from the Lord our God to leave us a remnant to escape, for we were bondmen, yet our God hath not forsaken us, but hath extended mercy to us."

Cruel as were this people, they possessed traits of character which might be an example to many Christians—by their honesty in dealing with each other—goods being exposed in public warehouses, with the prices affixed to each, and no one to attend to the sale. Any one might enter, make choice of an article, which they may take or leave, and leave the price charged in its proper place.

Their devotional hours are strictly observed. Carrying bread through the streets, they cry, "God is Merciful; he gives us bread." With water they cry, "God is generous; he gives us water."

Sending those men to them as consuls who had been their slaves was thought injudicious, as they never have any respect for those who had been in bondage.

CHAPTER XV.

Journal—An Ancient Race—Dey of Algiers—Officers—Ceremony of Introduction—Fast—Story of a Turk—Tunis—Bey's Palace—Swedish Consul—Ornaments—Slaves—Coffee handed—Ancient Carthage—Canal—Pieces of Antiquity—Bey's prediction of America—Costume—Adventures of a Female—Coasting Trade—Captain Cuffee.

A FEW sketches from the journal of a friend who transacted business at Algiers in 1799, between the Dey and the United States, may interest you.

"*Algiers, Feb.* 14*th*. Numbers of people come to the city from the mountains belonging to the Dey, who are supposed to be the descendants of Canaan, according to an inscription on a stone, at a fountain in the Punic language, 'Thus are we fled hither from the presence of that great robber Joshua the son of Nun.' Those are at the present a kind of Christians who never shave their heads nor beards, but who wear a cross marked with blue on their cheeks by way of distinction.

"22d. We were presented to the Dey and officers of the regency. We passed the grand gate, lined by Janizaries, and were conducted across a court, and ascended two flights of stairs crowded by Christian slaves, mostly boys richly dressed, who only pass through the gates one day in the year, the first day after the annual fast of Ramadan, and the first of the new moon in March, the day of liberty.

"Entering the apartment, the Dey was seated exactly like a tailor at his work on a bench covered with a rich cloth of gold, and with cushions of green and gold velvet placed around him. His attendants, ten in number, were superbly dressed, two being old men, the others being Christian boys.

"After taking off our shoes, a ceremony never neglected, a Turk presented us in rotation. He gave us his hand, with an immense diamond on his finger, to kiss, then asked a few foolish questions, and in some minutes we were dismissed.

"He appears about sixty, a venerable figure; a long gray beard flows down his breast. I am informed he has no education, and can neither read nor write. We were next presented to his prime minister with the same ceremony.

"He appeared to be a sensible, well-informed man, about sixty. His apartment was in the great court, which formed a recess surrounded by large looking-glasses and a prodigious number of curious clocks, carpets of the richest kind, cushions, &c. His secretary sat with him, and before them fine fountains were playing. We were next presented to the general of the horse and the divan. Coffee was not handed, as it was their great fast of Ramadan.

"*March 3d.* At the Dey's request, a Turk and Greek passenger to Tunis were received. The former was a native of Constantinople, about fifty-five, very religious and of gentle manners. He had been absent seven years from his family, twice shipwrecked, and was now on his way home. As he had sufficient property, he proposed to devote the remainder of his life to the service of his God.

"In conversation, when occasion required him to mention our blessed Saviour, he always said, ' Jesus, the son of Mary.' On asking him the reason, his answer was, ' that his religion forbid his calling him the son of God, and should he call him the son of any other person than Mary he would commit sin,' therefore he strove to avoid offending in either by avoiding religious subjects when he could.

"If not convinced, he was well informed and free from presumption. Thoroughly acquainted with the Old and New Testaments and

Jewish ceremonies, he had spent a long time at Naples and Rome, informing himself of their mode of worship. He had also been at Mecca.

"We were very attentive to him, and endeavored to make his situation as comfortable as possible; he often expressed a wish we might meet at Constantinople, where he would convince me he was not ungrateful. He prays much, and appears to possess the peace of mind of a person who had acted to the best of his judgment. For much information I am indebted to my Turkish companion, who has taken his passage to Smyrna.

"Before we parted he gave me his history. He was born a Jew of the line of David, and descended from Rabbis, and his education was well attended to, as he was born of rich parents. Some time past, his ill star led him into the house of an Aga or Turkish general.

"Being seen, he was taken prisoner and brought to the Dey of Algiers, where he was condemned to be burned alive or immediately change his faith. For a time he was undetermined, but the desire of life prevailed, which he purchased with his apostacy; and from that moment life has not been worth preserving. He hopes the God of his fathers, who knows his heart, will forgive him, but he can never forgive himself. This has been the cause of his long rambles from home. To use his own words, 'I tremble at the thought of meeting my family.'"

As the preceding story interested me, I took it from two places in the journal, which will explain the following dates. The Greek was a redeemed slave, with nothing remarkable in his character.

"*March* 14*th*. Went on shore at Tunis, and the next day went to Barda, the Bey's palace, about four miles from Tunis. We passed an aqueduct which conveys water to a castle situated on a high hill near Barda. The palace is of very great extent, surrounded by a vast ditch and wall of no great strength, except to repel the Tartars. Entering the great court we passed four gates, each guarded. Arrived at the last we left our post-chaise, politely sent us by the Swedish consul. This gentleman had charge of American affairs.

"Next we passed three courts filled with guards—Turks; then the great court, carrying our hats in our hands, for no one was allowed to go through covered. Here a difficulty arose. We had come in boots, and the Bey admitted no one booted, except commandants. Even for one, mats must be spread over his carpets.

"After spending an hour it was concluded yellow slippers should be provided. Thus equipped, we marched across the court one hundred and twenty feet square, with a fine piazza supported by marble pillars, and a superb fountain in the centre of a marble pavement.

"Two dragomen led the way, and I followed. Next Mr. ———. In this manner we ascended a flight of at least one hundred steps, which brought us to a grand saloon, where we met about sixty slaves, dressed superbly; from this we passed into a large hall, where thirty renegades wore arms and sables. Here were a number of Christian boys, slaves, handsomely dressed in uniform, and extremely clean.

"During this time a profound silence was observed, no one daring to speak above his breath, insomuch you could distinctly hear the ticking of clocks, and watches, which were very numerous along the walls. Many are extremely elegant, set with rubies and diamonds.

"In the same order we entered the Bey's apartment, which appeared like a guard-house placed in a watchmaker's shop, more than any place I could think of. He was seated on a table surrounded with cushions of crimson velvet. By him stood his prime minister and keeper of the seals.

"I observed during our stay in his presence these two persons never took their hands from the hilt of their sabres. We were permitted to wear our side arms, which I thought extraordinary. The Bey immediately pointed a seat for me close by his side on his right hand. It was a long board, the others in rotation. The dragomen stood. Coffee was handed in small china cups; each cup was in another of filagree silver, thickly set with diamonds, then placed on china saucers.

"These cups held about two tablespoonfuls, and were presented by Christian slaves, richly dressed. Little business was done, although the Bey appeared like a business man, and seemed to understand the politics of Europe. In three-quarters of an hour we were dismissed. As we entered here we shook hands.

"When we got down to the square and had on our boots, the renegade came to inform us that the master of the seals wished to see us in his own apartment, and the yellow slippers were resumed.

"Our introduction was much the same. But instead of standing, sabre in hand, we found him seated like a tailor on a cushion of very rich purple and gold. Coffee as before, and exactly the same ceremony observed. He appears a well-informed man; is a Georgian by birth. I am informed there are here eighteen hundred Christian slaves.

"Tunis is situated at least twelve miles from the harbor where the vessels lay. There is a small canal defended by two castles, which leads into a lake ten miles broad and fourteen long, supposed to be the sight of ancient Carthage. The lake is very shallow and fetid, seldom more than five feet deep, and in many places but three feet. Frequently in going up the river, one is stopped by getting on chimneys or terraces of the houses, which report says were sunk by an earthquake.

"Unfortunately, the water is so muddy one cannot see an inch below the surface. On the least agitation it is filled with green particles. Along the bank to the north and northwest are the remains of the ancient and once glorious city of Carthage, which Dido founded, and at which she lived and died.

"The Bey, at immense expense, is forming a canal through this lake. When finished, it will present to the world ruins equal to Herculaneum. Pieces of antiquity have been discovered, but the Moors and Arabs have such an aversion to statues they destroy them as a religious duty.

"Parts of Carthage are pretty certainly found. Those I have visited now are where the canal is so choked that a canoe could not pass through it. Some time ago, on blowing up ruins, a tomb was discovered; on it four figures, one representing the skeleton of a man in complete armor, were found. On his right hand, a lion passant; on his left, an ox passant; behind him, a ram in the same attitude.

"The figures were much larger than life, and of exquisite workmanship. The Arabs destroyed them all. To them, the likeness of an animate thing is an abomination. This was supposed to be the tomb of Scipio Africanus.

"Just returned from a ramble through the woods attended by a Moor. I passed some Arab huts, and observed in one the centre of a ruined column. There are many, but all broken; nor will their religious scruples leave a fragment large enough to remove. Some coins and valuable gems have been found, yet those very people in many instances shame Christians; for in everything they say and do, they seem to remember their God. Meeting them in the streets, roads, or fields, you hear the emphatic exclamations, 'God most high,' 'God is great,' &c.

"At Tunis there are slaves of all nations, and they are much better treated than at Algiers, wearing no chains or rings, never beaten unless they have committed great faults, and they are well fed. The streets are narrow and very dirty; several of them are arched over with small holes in the top to admit light.

"*March* 26*th.* Waited on the Bey to take leave. On entering his apartment, found his secretary and assistant busy in sealing papers. The two seals were fastened to the Bey's side by cords of green silk about twenty feet long. When the secretary has finished, they are carefully rolled up and put in his bosom. He never loses sight of these seals.

"He was very friendly to me, pressed my hand and hoped to see me again. He did not appear pleased with Mr. Eaton or satisfied with the presents; says they were not of sufficient value.

"Speaking of treaties, he remarked that of all nations the Swedes were the most favored by his ancestors, who were pleased by a box with a stone in it. But he wished for something more substantial and would have it; that we were a rich and populous nation, and would certainly one day possess the mines of gold and silver now in possession of the Spaniards. Then we could make him a present of one, at which he laughed.

"Talking about the French in Egypt, we observed, 'Bonaparte might march from Cairo to Tripoli.' He answered that an army could not march in less than four months, besides water was to be had in only two places. It was observed the devil might help him. He replied, on some occasions he did appear to be his friend.

"*April* 2*d.* Proceeded to Tripoli. This (*place*) is filled with business transactions and difficulty with the Bashaw.

"*April* 13*th.* Rode about a mile in the desert to view the ruins of a palace which belonged to his father, where three hundred and fifty Turks were killed in one day while feasting. Being one of the oldest families, he is one of the greatest tyrants, and waded to his throne through the blood of his relations. He keeps everything in his own hands, even the keys of the treasury.

"During his father's life, he was an exile among the Arabs in the desert, and married the daughter of a chief, who is living in the castle.

"*April* 26*th.* Arrived at Tunis; had an interview with the Bashaw and Sepotah, who are still displeased with the presents. They know what has been given to Algiers, and say, 'All their fine vessels are of American construction, while our presents are unknown to our court and people. A fine vessel would be seen, and the subjects and others know where she came from.'"

A gentleman educated in the old Academy of Wilmington, and for years American consul at Tunis, gave me a description of his introduction to the Bey. It being so similar to the preceding, I will only give a description of the apartments at a later day.

After passing through a court and ascending flights of steps, he entered a most magnificent saloon, the whole lined with mirrors, and hung with crimson velvet worked and fringed with gold. The entire room was festooned from the ceiling in elegant taste, and the richest carpets covered the floors. Three rows of benches, one above the other, were covered and trimmed like the hangings, and placed on either side the length of the saloon.

On these stood the guard in military costume, of three orders, the highest tier Turks, next Moor, next the blackest of the African race, each nation in their appropriate dress, splendidly equipped and of the finest figures.

The Bey seated above all, magnificently decorated in gold and crimson velvet, sparkling with diamonds and costly jewels. The flowing robes, turbans, and sashes were gorgeous altogether. This gentleman had never seen such a display of grandeur equaled, though he had been a traveler with many opportunities.

After this episode or digression, which may be interesting to some of our young readers, we go on with our domestic narrative.

During the epidemic of '98, a dismantled ship from Lisbon arrived here. In a storm near Cape Henlopen, they cut away one mast. Capt. Beard, who had sailed from this port in by-gone days, and one lady, were passengers, and the following adventurous story may give you some idea of the hardships and perils she sustained on the ocean.

We had left our home, and secured a retreat in the suburbs. In the same house these people spent a few days. The lady had kept a journal, which we were privileged to hear read. The captain was a man of unquestioned veracity, and affirmed to the truth of it wherein he was a participator, and doubted no part of her story.

Our heroine was well educated, gentle and affable in manner, though her aspect was as rough as that of the weather-beaten sailor, and her attire singular. Her birthplace was Liverpool. She had married young and settled in Halifax, and, happy in domestic life, years winged their flight amid peace and plenty until it pleased God to lay his afflictive hand upon her.

Death bore away an affectionate husband, leaving her a widow with two children, amply provided for.

The son had been sent by his father to England to complete his education. Two years after that event she inherited an estate on the death of a relative, and a desire to see her son was an inducement for her to visit the land of her nativity.

The daughter, in charge of a faithful guardian, was left at school. The voyage across the ocean was prosperous, and she was greeted with affection by the friends of her youth, and their joyous meeting cheered her saddened spirits, and by their assistance her business was closed with success.

Some remittances were sent home, and after six months she embarked. Two weeks had passed on the lonely ocean, and a tempest arose, and the skill of seamen who had often braved its dangers was baffled. Everything was swept from the deck, the ship abandoned, and much of her valuable treasure remained in the wreck, doomed to the fathomless abyss.

Tossed with a tempest, next day they lightened the ship, and when neither sun nor stars appeared, all hope that they could be saved was then taken away, and they had much work to come on by the boat. In anxious fear they spent days in the boat, until rescued by benevolent sailors sent from a vessel bound to a far country.

A change of garments and some pieces of gold, secured in a girdle, were her only treasure, far from kindred and home. A stranger in distress, she excited sympathy. Her passage was taken in a ship commanded by Capt. Beard, bound to Philadelphia. Every attention and kindness was paid by this worthy man to cheer her in her isolated condition.

The prospect of meeting soon her beloved daughter, who she knew must be suffering great anxiety respecting her fate, absorbed all her thoughts. Forgetfulness of the past left her unprepared to meet the sad fate which suddenly enshrouded her in the deepest gloom.

This fine ship was captured by one from a Spanish port, and the crew were marched as prisoners into the interior. Even this lonely female was subjected to rigorous and unkind treatment, which added to their disastrous captivity. Weeks passed almost in despair, when an event occurred enabling them to force their way clandestinely to a town on the Bay of Biscay, where, with a small sum each one had concealed, they purchased a boat, providing a scanty supply of food and water, and fourteen souls ventured on the perilous deep.

In a sailor's garb, this female took her turn at the oar, exposed to all the hardships of a boisterous sea, continuing for two weeks in the open boat, driven by storms on an unknown and trackless way. Often at midnight their canopy was a dark and frowning sky; no sound but the angry billows lashing the sides of their fragile barque, the only plank to screen them from a fearful eternity. They shuddered at the thought of being engulfed in the fathomless abyss, their fate known only to an omniscient God, for amid such terrific scenes no human confidence can overcome the shuddering weakness of mortality. A genuine spark of the Holy Spirit must be kindled within to prepare us for death, whether He approach by the tempest or still small voice. "I cried by reason of mine affliction unto the Lord, and He heard me, for Thou hadst cast me into the deep in the midst of the seas, and the floods compassed me about."

In their darkest hour relief came. They were rescued by a ship bound to Lisbon, whence a passage was procured to Philadelphia. Here a brig was just ready to sail for Halifax, in which she embarked. The captain had heard of this tempest-lost female, and was anxious to bestow every kindness upon her. After all her great disasters and fortitude under every discouragement, she was landed safe on the spot from whence she started just two years before.

In those days the coasting trade was very considerable, a number of vessels from the Eastern States and from Nova Scotia laden with plaster of Paris; and varieties of fish, quantities of excellent smoked salmon, and also potatoes were articles of trade. They discharged their cargoes at these wharves, and in return they loaded with flour, corn meal, and grain, &c.

One of the most noted traders was Captain Cuffee, a colored man. He owned several vessels besides the ship he sailed. Though manned by people of color, subordination and order presided on board. The captain was much respected by all those who transacted business with him, and he sustained a reputation for integrity and good demeanor.

He was not very dark; a large athletic man, pretty well proportioned, and his countenance portrayed thought and decision. He wore the simple garb of a Friend, and professed to adhere to Friends' principles. He was a regular attendant on their religious meetings.

He had often crossed the equator to the southern coast of Africa, and traded at Sierra Leone. He was a warm advocate for colonizing the people of color in their mother country. He thought it the only way to advance their prosperity and permanent good. His voyages to this town were frequent in the early days of the present century. James Brian, Stockton, and Craig were largely concerned in this business about the period we notice.

The first shipments of cheese which were exported from this country to England were sent there on adventure by Mr. Pedrick, now of New York, a young man brought up by Joseph C. Gilpin, at his store in Wilmington; and thus originated a business of great extent, and a most valuable addition to the agricultural exports of our country.

CHAPTER XVI.

Visitations of the Yellow Fever—Every House Crowded—Ship on Fire—Its first appearance here as an Epidemic—In 1798—Intense Alarm—Death of Citizens—Touching Scenes—A few Philanthropists—J. Miller—James Lea—John Ferris—Dr. Vaughan.

WANDERING far beyond our contemplated excursion, we have been led to traverse the ocean and explore distant lands.

Once more we resume the domestic part of our narrative. The sorrowful year of 1793 has been glanced at; in '97, pestilence again raged in Philadelphia, and many citizens sought refuge here. Shipping and dry goods merchants, &c., brought their Western customers until every nook and corner became filled.

Ships crowded the wharves. One day a ship next to the wharf was seen in flames, and the cry of fire caused universal alarm. There seemed no way for surrounding vessels to escape, but happily by cutting away the ropes and letting them float down the creek they were saved, and the fire was soon extinguished. "Every shipmaster, and all the company in ships, and sailors, and as many as trade by sea, stood afar off."

Many cases of fever occurred, but they were all traced to persons who had been in the city. One in our own family, a female relative, who had been from Philadelphia a week, was violently attacked, but recovered. A very worthy lady, daughter of Mr. Joseph Shallcross, fell a victim to the disease in her father's house, amidst the grief of sorrowing relatives; and many others died, though the disease was not communicated.

In 1798, Philadelphia had been unusually healthy. Pleasure and gayety prevailed, and yellow was the predominant color. Dresses, bonnets, shoes, gloves, &c., tinged the city with a yellow hue. But in July, in the midst of gay life, Death on the Pale Horse rode through the streets, suddenly scattering pestilence among the terrified inhabitants.

An ordinance was issued that every infected house should be designated by a yellow flag hung from the door or window, but many rebelled against this decree. In dress, the transition in color was instantaneous.

Hither many again fled for a temporary home, and business men renewed their occupations, and every place was filled. Now the opinion was fully established that change of air removed the infection, and each one felt his own security in being remote from the disease.

But, alas! that memorable day, the 5th of September, put many hopes to flight. Samuel T. Erwin, a respectable man of an old family, sickened and died with the yellow fever; also his wife and brother, who had never been absent. And it was said ten out of eleven in one family on McComb's wharf died. Mr. and Mrs. McC., estimable persons of great respectability, died; also the wife of Col. Tilton, opposite. In the next house, Major Pattens, and Mr. Miller, a young lawyer of promise, fell victims to it.

On investigation, rags had been stored, and the bags stood some time on the wharf. On these Mr. Erwin had sat to rest after fishing. The disease was most fatal along the wharf. From this crowded town they knew not where to flee, but it was soon deserted. "How doth the city sit solitary that was full of people!"

Touching facts of this season impress us with the idea that many during pestilence are hastened to an untimely grave. Mrs. H. had been faithfully attended during her sickness by affectionate relatives. Her grave clothes prepared, even dressed and laid in the coffin, when signs of life appeared and she was removed to her bed. Next day at the very hour she expired.

An extraordinary case occurred in a dwelling on Hemphill's wharf. J. Provost and wife were both subjects of the fever, and the committee for the relief of the needy were applied to. They sent the only help in their power to procure, two worthless colored women at two dollars per day for nursing.

These soon reported their death. Men of similar character brought their coffins in a cart, and were hurrying them to the grave, when a humane man, though unable to do much, having lost an arm, noticed the cart, and went to oversee those people. His daily visits were to houses of mourning, yet this one had been passed by. He was induced to prevail on a timid old lady to follow him to the lonely abode of contagion. His forebodings seemed to warn him that death was not there.

Ascending the stairs, their footsteps alarmed these miscreants while dragging the apparently lifeless man from his bed, though still warm. In the same room lay his wife, sensible but speechless, waving her hand. An effort to place her in the coffin had aroused her to resist at the moment these good Samaritans entered.

By bathing them, changing their clothes, and administering suitable nourishment, they soon revived, and both lived for years useful members of the Methodist Society, and would often recount the scene with gratitude to their Heavenly Father and to these kind friends, and tell their marvellous story.

Mrs. Provost said their harsh treatment aroused her feelings at her sad fate with indescribable awe. Her feeble resistance alarmed them. Turning to her husband in the most inhuman manner, they had resolved to bury him dead or alive.

In this deplorable state there seemed to be no hand to help, no power to resist wretches who for a scanty pittance were crushing them out of life into an endless eternity.

The benevolent individuals who rescued them were Mrs. Susanna Sellers, an old inhabitant, and Mr. Miller, a Methodist local preacher, whose good deeds during that season of calamity ought to be had in everlasting remembrance. This disease was most prevalent along the water. In the village of Brandywine many died, two being sons of Joseph Tatnall, Esq.

A lapse of four years had wiped away the tears and sorrowing for the dead, and with many this melancholy season was buried in oblivion. A new century had dawned upon us. In 1802 this pestilence renewed its visit to Philadelphia, and again our town was an asylum sought in terror, where business was resumed with apparent safety. This season intercourse between the places was prohibited by order in council, yet a convalescent subject stealthily retreated from Philadelpha to her mother's in Wilmington. The spot was most unfavorable, below Second in King street, a mere alley, between stables and cellars of stagnant water. From sudden exposure the subject relapsed.

Dr. E. Smith, an eminent physician, pronounced it a most malignant case of yellow fever, and advised the immediate abandonment of the neighborhood to arrest its progress. But an apathy seemed to seize the people, as well as the police. Instead of inspiring caution, those who dare not doubt his judgment were willing to attribute his salutary advice to timidity.

The brief space of a few days infected the whole square, and Death bore away his victim from every dwelling. "Who now was calm? who now resolute?" All was terror and despair, panic-stricken people flying they knew not whither. "Sound an alarm, let the inhabitants of the earth tremble, for the day of the Lord is nigh."

Naught but afflictive scenes were presented. A family in Front street near King excited the deepest sympathy; it consisted of the aged parents, three daughters, and a son, all previously in good health. The eldest daughter was married to a seaman and lived with her father; she was first seized with the malady, and the third day was borne to her grave.

In two days more, the remains of the three other children, their only offspring, were conveyed to repose side by side in the Methodist Cemetery.

There were none to follow them to the tomb, save the bereaved parents and a feeble old man. Here they waited long in hope of assistance, but none came, and the coffin lids were warped by the scorching sun.

It chills the heart to relate the thrilling scenes. The agonized parents were obliged to consign the remains of their beloved ones with their own hands to the narrow house appointed to all living. Advancing to the open grave, the father stood aghast, unable to yield to the stern necessity.

But the mother, like a machine put in motion, performed the duty. No expression of sorrow clouded her brow, no tear bedewed her cheek.

The feeble old man stretched out his palsied hand to aid in staying the rope. Death he had long viewed as an angel of mercy to bear him from earthly sorrows and guide him to endless bliss. But this awful solemnity overcame the weakness of his nature. The rope slipped; his trembling limbs bent until he fell on the grass.

Now death appeared as the King of Terrors; he saw him in majestic awe enter the humble abode, with the stifling breath of pestilence, to take from these bereaved parents the only hope and support of their declining years.

The mother's account of her own state was most affecting. Her eldest daughter's disease was at once pronounced malignant. Then terror seemed to seize her whole soul. She was all feeling. Tears swept down her cheeks like a flood, day and night, until everything was misty.

The others sickened, and as the eldest was borne down the stairs, tears no longer bedewed her cheek, and her whole sense of feeling was suddenly benumbed. She nursed the other three, for no help could be procured. Her duties were performed by day and by night, with no power to feel even extreme fatigue or to reflect on her forlorn situation. This stupor spared her much anguish, and she doubted not was wisely ordered by an overruling Providence to prepare her for the sad task. Weeks passed in this state of torpor ere her sad bereavement was mourned. Osborne was the name of the family. He was a harmless, goodly man, long known as a tallow chandler in this town. They were members of the Methodist Society.

Many victims of this mournful visitation claim our notice, and no doubt many are buried in oblivion. Mrs. Springer, the widowed daughter of the Rev. Petrus Tranberg, was left in charge of three orphan grand children, for whom she had happily chosen a faithful guardian, James Lea, whose ancestors were among those of olden days.

The eldest of these orphans married young, and in the absence of her husband resided with her grandmother. One and another sickened, until the whole family were subjects of the epidemic.

In this sad case the guardian made his daily visits, procuring for them every comfort: even the chamber of death was the scene of his devotion to see that all was conducted in order. Then he followed each one of them to the grave.

The youngest female, and an infant of few days, were the only survivors, and on consigning the last remains to the dust his ward was received into the bosom of his family. Their own younger children were sent into the country.

Mr. Lea was indeed a father to the fatherless, while his excellent wife felt a mother's care for the helpless babe. With paternal affection they guarded they guarded the youthful days of their ward, who was married in their house, and left it as Mrs. G., ever retaining a grateful affection for these warm-hearted friends of her youth. "To him that is afflicted pity should be showed from his friend."

While gloom enshrouded the town, and noisome pestilence exhaled vapors that led to the gates of death, the destroying angel led his captives to the tomb. Neither bloom of youth, robust health, nor the desire of a little "time to prepare to meet their God" availed. His inevitable grasp closed the earthly scene.

When the contagious atmosphere blew into a dwelling and prostrated an inmate by the afflictive hand of the Almighty, hope too often winged its way, despondency seized the mind, energy languished, and the victim became too feeble to apply remedies at the favored moment, either to mitigate or remove the malady. It was thought this extreme fear hastened many to the tomb, amid silence and loneliness. Friends were few; no soothing hand was near to administer relief.

Yet two or three philanthropists did enter the chamber of death to commiserate the sad heart and shed a ray of light over the darkest hour. With the course of years they have glided down the stream of time, and their "places are no longer known." But as the evergreen retains its verdure, so a few still sweetly cherish the remembrance of their works of mercy, and we record our tribute of affection to departed worth.

All hearts were faint, and every voice seemed to echo "whither shall I flee?" "Escape for thy life, look not behind thee; neither stay thou in all the plain, lest thou be consumed." On the eve of leaving home disease beset our way, and I became a subject. On the morrow my mother was attacked, and Dr. Vaughan's soothing manner and devoted attention, and a sympathizing friend, Mr. James Lea, in his daily visits, provided every comfort. Such kindness shed a ray of hope over the darkest hour of affliction.

One more esteemed friend demands a grateful memorial of affection. This was Col. Thomas Kean, an officer in the Revolution, and a worthy and useful citizen, who was engaged in commerce till near the close of this eventful period. Death seemed to spare him till the eleventh hour, and in an unexpected moment bid him leave his earthly cares to mingle with the dust.

Many sympathizing friends mourned his departure. He was an affectionate husband and father, and a sincere friend, ever ready to visit the widow in affliction and to soothe her cares.

His widow survived him for years to mourn this afflictive dispensation. And when the full term allotted to man had passed away, she was called to "resign her fleeting breath," and "her spirit to ascend to God who gave it," and her body to return to dust.

Having long confessed her Saviour before men, she could with confidence lean on him to guide her through the valley of the shadow of death to realms of endless bliss. "Thou art with me; thy rod and thy staff, they comfort me."

The visits of John Ferris, too, we hold in grateful remembrance. But his philanthropy claims public notice. Wherever the pestilential breath blew in sickness, death and sorrow, there he was found, by day and by night, to administer relief. All were objects of his peculiar care, whether in the stately mansion or lowly cabin.

Even death seemed to have respect to his services, and to leave him a little longer to follow up these acts of mercy till the pestilence was stayed. Yet he also was borne away as the last victim, a martyr in the cause of humanity, and none was more deeply lamented. "When the ear heard me, then it blessed me; when the eye saw me, it gave witness to me."

In the most aggravated state of the disease in 1802, a single physician prescribed for all who were afflicted. Dr. John Vaughan most assiduously fulfilled the arduous task. Other practitioners were either sick or absent. But no omission of duty chilled the patient's heart, lest the lamp of life should grow dim or cease to burn through medical neglect. Nor did a hasty prescription or hurried visit create alarm or despair.

His tranquil manner and affectionate sympathy soothed the dark hour of affliction; like "a burning and shining light," he exhibited the Gospel principles of a practical Christian. But after this, when a few more years had glided by, death bore him away in the prime of life; tears of sorrow flowed o'er his grave as the memorials of grateful hearts. He also left a young family, in remembrance of his private and public services and sympathy, to mourn his loss.

CHAPTER XVII.

Walnut Street--Old Trees--Amusements--Fairs--Folly Lane--Anecdote--Dr. David Bush--R. M , Esq.,--D. E. N. B.--Gov. M'Kean--Separation--Adventures of a Young Lady.

To perambulate the streets, we sally forth from a point where events mostly end--Amen corner, Front and Walnut streets. Here Captain Mendenhall resided sixty years ago. His father-in-law, Joel Zane, a respectable Friend, lived next door, and predicting things were to remain just so, called it *Amen Corner*.

Thence to French street was a beautiful square. The houses on the upper side were elevated with a graceful slope to the water; and from this open space, covered with rich grass, there was a full view of the shipping. Lombardy poplars and weeping willows shaded the fronts with a beautiful effect, and fine meadows banked in on the left. In days of yore there was a row of noble walnut trees opposite, and stumps yet remained, with spikes driven in to fasten boats. A dock ran up to Front street, and in flood tide these boats landed their freight.

In olden time this was noted for youthful sports. Under the majectic walnuts on the green sward, they would play at "Prison base" or at "Old witch by the wayside." Fairs were also held, and at them there was always a large assemblage, a joyous mingling of lookers-on and performers. The musical instruments were the violin, bugle, flute, fife, bagpipe, and banjo. There was dancing, too, and many a sober one took a peep at the Dutch lads and lassies dancing hypsey-saw. Fair days were merry days. Moonlight nights were chosen for

> "These healthful sports, that graced the peaceful scene,
> Lived in each look, and brightened all the green "

An aged gentleman said "that about the year 1765, the country people were supplied with spring and fall goods at these fairs, held in all the villages, and attended by young and old. Some went to buy, others for fun and frolic. On a fine day, young men came by hundreds, with a lassie 'alongside;' and their shirt sleeves were nicely plaited and crimped as high as the elbow, above which it was tied with a colored tape or ribbon, called sleeve strings. Their coats were tied behind the saddle. They wore thin-soled shoes for dancing, and two pair of stockings, the inside ones white and the outer blue yarn, the top rolled neatly below the breeches knee-band to show the white, and guard them from the dirt of the horse's feet. Boots were not worn at that time; a man booted and covered by an umbrella would have been 'exposed to scoffs.'"

Then this gentleman relates a few circumstances to mark the changes. The first green silk umbrella seen was brought by Capt. Bennett from Lisbon for his wife; the second by John Ferris for his wife Lydia, by the same captain, and the third by my father from the West Indies. I remember being so much ashamed of it that I only held it a few moments over my head while walking by his side, one day in the year 1770. The gentleman alluded to was John Shallcross, Esq.

Somewhere about 1787 or '9, my mother received from her friend in the West Indies a present of two umbrellas, one large green silk one for herself, and a smaller-sized red one for me. My schoolmates all came to see it, and it was uncovered and hoisted with the greatest care, and exhibited to many who had never seen the like. It was a topic of conversation among the young, and this elegant present was viewed as an emblem of pride.

At these fairs, stalls were erected in the streets—I think in Fourth street. From the upper market down, dry goods of every variety were displayed, and everything good in season was there, feasting being not the least part of the attraction. There was plenty of customers, who saved their money to make purchases at the fair.

As memory may recall incidents in passing up the streets, we will briefly trace them. Some who were once the busy tenants in this square have long been slumbering in the ocean. Captain Proale owned the house southeast corner of Second street—then called Folly lane, where stood five tenements, one in an orchard, where Rose Valentine supplied children with apples.

The upper cabin was Peter Steinmetz. An anecdote of him is somewhat amusing. It was on the eve of winter, and deep snow covered the earth. Peter and Debby were convalescent; a long illness had increased their poverty. The physician, Dr. Bush, knew their inability to procure fuel, and was about to devise means to furnish this comfort. He was benevolent, but fond of fun. Being summoned on a jury, where twenty-four persons were able to give a pittance, with much feeling he stated Peter's destitution, and described a most extraordinary animal he owned--a native of the east, he thought, from its long beard and moustaches (very rare in those days). It could stand on two legs, was very sagacious, had an expressive countenance, and delicate taste, so tame as to eat out of the hand, yet had strength and spirit to knock down an offender. Peter had no suitable place for it, nor means to provide food. Traveling menageries were unknown, and wild beasts rarely exhibited.

The company agreed that such a rare phenomenon ought to be preserved. As the doctor's stratagem succeeded, he proposed that they should go the same evening and see it. Each one paying a half dollar, would induce others to go. Care had been taken to warn Peter. The animal was kept in the cellar, and one at a time had to descend the shackling steps.

The first one was an irritable man, who saw an old goat, with a long beard, that had been a terror to children for months. He became so exasperated as to threaten to level poor Peter, annihilate the goat, and was ready for fisticuffs with the doctor, who had much pleasantry and tact in such sports; and begged him in wrath to remember mercy, and not stand alone as the object of ridicule, but let each one take their share.

He saw this was true policy, and joined heartily in the trick. The joke was the gossip of the day. But the best end was a supply of fuel for those industrious poor.

In 1796, the property once Capt. Proale's, on the corner, was purchased by Robert Montgomery, Esq., a wealthy gentleman. The dwelling was enlarged, out-houses and stables built, and a beautiful flower garden tastefully arranged. At this day, the location might seem a strange fancy, when the face of nature is so changed by raising the street and crowding it with small tenements, which intercept the water view. Then it was a rural spot.

Mr. M. had made the tour of Europe, and participated in the elegancies and luxuries of foreign climes. His early years were mostly spent in France, where he had been educated, and had married an accomplished lady.

Emigrants from that country had sought an asylum in this town, from the horrors of the revolution there, among whom were those of the best society, and the attraction was to mingle with those of congenial tastes.

Were one of our youthful aspirants to visit these premises, and be told that the former owner had money enough and to spare, that the

Governor of Pennsylvania and his family were his guests four months, and that in those days governors were distinguished men, not drawn by lot, but selected for talents or noble deeds, how would they wonder!

The Governor's family were here during the prevalence of the yellow fever in Philadelphia, in '97. At that memorable period an English officer arrived. Mr. M. was at the hotel, and recognized him as a classmate in France. His domicil was overflowing with guests, and there was not a spare nook at the hotel.

Mr. Montgomery ranged the streets from door to door to find a lodging for the stranger and his servant. As no other place could be obtained, a lady fitted up a cot-bed in her parlor for Edward Nathaniel Bancroft, Surgeon-General to his Britannic Majesty's forces in the West Indies. His name and rank were marked in full on his trunks with brass nails.

You may not be aware that British influence was said to prevail at one time. Now it was reversed—French ascendency being "the ton." So the prudent surgeon had his badge of honor *covered*, lest he might fall into rude hands. This minute sketch is only the prelude to an interesting narrative of the family of the surgeon's uncle, whom he came to visit. Their story will be related in turn.

Mr. M. married very young, and having no children they adopted an infant in France. The eventful story of her brief life will no doubt be touching to her surviving schoolmates, should it happen to fall into their hands, as she was much endeared to them.

Discontent and imaginary trouble may overshadow the mansion of the rich and exalted. They are not the peculiar birthright of the poor, nor their inevitable lot, but when discord invades the gilded hall, too often it ends in hapless woe. This rural abode, that so much pains had been taken to beautify and render attractive, where pleasure seemed to preside and crown the joyous inmates with youth, health, and worldly possessions, and so lately arranged for a permanent residence, was suddenly abandoned for one more in fashionable life. Philadelphia presented amusements and gayeties, and thither they removed, entering fully into the pleasures of city life, which soon grew wearisome. Ere this once happy couple reached the prime of life, they separated by mutual consent, never to meet on this side of the grave.

No apparent reason was offered for the rash resolve, save that one preferred America, the other France. Neither would yield. Apportioned with a large annuity, Mrs. M. set sail for her native land.

Regardless of absent friends, she entered with spirit into the frivolities of Paris, while Mr. M. dissipated away his days in Philadelphia.

Neither pains nor expense were spared on little Miss, their adopted daughter—she was placed with Mrs. Rivardi, principal of a fashionable boarding-school in Philadelphia. Her education was strictly attended to, and application with good talents in due time presented her to society an accomplished lady. But alas! unpropitious circumstances rendered her father's house an unpleasant home, and her friends interposed and counselled her to reside with her adopted mother in Paris. Her acquiescence was readily gained, but her father reluctantly consented, though he promised her ample support.

The non-intercourse law, then in force, was for some time a hinderance to her departure. At length, a vessel was to sail to England with dispatches, and to touch at port L'Orient. The commander was a gentleman, and promised her protection, and to resign her to the care of the American consul. Having just attained her seventeeth year, she was of prepossessing appearance and courteous manners. She traversed the ocean with strangers to seek a new home.

After a prosperous voyage she was landed at the destined haven, where unforseen events compelled the kind captain to resign his charge to the care of a stranger, who escorted her to the hotel of the consul. Unfortunately, that officer was absent, and it was a time of much political intrigue.

It was soon noised abroad that 'an interesting young girl had been landed from a brig bound to a country with which intercourse was prohibited, and without a protector. To arrive under such circumstances was too mysterious to be solved, and suspicion, ever on the wing, soon decided that she was a spy, and those on the watch-tower saw their path of duty plainly to cite her before the city authorities.

This intelligence overpowered her, as she had no one to ask counsel of, nor from whom to claim protection. In a moment, shrinking nature gave way, and she swooned. Even her accusers were alarmed, and felt pity for the destitute orphan.

How sad a transition in a short time! All her life she had been flattered as an heiress, indulged in luxury, with attendants at her bidding. Suddenly, she was a forlorn stranger, and summoned before the municipality to answer to the charge of an unknown crime.

At length she was aroused from this shock, and conscious innocence sustained her in the hour of trial. With undaunted energy, she answered every question, and stated her story fluently in the

French language. Her eloquence and guileless manner were the admiration of this vast assemblage.

Then fearlessly she denounced such harsh procedure, and refused all proffered attention. As she was about to be relieved from this embarrassing scene, the astonished consul entered. In compliance with her request, she was instantly removed from this detestable place, and they were soon on the road to Paris.

Buoyed up with enthusiastic delight at the hope of meeting one she loved best on earth, whom she had been taught to call by the endearing name of *mother*, who had watched over her in infancy with affectionate solicitude, whose long absence had been so sincerely mourned, now anticipating the happiness of embracing this beloved one, to whom she could confide her sorrow, and tell her sad adventure at L'Orient, realizing the sympathy of her warm heart by a kind reception, she banished all care from her thoughts.

Alas! on entering the halls of this visionary Paradise, her airy castles crumbled! No affectionate mother greeted her arrival, or listened to her tale of sorrow.

A cold, heartless woman censured her rash imprudence in venturing on the voyage alone, and still more for leaving a rich father, in whose affection there were those who were ever ready to supplant her. Having no security for her pittance, she might be left to earn her daily bread, or receive it from the cold hand of charity. No assistance need be expected from *her* scanty income, barely enough to supply her own wants, therefore no obstacle must delay her return.

Grieved and bowed down by slighted hopes, a speedy journey brought her again to Port L'Orient, whence she embarked in the same vessel homeward bound with dispatches.

Unable to suppress her agonized feelings, she revealed her sorrow to the benevolent officer, who sympathized with her, and by every attention strove to soothe her wounded spirit. Her father's reception of her in Philadelphia was most affectionate, for she was tenderly beloved by him. Yet his house was a desolate home, and happiness no more was an inmate of her bosom; no pleasing anticipation of the future cheered her lonely hours, or buoyed up by her drooping spirit.

On a winter evening, with a slight cold, she went to the Museum. It was lighted up, and all was gayety. The worthy captain met her, and apologizing for his inattention, promised her a visit through the week. Her father was suffering from an attack of the gout, and she felt assured his visit would give him pleasure. Time passed cheerily as they promenaded the crowded assembly, until ten o'clock.

To comply with his promise, and pass a pleasant evening, he went to Mr. M.'s mansion. In the hall he met an elderly female. The answer to his inquiry was, "Mr. M. is as well as can be expected." In the drawing-room he was asked, "Do you wish to see Miss M.?" When taken into the room, the spectacle which met his gaze was overpowering. So lately as the last Tuesday, he saw that lovely animated form as she passed with him through the crowd. Now it was only Friday, and the spirit had fled forever! Here was only the lifeless corpse!

> "To-day we frolic in the rosy bloom
> Of jocund youth—the morrow knells us to the tomb."

This mournful event was an exciting subject of conversation for months in Philadelphia.

CHAPTER XVIII.

Methodist Meeting-house—John Thelwell—Stone Meeting-house—A Noted Lawyer—White Hall—Vandever's Island—Old Swedes' Cemetery—Remembrances of the dead.

FOLLY LANE, now Second street, is now filled up with respectable dwellings. Two young men of enterprise, Bonny and Bush, some years since erected a foundry and machine shop, that gave rise to the improvement. The former was cut off in the spring-time of life, and though a stranger here, was esteemed a useful and worthy citizen. The northeast corner was long a noted spot, but not for the style of the dwelling or its valued inmates. Its title was the *four-story*, being a unit for many years.

The next place of note was a humble Methodist meeting-house founded by a meek and lowly people, who would shudder at the popish name of a church, though they did decorate it with evergreens on Christmas, and kept the day as a religious festival. It has been so often enlarged that hardly a relic of the original is left. Now it can vie with many buildings in large cities, and is called *Asbury Church*.

Opposite is the parsonage of the Swedish church, and the residence of all the rectors to the year 1828. In the rear was a fine garden kept in the best order, and a draw-well of excellent water.

Capt. Dawson, a respectable pilot, owned the property above. Having a competency and no children, he and his worthy wife were patrons of the Methodist society in time of need. But we must not pass this primitive place of worship without a tribute of respect to John Thelwell, its devoted patron from its early dawn, and faithful until death. "The Lord shall count, when he writeth up the people, that this man was born there." It would be easier for us to say what he did not than to recount his numerous duties. He was a ruler, an exhorter, and an efficent class-leader with these people. He was clerk of the market, too, and once he weighed a woman's butter which was wanting in balance, and was about to take away the basket. She being keen-sighted, and he having but one eye, she took the advantage by daubing a pound in the other eye, and thus made off with her effects.

He held the office of bell-man from time immemorial, as crier. Many at this day remember Daddy Thelwell and his big bell, tingling as he passed, and warning the burgesses to attend their meeting in the little town chamber over the end of the lower market-house. Also for sales of property and goods at auction. Those are yet living who heard the joyful sound of his old bell ringing in their ears, arousing them from repose, his voice echoing loud and long, "*Cornwallis is taken! Cornwallis is taken!*"

Could you believe, after being faithful to all these duties, he should be a schoolmaster, and of some note, too?

The more ancient horn-book, scarcely now remembered, became out of use in this country, and ceased to be imported from England, when we undertook to teach ourselves learning after the Revolution. It was soon below our expectations, for it only contained the alphabetic letters, the numerals, and the Lord's prayer. These, fastened on a small thin board, about the size of a small spelling-book page, were securely nailed to it with a strip of bright brass for a margin, and covered with a plate of horn so transparent as to render the text clearly to be read, yet fully defended from the unwashed fingers of the pupils.

One of the British poets has immortalized this elementary guide to all the future learning of our advanced age by an elegant poem, of which we venture to insert the introduction and conclusion:—

" Hail, ancient book, most venerable code,
Learning's first cradle and its last abode ;
The huge unnumbered volumes which we see,
By lazy plagiarists are stolen from thee:
But future times to thy sufficient store
Shall ne'er presume to add one letter more.
Thee will I sing in homely wainscot bound,
The golden verge encompassing around
The faithful horn in front from age to age,
Preserving thy invaluable page."

"In idle pages no errata stand
To tell the blunders of the printer's hand."

" An ancient peasant, on his latest bed,
Wished for a friend some goodly book to read :
The pious grandson thy known handle takes,
With eyes lift up this savory lecture makes.
'*Great A*,' he gravely read, the important sound,
Made hollow walls and empty roofs rebound ;
The expiring ancient raised his drooping head,
And thanked the stars that Hodge had learned to read.
——'*Great B*,' the yonker bawls. 'Oh! heavenly breath :
What ghostly comforts in the hour of death !
What hopes I feel !' '*Great C*,' pronounced the boy.
The grandsire dies in ecstasy of joy."

But the intruding successor to teach the alphabet—spelling, reading and grammar—was Dilworth's spelling-book, with small print, like old worn-out newspaper type. This generation would not now bend their minds to study such dim lights. Most boys and girls here were his pupils, at least during part of their school days.

At the foot of Quaker Hill, Mr. Thelwell had commenced teaching, but was soon promoted to the little Senate Chamber over the market-house, and this, at the corner of Third and King streets, was long his room. The boys' entrance was front, the girls' up an alley. Even in in those *primitive days* there were some unruly children; but he adhered most strictly to the letter of Solomon's advice, and "never spared the rod." The rattan or ferrule seemed to be in perpetual motion, and were as common in his seminary as gymnastics are at this day, and woe to the boy mounted to receive the reward of his exploits or omissions! But wondrous strange if after such an exhibitiion he should return to school subdued. It can only be accounted for, that Independence was not fully understood in the young Republic. Certainly it was not carried out as in this day.

The Bible was used for the senior class, and also Gough's Arithmetic, with sums in simple division that would fill a large slate, and puzzle many a brain, and cause showers of tears. This school was opened every morning by prayer and singing a hymn.

> "The village all declared how much he knew;
> 'Twas certain he could write and cipher too;
> Lands he could measure, times and tides presage.
> And e'en the story ran that he could gauge.
> But past is all his fame. The very spot
> Where many a time he triumphed is forgot."

Miss Debby Thelwell, the eldest daughter, assisted and kept the girls in order; she was a very worthy woman, but with no literary pretensions. Miss Polly rarely entered; she was timid and more refined. After the father's death, the sisters united, and taught young children for many years. In old age, this worthy family were removed by death from useful employment, having contributed their share of good to this community.

The first assemblage of Methodists in this town worshiped in an upper story of Capt. Joseph Gilpin's store-house on King street, and the next place was J. Thelwell's school-room, corner of King and Third streets.

Eastward of Fourth street there were no buildings, and the street downwards was called Ferry Lane, and on the north side there was a row of old houses. The two lower were owned by Joan and Rose Hugal. Rose was a celebrated cook, and their garden supplied many families with quinces for preserving.

In 1801, on election day, the voters then went over to New Castle. About noon a fire broke out in the second house of this row. A small engine and buckets were the only aparatus, and great was the alarm. In the absence of men, women acted their part, in passing the full water buckets up one side and the empty ones down the other. A lane had been formed by them down Walnut street to the creek. It was a laborious task, but it is mentioned among other trifles to show the ways of things in olden times.

Corner of Fifth street was "the stone meeting-house," so called in those days. It was built by the converts of the celebrated George Whitefield, who seceded from the congregation, and were called *New Lights*. Rev. William Smith, who was their pastor, died in New

Jersey. He was succeeded by our worthy friend Dr. Read. Both these pastors preferred keeping their light trimmed, and to follow the old paths.

Under the pastoral charge of the Rev. E. W. Gilbert, it was much enlarged, and a free school built by general subscription. When a new church was erected, the minority clung to this, but in wisdom soon reunited to their brethren.

The Baptists are the present owners. Down Hanover street was called Chicken Alley—the alley below, Dogtown.

Broad street hence was called Church Lane. On this spot, half a century ago, the reply of a boy eleven years old, to a noted lawyer of that day, was deemed so appropriate that to show the force of his wit it may be proper to sketch his character.

A lawyer had suddenly appeared in this borough, and made himself of great notoriety by going from door to door to search out old deeds, proclaiming himself to possess extraordinary powers to prove the titles of other days. If an old musty deed of past generations could be raked up, for a very small fee, *paid in advance,* your name was honored on his list of clients. Many a one was caught by surprise, and quite a sensation created in the vicinity.

The whole tribe of Brandywine millers were to be dispossessed and a poor little English barber was made the "heir apparent" in right of his wife, who was of Swedish descent. Wills he dragged into court, and instituted many petty suits, besides this mighty one. The barber was very much elated at his prospective wealth, and felt very consequential.

On the decisive day, he was seated in the Court-House, to hear the issue, full of hope and breathless expectation. The decree was announced against all such claims, and the poor deluded man fainted away, fell on the floor, and scarcely revived. Thus the lawyer's professional race was ended, and many called him a swindler.

A deep snow covered the ground, and here was a narrow pathway leading to the old church, where this lawyer met the boy, and said, "My little friend, I suppose you call this the straight and narrow way?" "I think not," said the boy, coolly. "Why so?" said the lawyer. "Because," answered he, "*I meet Mr. Hall here.*" The reply made an impression. He went to his lodging, and told his wife he had never met with so pointed a reproof.

In old time White Hall near the Brandywine was a mansion of plenty. The owner, Capt. Joseph Stidham, commanded a company of militia during the Revolution. He was young, wealthy, and liberal. In the prime of life reverses strewed his path with cares, and he died poor.

A large portion of this district was in brickyards, where the best brick was made, and exported by the proprietors. Thomas Cox and Wm. Kirk, their descendants, still own part of it. Near by was the old King's road to Philadelphia. A toll bridge just above the railroad was the private property of Peter Vandever, and in those days a large revenue was drawn from it. The Vandever family was respectable and wealthy. Their ancestor adopted the religious views of Luther, and fled from the persecutions in the Netherlands to this wilderness, in the 16th century, and settled on the Brandywine, calling their place "Vandever's Island."

And it long retained the name, as part of this estate is still in possession of a descendant. The ancient dwelling stands as a relic, which was erected before the old Swedes' Church. The maternal ancestors of this family were Swedes.

An anecdote of an old man in their service is somewhat amusing. The governor and his suite, on visiting this lower province, were complimented with a free pass, and the old man knew he was not to receive toll from his excellency. But he was unwilling to let so many pass without paying toll, and stopped them, exclaiming, "Do you all pretend to be governors?" and exacted toll from the suite.

On another occasion the young men had been to Jersey in a canoe to shoot ducks, and were presented with a superior pumpkin, large and round. On their return the night was dark, and they left the boat for for the man to secure.

He jumped in, and his weight pressed one end into the water. The pumpkin rolled forward, and struck him with such force that he ran away alarmed; but reflecting that he might be called a coward, he resolved to prove his courage by a second trial, and let the rascal see that he had missed his mark by insulting him. Assuming the courage of a hero, he advanced boldly, and sprang into the canoe so suddenly that it brought down his antagonist with such force as to give him a severe blow. To his surprise and terror, he discovered that it was a monster without arms or legs, therefore it be must something supernatural and irresistible.

This island was partly encircled by marshy land, and when banked in, tilled and drained, became fertile meadows for pasture and grazing. Here and there were built cabins called marsh-houses, occupied by one who tilled the ground or guarded the cattle.

At the end of Marsh Lane, near this old mansion, lived a colored man, a son of old Jerry Harman. In 1838, the last time the bridge was carried away, he saw the water rise, and hurried on, crossing the bridge, and feeling it move, sprang on terra firma just as it passed away.

As he approached his cabin, he waded through deep water, and found his wife with two small children in the greatest consternation. They all climbed to the loft, and the water rising rapidly they made their way to the roof, clinging to it in fear and trembling. Soon a mighty rushing wind tore it from the hold, and swept it through the air over the water more than sixty feet, and landed it on the railroad, with these four human beings, just as the darkness of night was closing in. "I will bring thee up out of the midst of the rivers; thou shalt fall upon the open fields."

Swedes' Cemetery.—Thus our wanderings have again brought us to hold, as it were, mental converse with the dead.

> "When eve is purpling cliff and cave,
> Thoughts of the heart, how soft ye flow."

We enter the ancient burial-place, to linger amid the moldering dust, and in a day-dream ponder over incidents which our fathers have told us of the lives of by-gone generations, and those of more recent date.

> "Then all by chance or fate removed,
> Like spirits crowd upon the eye;
> Those whom we liked, the few we loved,
> And the whole heart is memory."

Under yon old walnut tree lies that "young man who was dead and is alive again." Near by, a fair maiden, whose bridal robes were cast aside to shroud her for the grave. On the south, the two young men, a bridegroom and a brother, whose joyous hearts gladdened to to see the beams of the setting sun glittering on the water, and the breeze fill the sails to waft them over, unconscious of the rising tempest, which ere nightfall hurried them into an endless eternity, and turned the house of feasting into a house of grievous mourning.

That old tombstone near covers the rich and honorable West India merchant, E. M. Gray, whom neither wealth, fame, worth, nor medical skill could save from the iron grasp of death.

Yon monument on the south side of this venerable cemetery commemorates the virtues of a native of Strausburg, France, John James Ullmann, Esq., a gentleman of varied and extensive information and scientific attainments. Born of an ancient and honorable family, in that antique city, his education was of the highest grade which Europe could afford. Being at the University when the brilliant discoveries of Lavoisier were astonishing the scientific world, his natural aptitude for investigation found an ample scope in chemistry, then just assuming its modern form. His familiarity with the languages of Europe was remarkable. He spoke and wrote most of them with fluency, and he was also considerably acquainted with the Asiatic languages.

Mr. Ullmann was for those days a great traveler; he had traversed Europe and much of Asia. The institutions of America were familiar to him, as in early life he had conceived a great admiration for their republican characteristics. He resided in India many years, and transacted business with some of the most eminent merchants of this country, by whom he was highly esteemed. In the prime of life he retired from commercial pursuits with an ample fortune, having married an estimable lady, the daughter of a French naval officer. He came to the United States, and selected Wilmington for his residence, and was for years a loved and honored citizen. He alway was reputed to be a *millionaire*. While in apparent health and vigor, he was cut down by apoplexy, in the twinkling of an eye, leaving a widow and seven young children to mourn their sad bereavement.

Mr. Ullmann was a man of polished manners and noble appearance, and possessed great conversational powers. He was emphatically a gentleman of the "old school." Alas! that there should be so few successors to that class of men.

We have ofttimes stood by the open grave and seen an affectionate father consigned to his last earthly abode. "Leave thy fatherless children, and I will preserve them alive, and let thy widows trust in me." And the mother in the bloom of youth called to resign the tenderest objects of her fostering care, and we did "weep with those who wept" at the thrilling sound "earth to earth." Many of the young and lovely lie here. How often has the "first-born" been a sacrifice to the Lord. Many such touching scenes might be stated were we to speak of that only which we know.

The monument near by commemorates a first-born, Ferdinand Bauduy, who, from his earliest years was a child of promise, and trained in virtue's ways, and the end of his collegiate course was crowned with honors, and he ready to act his part in a world of cares at an epoch in the manufacturing interest which then allured enterprising men.

He turned his attention to the art of dyeing cloth, for which France was famous, and thither bent his steps. After he had attained the artist's skill, he returned full of life and hope, to commence a useful career on the Brandywine, where he married an estimable young lady, the companion of his early days, and the daughter of E. J. Dupont, Esq.

The sun of prosperity seemed to gild his outset, and cheer the manufacturer at his labor. But ah! the cruel spoiler invaded his domestic circle, and bore away one so beloved by kindred and friends. "In the midst of life we are in death." To the business concern it was "as the shadow that steals over noonday," and the sad event was lamented by all in the vicinity, for he who was an ornament to society and bid fair to be a useful citizen was no more.

Those three tombstones are remembrances of earthly happiness. One in the centre covers the remains of a venerated father and his affectionate daughter; a wife and mother, who suddenly passed from earthly joys, and on this tomb the sun that lighted and cheered her circle, set to rise no more. A few brief years passed away, and both her sons died also, and here lies their sleeping dust side by side.

> "The parent, ever honored, ever dear,
>   Claims from the filial breast the pious sigh:
> A brother's urn demands the kindred tear,
>   And gentle sorrows gush from friendship's eye."

This small tribute of affection springs from daily observation. They were the most obedient, happy, and interesting children we have ever known. E. M.

The pyramid near commemorates Mons. Hammond and his only child, a lovely boy, borne away at an interesting period, to the great grief of his parents. The father was summoned in the prime of life to become an inmate of this narrow apartment, to mingle with the dust of his son.

M. H. settled here with other emigrants, and was a highly respectable citizen and kind master. He manumitted a valuable slave, Andrew Noels, and gave him five hundred dollars to purchase a house.

Here our attention is arrested by youths of kindred ties. There is a remembrance of the young and lovely Cora Garesche, who in the midst of her bridal preparations, in an unexpected hour, was conveyed to an eternal home; and a younger sister, that, lately a bride, is embosomed in the same soil.

On this spot the family have mourned many youthful bereavements.

The account already given concerning Major Peter Jaquett has comprised many of the incidents of his family and of his private life; but the inscription on his tomb, in the burying-ground of the Swedes' Church, intended to hand his Revolutionary incidents to posterity, is so remarkable and historical that it is probable it would be considered an omission not to preserve it in these reminiscences, as it was directed by himself to be handed to the future notice of posterity.

SACRED TO THE MEMORY OF

MAJOR PETER JAQUETT,

A distinguished officer of the Revolutionary army, who died at his residence—Long Hook Farm—near this city, September 13th, A. D. 1834, in the 80th year of his age, having been born on the 6th of April, 1755. On the 4th of January, 1776, he joined the Delaware Regiment, and until April, 1780, he was in every general engagement under Washington, which took place in Delaware, Pennsylvania, New Jersey, New York, and the Eastern States. He was then ordered to join the Southern army under General Gates; and with the brave De Kalb he was in the battle of Camden, of the 16th of August, in which the Delaware Regiment, consisting of eight companies, was reduced to two only, of ninety-six men each, the command of which devolved upon his brave comrade Kirkwood and himself, as the oldest officers left of this gallant band. He was also in the battle of Guilford Court House, the second battle of Camden, and in the battle of Eutaw Springs. He assisted in the siege of '96, and capture of the village of that name; and was also in every action and skirmish under General Green, in whose army he remained until the capture of Lord Cornwallis at Yorktown. He returned to his native State in 1782, and in 1794 married Eliza P. Price, daughter of Elisha Price, of Chester, Pa.; and, as a farmer, he lived upon his paternal estate until his death. The brave and honored soldier—the kind and obliging neighbor and friend.

BENEATH THIS STONE ALSO REPOSE THE REMAINS OF

ELIZA P. JAQUETT,

Wife of Major Peter Jaquett, who was born November 25th, 1769, and died May 5th, 1834. She was an affectionate and devoted wife, a kind and humane mistress, and a warm and untiring friend. In early life she became a regular member of the Episcopal Church, to which and its ordinances she always remained devotedly attached, trusting to her Saviour alone for pardon and forgiveness, and in his gracious promises for the hope of a blessed immortality.

Many interesting epitaphs, which would swell our pages, are passed by. But the tombs of two young mothers attract our notice. One, whom we knew well in her early days as Margaret Stevenson; when Mrs. Higgins, like a lovely flower she drooped and faded from the sight, leaving her three young children.

Another of more recent date demands a passing tribute, because of the same communion and of few years. In the midst of worldly enjoyments, Mrs. Mary Bradford avowed herself on the Lord's side. And when death bid her at so early an age leave three infant children and a deeply afflicted family, they were sustained by the glorious hope that while they were sorrowing over her grave she was "an heiress of immortal bliss."

We conclude our meditations amid the tombs with a memento of respect to Wm. B. Brobson, Esq., a friend of many years. But what shall we say? His literary attainments are well known. His devotion to promote the interest of his church is acknowledged, and his removal from earthly scenes lamented. There seems no more for us to say, but to fill up a meagre skeleton with an interested token of remembrance and respect.

The influence of Mr. Brobson more than others elicited our consent to put forth this volume. He thought too little was known of the early days of this ancient town; and that the reminiscences accompanying it should be rescued from oblivion.

The interest he felt in his birthplace gave a zest to the little incidents which are carefully related in truthfulness. We were often amazed that his comprehensive mind could regard the trifles we were ready to toss off. He said, "Add all you can that relates to olden time. From such hints information is gained." The parts read to him inspired a confidence to go on; but it is sincerely regretted that the entire manuscript was not read to so competent a judge, efficient and friendly in detecting its omissions.

OLD SWEDES' CHURCH,

THE CHRISTIAN HOME OF MY CHILDHOOD,

FAREWELL.

MY LAST EARTHLY RESTING-PLACE,

FAREWELL.

CHAPTER XIX.

French Street—Mrs. Way—I. H.—Capt. E. Brown—Allen McLane, Esq.—J. Stapler, Esq.—School—Gov. McKinley—Town Taken—Anecdotes—Escape of Capt. M. and Capt. K—Fleet—A Young Lady—De Sourci—Monsieur Garesche—Betty Jackson—Change in Scenery—Old Mansions.

From Water St., we will walk up French St., and note persons and events of olden days. As some occupations were connected more than others with commerce, they will be noted in passing. A. Davis, sailmaker, lived in yon high-roof frame on your right; and William Fussel, biscuit baker, in the old stone house above Second St., which is now a pottery. He was a very worthy member of the Friends' Society. On the northeast corner of Second St. was a school of long standing for girls.

"There, in her noisy mansion, skilled to rule,
The village mistress taught her little school;
Well had the boding tremblers learned to trace
The day's disasters in her morning face."

Mrs. Elizabeth Way was a celebrated teacher of needlework, so important for misses in those times that even the art of shirt-making was strictly attended to, and fitting and cutting were taught here. All were closely inspected by the mistress, and must be done with neatness and care. Most of the older females, brought up in this town, have been her pupils.

Mrs. Way was a very respectable and worthy woman; she had received an education superior to most women of her day, and was endowed with a strong mind and strict principles of morality, yet an irritable temper was a drawback to her usefulness, and it was annoying to some of her pupils. She was a disciplinarian of the old school, and strictly adhered to the wise king's advice. A bunch of switches or cat-o'-nine tails were freely used to correct the naughty.

Leather spectacles were worn for slighted work. Much attention was paid to the position, for, if the head leaned down, Jamestown burs strung on tape were ready for a necklace, or if the person stooped a steele was at hand. This was the length of the waist, and held up the chin by a piece extending round the neck, and a strap confined it down. It was not very comfortable to the wearer, though fitted to make the "crooked ways straight"—but a morocco spider worn on the back, confined to the shoulders by a belt, was more usual.

The celebrated painter Benjamin West had been the companion of Mrs. Way's childhood and youth. As absent friends, they kept up a correspondence in age, and it seemed much pleasure to her to relate anecdotes of his early days.

Isaac Hendrickson, of Swedish descent, and then one of the most respectable shipping merchants, married her only daughter, a handsome and lovely woman, and highly esteemed. He owned the opposite corner where they lived. Mrs. Way was aged, and had declined teaching to reside with her daughter. Her only son, a young physician, was also an inmate of this family. Mrs. H. and the Dr. both fell victims to the fever in 1798. This sore calamity "brought down her gray hairs in sorrow to the grave." "If I am bereaved of my children, I am bereaved."

Capt. Elisha Brown, a worthy townsman, purchased this house, intending to reside there on his return from the last voyage he expected to make by sea. It proved the last, for neither vessel nor crew were ever heard of. A widow and two children mourned the loss of an affectionate husband and father. "He shall not return thither any more."

Col. Allen McLane, an officer in the revolution, and long collector of this port, was the next owner, and was here, the custom house office, long after his death. The house above is an old relic, once the property of John Stapler, donor of the land occupied by the almshouse.

The Tranberg house has been minutely described, yet a little incident of the revolution may be in place. While the British had possession here, two officers, in passing, espied the portrait of Col. Benzell, and stopped to inquire his history. They were politely informed that he died in his majesty's service, commander at Crown Point, and this was the home of his widow. "Madam," he replied, "let it hang in sight, and your family will be protected." They were protected.

Mrs. Phebe Vining lived on the southeast corner of Third street, and this house was for many years afterwards the residence of J. A. Bayard, Esq. It was occupied next by Gov. Bassett, his father-in-law. The northwest corner, now a coachmaker's shop, is of great notoriety; and here we pause to recount deeds of the Revolution, and from which you must conclude this was the court-end of the town.

Somewhere about 1760, in an orchard near this corner, was a frame building, where a learned Scotchman kept a classical school, and he was styled Master Wilson. Having but few pupils to study the languages, his large number was made up of boys and girls, varying in ages.

There Dr. Nicholas Way was partly educated, and Samuel Canby, and many others. My mother was also a pupil at the same time, and it was so unusual for girls to be taught arithmetic farther than simple division, that even thus far in figures was deemed absurd. "For what use," said these primitive villagers, "can it be to woman?" But my mother's fondness for this branch induced her parents, by the master's advice, to let her proceed through the "double rule of three," and for her perseverance she ofttimes had to bear the taunts, and be called "a tom-boy with her big slate."

Dr. James McKinley occupied this frame, which was moved back, when he built this mansion, now a relic of other days. A neat garden with choice fruit ornamented with flowers, especially tulips, then rare, extended to King street, and it was kept in order by his faithful servant Fortune, a native of Guinea, who lived to a great age. The clean walk of white Irish gravel, brought by Capt. Jeffries, and spread the length of the square, is remembered. Here the celebrated A. H. Rowan often paced, meditating on the land he never expected to visit again, while many a sigh escaped, and, on hearing the tune of "*Erin go bragh*" whistled or sung, he would abruptly depart.

Dr. McKinley pursued his profession until death ended his career, in 1796. His remains lie in the old Presbyterian cemetery, and his bounty to that church is commemorated on a pillar at the gateway. A widow was his only surviving relative.

Dr. McKinley, in '77 was governor of this province. After the battle of Brandywine, the British quietly entered the town at night, when silence reigned and the agitated spirits had sunk to sweet repose. His excellency was disturbed by the sound of voices and pattering of feet. On raising the window, his surprise was overpowering to see his mansion surrounded by so strong a guard, and to feel himself a prisoner.

The following morning was market morning, and the scarcity of provisions drew people thither early. Two females met, and expressed their indignation at seeing red-coats parading the streets with freedom, and censured the police for permitting it. A British officer overheard their confabulation about what ought to be done with his majesty's soldiers, and stepped forward, gently touching the elder lady's arm, said, "Madam, do you know that you are all prisoners? Be advised to return to your homes." The admonition was promptly obeyed. Miss Peggy Allison, a worthy lady, long known and respected, who died here in old age, made the severe remark to Miss Hannah Shallcross, a belle of her day.

Capt. H. Montgomery had removed his family to Salem, N. J., and proffered his services to Gen. Washington previous to the battle. His wife's sister, who was a widow, had resolved to remain by her property in town. He lodged there on the memorable night, and offered to market for her in the morning; and was leisurely passing on, at gray dawn, when he espied the governor's house surrounded by red-coats. At once he thought of his precarious situation, for he was aware of their threats to send him to England should they capture him; and his fate seemed clearly sealed, for he knew that any attempt to escape would be in vain.

Therefore he dauntlessly walked up to the commanding officer and bowed. Happily for him his dress was a complete suit of black, having no other change in town, and the officer fancied that he was a Presbyterian Minister, and saluted him politely, saying, "Sir, you see the town is taken, and you had better retire until later in the day, when order will be established, and you can walk unmolested."

The captain thanked him and turned. When his name and residence were demanded, he pointed to his lodging, but evaded the name. The officer made many inquiries; how far the fleet could come up on tide, the distance of the channel from the shore, &c. The captain promptly answered, and having observed the favorable mistake, it diffused a cheering hope of escape.

Capt. Kean, of the militia, was also here. A protracted ague had left him sallow and emaciated, and he was depressed and exhausted by fatigue. A report that a file of soldiers were in search of two rebel officers induced them to keep out of the way by secreting themselves, and ofttimes changing place. Their last resort was behind a stack of chimneys in a garret of the custom-house, before noticed.

While they were in this predicament, the soldiers ascended and flourished their swords around the chimneys, and more than once were near cutting them. The garret was empty and dark. At length they gave over the search, exclaiming, with oaths, "it was a poor place, although the exterior was so good looking." Mrs. Littler, the hostess, said they were young housekeepers, and very poor, and this was only a temporary residence. The truth was, their furniture had been removed.

The abode of John Stapler yet stands next door. He was a plain Friend, and firmly adhered to royalty, yet true to the rebels in this dark hour. His aid was solicited, and promptly granted. Many plans were cogitated, when Capt. Montgomery suggested to procure a large vest for Capt. Kean, and pad it to give him the appearance of corpulence.

The scheme was approved, and Friend Stapler borrowed one of John Benson, a remarkably corpulent man, that took a pillow to pad, and dressed him in a plain Quaker garb of his own, with a low-crowned and broad-brimmed hat. Under the wing of royalty, and for his staff a would-be parson, the trio sallied forth for the invalid to breathe fresh air, and he was really much refreshed by the hope of escape.

A British officer met them and sympathized with the afflicted gentleman, inquiring how long he had been dropsical. This was a happy hit, and his kindness was most encouraging. Permission was asked to extend their walk, which was cheerfully granted. Late in the afternoon a third sally out was effected. The sentinel had seen them in conversation with the officer, and, besides, he had been ordered to let them pass.

No sooner were they out of his sight than the pillow was dropped, and they made their way with a quick step to Brandywine, saying, "Arise! let us flee! for we shall not else escape! Make speed to depart, lest they overtake us suddenly and bring evil upon us!"

The boat was on the other side in charge of an intoxicated man, which caused delay in getting over the creek. At length they succeeded; but an evil-disposed woman had given information who they were, and as they put off the boat the soldiers made a rush to the shore, and with threats ordered them to return, firing their muskets.

But one held the boatman while the other paddled over rejoicing, and tied the poor fellow to a tree, and took refuge in a corn-field, which screened them for a time. With cautious footsteps they paced through the rustling corn, until night discomfited their pursuers. Then wading through marshes and leaping ditches, ere the morning dawned they reached the Delaware shore.

Part of the British fleet lay in the stream, and this they must pass through. It was a sad dilemma. There was no time to deliberate or for any precautionary measures. An old batteau was fastened at a fishing-place. As it was their only resource, they hastily sprang into it, and were no sooner off the shore than, to their horror, they found it leaky and one side broken.

To cross in so fragile a boat they knew was hazardous; but there was no alternative. Capt. Kean, in his delicate health, lay in the bottom merged in water, baling it out with his hat, while his most strenuous efforts could scarcely keep the shattered bark from sinking, and Capt. Montgomery paddled over the river amid the enemy's ships. They were twice hailed, but, silently pursuing their way, gave no answer, and the officer on board the ship thought it might be a delusion.

This dreary night the sky was veiled in darkness, and they were on the deep with only a decayed plank to cling to. Their feelings were of intense concern, though they had so lately faced the mouth of cannon. They were almost ready to conclude that their fate as prisoners on the preceding day was less gloomy, or had they been taken by the enemy's ships safer. But as the morning dawned, they landed in triumph on the Jersey shore, and viewing the planks that had borne them over, they acknowledged a superintending Providence.

Once more their way was through a corn field, and as they reached a copse of wood, they saw a cabin, and sought admittance. A well known voice saluted them with a hearty welcome. Thomas Crow, a worthy townsman, had fled from the foe, and found in this humble retreat a safe asylum for his family, where liberty and kind friends were hailed as joyous blessings.

Authentic anecdotes of revolutionary days are sought out with such earnestness that we are induced to state all that have fallen in our way. Previous to the battle, a woman meanly attired called at the residence of Joseph Shallcross, requesting a private interview with the host. On entering the room, she presented Mr. Shallcross with a letter from Gen. Washington, wishing to obtain information of the enemy. The letter was quilted in her petticoat, and an answer was returned in the same way.

This gentleman was a member of Friends' society, and so deeply interested in the cause of independence, and in energetic efforts to attain it, that was ofttimes said he only omitted to shoulder the musket.

The following story was related by the lady to many of her friends. Two officers, one a captain in the regular army, the other of the militia, on the night the town was taken, lodged at the house of their mother-in-law, Mrs. Hansons, north-west corner of Shipley and Hanover Sts. Mrs. Hanson was a widow with two single daughters; one of them was very handsome, and quite a belle. They were members of the Friends' society. One of these females was awakened by the sound of voices and footsteps, so unusual at the late hour, that she raised the window, and was exceedingly alarmed to find the house surrounded by red-coats. She aroused the family, who quietly assembled in the parlor to devise some means for the escape of the rebel officers. One was in full uniform, and had no change of clothes. This was most perplexing. Many schemes were proposed and new difficulties presented.

Miss Nancy made her proposition, and it was instantly adopted. In the third story was a large hearth, and the bricks were taken up and the sand removed. The military suit was folded and wrapped in paper, and laid there, carefully replacing the bricks. As the morning of a new day dawned, they were puzzled how to obtain a suit for the officer; but this young lady also undertook the enterprise. She appeared at the front door very neatly dressed, and attracted the notice of a British officer.

He politely saluted her, and she freely communicated to him the embarrassing circumstances of the family—that an invalid relative had taken a ride for change of air, and was unavoidably detained, and that an article from an opposite neighbor was wanted which was important to his comfort, but not one was willing to venture across the street. Feeling it a duty to make the attempt, she requested his protection, which was graciously granted.

As she entered the domicil of her friends, they exclaimed with uplifted hands at her imprudence. There was no time for explanation. She solicited a suit of clothes packed in as small a bundle as possible, and taking it was escorted home, inspired with confidence by the successful adventure. She thanked the polite officer, and invited him with a few of his friends to partake of a cup of coffee prepared by her. The invitation was readily accepted, and while seated with them at the table an additional request was made. She informed the commandant that the carriage had been ordered at an early hour to convey the sick gentleman home, and she would presume to solicit his interference once more to prevent detention.

Assurance was given that they should not be molested. The mother deemed it most prudent for her adventurous daughter to accompany those officers whom her ingenious schemes had released. So she stepped in and took her departure. "Wherefore, now rise up, and as soon as ye be up early in the morning and have light, depart."

They drove rapidly to the old ferry, and were scarcely in the scow when they were pursued, and muskets fired as they crossed the creek. The balls whistled over their heads, and they made a most lucky escape to Dover, where this young lady was proclaimed a heroine of the eventful day, and in a few years married Major D. G. Adams, an officer of the Revolution, noticed in the reminiscences of the old Swedes' Church. Col. Tilton and Capt. Bellach were the officers rescued.

At the corner of Fourth street was the Erwin family, worthy people of olden days. The ancestor was a cabinet maker, and owned much property. One of the daughters married Israel Israel, who in the Revolution lived on the Delaware shore, much exposed to the enemy. In the absence of Mr. Israel, they made an attempt to carry off his cattle. When his wife knew their design, she rushed forward with only a boy and dog, and threw down the bars, and drove the cattle beyond their reach. The upper corner was once the seat of fashion, when the Vining family flourished there.

In Sixth street near French was an humble cottage, once an asylum for La Marquise De Sourci and her only child. This desolate female, born in high rank, accustomed to luxurious plenty and elegance, attended by the nobles of her land, was forced by the horrors of the French Revolution of 1789 and '90, penniless, to seek a home amid strangers.

All that was left of her former grandeur was this tender bud of nobility; and without the means to complete his education, he too might droop and languish on a foreign soil, or become dependent in adversity, or to fall a prey to the canker-worm of intemperance, which blighted so many fair blossoms in this young Repulic.

She was sensitive to her sad fate—that honors, riches and friends had passed away, yet no retrospective caused a murmur within these humble walls. Their energies were aroused by an ardent desire to seek employment, and self-respect seemed to enchain the thoughts of the noble-minded youth to exert his ingenuity even in a small way for the support of his decrepit mother.

A broken back rendered exertion on her part laborious; her diminutive person was unprepossessing, yet she was an accomplished lady of great refinement and elegance of manners.

A vine of dwarf gourds grew in the gardens, which, when ripe, young De Sourci gathered, and made of them globe boxes. The outside was ornamented by cutting figures, and staining and varnishing it. He carried them round the town, and found a ready sale, and the first one he completed is now in possession of a lady in Wilmington. It was either sold or presented by him to her mother, Mrs. Bedford.

Being encouraged in this effort, he most assiduously applied his talents to invent novel articles. Among these was something in the shape of a grasshopper to skip over the ice. This was a great amusement, and drew crowds to see the novelty glance over the Christiana. He was also famous for skating, but soon his attention was turned to building boats of small size, and these, too, sold well. Then he built one of larger dimensions, and rowed it up the creek. This one he soon sold, and another also, for he never wearied in his labors. They were all the work of his own hands.

At last he built one so large that he could cross the Delaware, and bring sand from Jersey to sell for building. The wonderful exertions of this meritorious youth, and his great success, was the theme of conversation. The sudden transition, from the loss of luxury and splendor to abject poverty and assiduous toil, would have been too overwhelming for most minds. Few could have sustained their equilibrium under such circumstances.

In the midst of his prosperous career, his heart glowed with affection for his widowed mother. To her he was devoted, and for her he seemed to live. When the toils of the day were ended, the little treasure he had earned was poured into her lap, and her cheerful smile of parental approbation was an ample reward. Independence secured happiness and contentment in their humble abode, where comparative comforts were few. They received the kindest attention from those of their own nation, who would willingly have provided for all their wants, for many wealthy French families were here at that day.

How mournfully thrilling is the conclusion of our story. This little boat, once too heavily laden, was overtaken by a storm and upset on the Delaware, and as the blossom droops and dies beneath the shower, so poor De Sourci bowed to the waves and died.

This sad event cast a gloom over the community, for he was generally known, and regarded as an estimable young man. Boats filled with anxious hearts searched day after day in vain for his remains. There was something touching in the deep maternal sorrow of this widow, fallen from greatness, and now bereft indeed. As "God directs the good man's steps," this sorrowful scene awakened the sympathy of her steadfast friend, the benevolent Dr. Bayard. Under his hospitable roof, her afflictions were soothed with the tenderest care, until death released him from his charge. Hence the Marchioness De Sourci was borne from his mansion to the old Swedes' cemetery, to lie by his side until the resurrection morn; "for the trumpet shall sound and the dead shall be raised."

In later years, a blind man lived with his grandmother, Mrs. Ann Sperry, an old inhabitant, and a very worthy member of Trinity Church. She was desirous to have a large poplar tree which was before her front door cut down. This blind man climbed the tree with a rope, which he tied to the top, holding on as he descended, then fastened it to a post at the corner of the street below. He cut it around with his axe, frequently trying the rope, until he found it give way. Then, by keeping at a proper distance, he accomplished the work by his own hands. T. Moore, who still lives near the spot, saw him achieve this feat. Thomas Byrnes could readily find any place in town, and was a most regular attendant at the old church, and always occupied the same seat in it.

Dr. Didie's old house is a relic of other days yet standing. He was a French physician, held in great estimation by the emigrants.

Adjoining was the well that gave rise to the story related of the sailor. An open square was then opposite; now a large Wesleyan seminary occupies the space, ofttimes numbering one hundred boarders. Within ten years, these two squares have been filled with handsome houses. Then comes an old establishment, known as the Garesche house. Two houses were purchased by Mr. Garesche, a French emigrant, and united by making great improvements. An ornamental garden, arranged with taste, extended to Walnut street; then it opened to the next square below, and the whole was a grass lot bordered with Lombardy poplar trees. Fruit trees were interspersed through the square, and with fanciful walks. Near the centre was a brick building of octagon form.

In winter it was used as a hot-house, and in summer as a saloon, where many joyous hours were passed, for in those days the French families entertained very handsomely, and they constituted a large and refined society of themselves.

On the top of this saloon was a summer-house of lattice work, encircled by a balcony, with seats and stands for flower-pots, tastefully arranged. The whole was in perfect keeping, and an ornament to the town while in possession of the respectable and wealthy owner, whose remains, with many others of the same family, are mingling in the dust of the old Swedes' cemetery.

The corner above was the residence of Dr. Bayard, whose benevolent character has been portrayed.

Long before, and succeeding the Revolution, an establishment just above was celebrated for its nice refreshments, where everything was the best of its kind. There were all sorts of beverages, and every variety of cakes and fruits. Tea parties were common here, for order and neatness presided over the domain of Betty Jackson, a colored woman of more than ordinary capability.

As the queen of her class, she knew how to rule, and her subordinates were submissive and attentive. Those who came to purchase cakes walked up the alley. Her best parlor was fitted up for exclusives only, and we remember

> "The white-washed wall, the nicely sanded floor,
> The polished clock that clicked behind the door;
> The pictures placed for ornament and use,
> The twelve good rules, the royal game of goose;
> The hearth, except when winter chilled the day,
> With aspen boughs and leaves, and fennel gay;
> While China tea-cups, wisely kept for show,
> Ranged o'er the chimney, glistened in a row."

From the balcony on the east was a flight of steps that ascended into a noble willow. Here a platform seated twelve or more persons, where you had an extensive view of the Delaware for miles. Beneath was a tasteful flower garden, from which many a bouquet was selected. The scenery was very attractive.

Betty died in old age, much respected, leaving valuable property; and it is creditable to say part of it still belongs to her descendants, who occupy the place. Her eldest son, Jeremiah Shad, was many years one of our principal butchers, famous for curing meat, and died respected as an industrious, useful man. Her youngest son, Gabriel Jackson, was like his father, a ship carpenter and master builder. He built the brig Keziah, which was long in the Irish trade, and brought its hundreds of passengers to this town.

Above this place, some fifty years ago, the colored people built their first meeting-house of stone, called Ezion Geber. It has been enlarged, with a cemetery kept in order, and under the Methodist government.

A party seceded, who now have a large brick meeting-house. They are independent, though Methodist. For years Peter Spencer, an exemplary colored man, was their ruler. His tact to govern was wonderful, and his influence unbounded. When death summoned him from his useful sphere, all classes of citizens lamented his departure. This has also a large cemetery, kept in neat order.

Hence to Brandywine were fine orchards, rows of cherry and pear trees along the fence, with plenty of small fruit by the wayside, where the winged families tuned their notes. Lots of luxuriant wheat yielding immense crops, green corn waving its lofty tassels as the wind whistled through, made one feel that surely peace and plenty reigns here.

But the art of man has changed the face of nature, driven away the feathered tribes, and given place to new tenants.

Two relics occupy the last corners of French street. One is surrounded by noble buttonwoods; and ancient shubbery and ivied walls proclaim antiquity. Alas! the worthy inmates once so busy in setting those mills in motion, giving life and energy to the scenery, and dispensing blessings among the industrious poor, and the cotemporaries of the Shipleys and Pooles, are slumbering in narrow cells of their frail mortality.

Meanwhile the trees, shrubs, and tiny sprigs of ivy, planted by their hands, are luxuriating in verdure and flourishing around their mansions. They cling so fondly to the old home that they creep into every crevice, and entwine on the walls as if to commemorate the sleeping dust of those by whose fostering care they were nurtured in tender years, and trained in the way of vigorous beauty.

CHAPTER XX.

King Street—Capt. Giles—A thrilling story—Gilpins—Anecdote—Mrs. Wallace—Eli Mendenhall—Capt. Jeffries—William Cook—Trinity Chapel—Dr. E. A. Smith's family—Capt J. Nicholson

KING STREET claims our notice, to bring out things new and old. The frame house corner of Water Street belonged to the Bush family. In colonial days, the north-west corner of Front Street was the residence of Capt. Giles, a rich merchant, who had seen much of life on the ocean, and had lived years in village simplicity, but neither had subdued his ambition. He gloried in his English ancestry.

His only son was a youth of noble appearance, good demeanor, and the pride of his father's heart; and his only daughter, for whom he designed an honorable alliance, was to share his possessions. Her person was comely, and one placed in such auspicious circumstances rarely fails to attract admirers, and many offers were rejected until young Malcolm paid his addresses to her.

His deportment was manly, and his person prepossessing, and he too was an only son, who would inherit much of this world's goods. He was no stranger, for his home was at Monckton Park, only across the stream. His suit was crowned with success, and pleasing to both families, so an early wedding day was fixed, and numerous invitations were sent out, and great preparations made to entertain in all the pomp that a village life could display.

The anticipated evening arrived, and was passed in joyous festivity. The Swedish minister performed the ceremonial rite, and the young villagers were bewildered by the splendor, for such notions of elegance had never before disturbed their rustic habits. Festive gaiety and new amusements filled each day for two weeks.

On a fine morning, a few young men fitted out a boat to sail on the Delaware, intending to return by early tea-time, as company was to assemble in the evening. About the hour they were expected to be homeward bound it grew dark, the clouds lowered, and the lightning flashed in vivid streaks. Thunder louder and louder proclaimed the majesty of Omnipotence, while the wind howled in terrific grandeur.

The doting father paced the floor intensely anxious, for he well knew the perils of deep water where there were no skilful hands to manage sails or oars. As his alarm increased, the household were thrown into paroxysms of frenzy. Ere nightfall the storm abated, and hope revived. Experienced boatmen were dispatched, but no tidings came to the loved ones. Midnight passed over in solemn sadness.

By morning dawn an express arrived from a brig in sight that the crew had witnessed the awful catastrophe of a boat upset in the height of the storm, and not a soul spared to tell the thrilling story. By timely exertions a few bodies were grappled from their watery grave, among whom were the bridegroom and his brother. Their funeral rites were solemnized in the old Swedish cemetery, by the rector who had so lately officiated at the wedding.

What a sudden transition! Now the house of feasting was changed to the house of mourning, from the brightest sunshine to the deepest woe. The hopes of two families were no more, and ere the orange blossoms that adorned the bride were withered, the widows' weeds were worn to mourn the youthful husband of her affections, and a brother who had been the idol of her heart. This melancholy event cast a gloom over the town.

In a few years Capt. Joseph Gilpin married this widow, and long occupied her father's house, of which he became the owner.

A young lady to whom Capt. Gilpin had paid some attentions felt disappointed on hearing of the gay wedding, and of his bright prospects in marrying an heiress. She inquired of her informant "what was the amount of her supposed inheritance." He replied "Twenty-four hundred pounds." This was sterling money, and a great sum in those days. She sighed, and said, "Do you believe it is so much? Why, then, it must be in logwood." Capt. Giles at that time had a large quantity of this article on hand, which had declined in value, and this little incident is to show, as we proceed, that great traffic was carried on here in dye-stuffs.

Capt. Gilpin was considered one of the handsomest men in the country, and in advanced age moved to the west, more than half a century ago. In 1831, at the age of eighty-five, he applied for a pension for revolutionary services. At the same time his brother, Israel Gilpin, aged ninety-three years, presented a petition for like services. The latter raised the first military company in this town to join the revolutionary army, of which he was the captain.

Next door, in Front street, was long the residence of Capt. Walker, who followed a seafaring life, but died at home, full of years. His nephew was lost at sea, in the noted brig Friday.

At the southwest corner of Second and King streets was long the residence of Edward Gilpin, a most worthy gentleman. He removed to live with his sons at Philadelphia, where he died in 1844, at eighty-four years of age. He had a large family of children, among whom was Charles Gilpin, Esq., the present mayor of Philadelphia.

Capt. Samuel Bush has been noticed in tracing the line of packets to Philadelphia. Fronting the market was the residence of Mrs. Bail, a widow, well known and highly appreciated—and for its novelty, a story will be related respecting the romantic adventures of one domesticated in her family.

It was the birth-place of this heroine, and she was caressed by every kind hearted member of her home. But as soon as her capability to act for herself was known, she presumed on their affection, and discovered a shocking propensity to pilfer.

Being an epicure, she spared nothing that suited her taste. This so annoyed the females of the household that it chilled their affections, and they agreed to part with her, and send her to a place provided in the country.

However, Miss Perseverance preferred her old home, and returned, resolving to remain there. This was perplexing, and a difficulty ensued to procure a distant home, which was changed again and again—but she determined not to give up her birthright for a mess of pottage.

At length Captain Hampton, a friend of the family, who was loading a brig here, belonging to Philadelphia, proffered to take this worrying inmate to the West Indies, and if she proved worthy by kind treatment, he would retain her in his service; but if perverse, he might leave her to her fate in a foreign land. At all events, her old home was no more to be troubled by such an incorrigible spirit.

The morning of taking a final leave was rather an exciting scene, as she was to embark on the wide ocean, and perhaps be left to seek a home among strangers. However, she was happy and useful on board the vessel, and became a pet with the sailors.

The brig made a prosperous voyage, and was no sooner safe at Chestnut street wharf than Madam Pussey secured her passage in Capt. Bush's packet, and next morning paid her respects in Mrs. Bail's parlor, to the astonished family; and though a mute, she manifested the most joyous feelings by her expressive signs. Henceforth her faults were overlooked, and her days were ended in peace in her youthful home.

On the south side of Second street market was an old house long the residence of Thomas Wallace, a block maker, who was also connected with commerce. A little incident of this family in the Revolution will point to things in troublous times. The industrious habits of these people procured them all the necessaries of life, and something to spare. They were never in want, but when the British took possession of the town, they had only continental money, and this was worse than useless, because care must be taken to conceal it. Now they were destitute.

Mrs. Wallace went to a kind neighbor, Mrs. Shallcross, and requested to borrow twelve shillings in hard money to supply their pressing need. This was readily granted, and soon after, she informed Mrs. Shallcross how abundantly they were supplied with hard money by an accidental circumstance.

The British soldiers drew flour in their rations, and it was so difficult to get it baked that one of them came and implored her to bake it for him. In pity, she made him good bread, and he insisted on her taking half of the flour, as there was more than sufficient for him. This was noised abroad, and crowds came to beg her to make bread, and as she could readily sell all there was to spare, it soon filled her pockets with hard money.

The daughter married Capt. Baker, who was lost at sea, neither vessel nor crew being ever heard of.

On the opposite side was Eli Mendenhall's card manufactory, and in every family a wheel was used some part of the day, for hired girls spent their evenings in spinning. Mr. Mendenhall did a large business. Old women and children earned money by setting cards, and when this business was superseded by machinery, it was deeply deplored as the means of depriving such persons of their daily bread. Mr. Mendenhall also kept a dry goods store on one side, and a grocery on the other side, and in old age he died an honest, estimable man.

Thomas Crow and Jonas Aldrick, both watchmakers, were on this square in days gone by, and were worthy men. The latter was of Swedish descent, and his ancestors were colonists.

Midway of this square, in King street, was the residence of Capt. James Jeffries, who sailed long from this port, and was a very respectable shipmaster and owner. The ships Wilmington and Neptune were owned in part by him. After a useful life spent on the ocean, he retired to his farm in Chester county, there to end his earthly career.

Here too was the house of Capt. Jacob Brinton. He sailed a brig which was owned in part by our worthy friend James Lea, whose two sons, promising young men, were on board, and no tidings of them ever reached their friends, or clue to guess their fate.

On the south corner of Fourth street was an old printing establishment, and it was also the private dwelling of John Adams.

Opposite was long the abode of a good simple-hearted man, a ruling elder of the second Presbyterian congregation, active in their temporal concerns, without losing sight of the spiritual, always anxious to keep the flock in the straight and narrow path. In old age he was well known as Daddy Cook. "And when Jacob had made an end of commanding his sons, he gathered his feet into his bed, and yielded up the ghost."

In 1816, a large lot was purchased of James Davis, for fourteen hundred dollars, at the corner of Hanover street, once the property of Mrs. Anna Dorothea Vertz. Here a cellar was dug to build a church, and the stone hauled. One of the evils of war was a deranged currency, which, with the failure of energetic measures, stopped further progress. A small building, however, was used as a lecture room. In this the first Sunday school in the town was opened, and its history will be given with that of the old Academy.

In 1829, Trinity Chapel was built, the Rev. Isaac Pardee being then rector. It was furnished complete, including organ and window blinds, by the energetic measures of females, who also paid for finishing the Sunday school room. Many departed ones were associated in this good work, a few of whom have been noticed, and we are pleased to record a tribute of gratitude to the memory of Miss Antonia Nicholson, who though in feeble health, plied the needle by night and by day in making fancy articles, the sales of which produced ninety-seven dollars profits, which were given by her to this object.

Some years afterwards the building was enlarged by subscription, and the interior much improved. It was furnished anew, a larger organ purchased, and gas lights were introduced for the first time into a church in the city by female energy—then under the pastoral charge of Rev. J. W. McCullough. But a want of taste was evident in the exterior.

Lately it has been improved by a tower and a fine toned bell, the gift of Mrs. Agnes Stothart. A commodious parsonage has been built adjoining, and it is now in the pastoral charge of the Rev. E. M. Vandeusen.

Hanover street Presbyterian Church is the largest in town—it is beautifully situated, but like our own, the exterior is deficient in taste. It has been lately improved. The congregation is large and regular in attendance, and very liberal in their contributions to promote every institution connected with their church.

The corner of Broad street, now Seventh, was the residence of a surgeon in the Revolutionary army, Dr. Ebenezer Smith, long a valued practitioner here. An anecdote of his father, which happened in perilous times, and related by the doctor, may amuse you. The old gentleman was a Presbyterian minister, strict as a Pharisee in his views of religious order and decorum. Punctual to time, on Sabbath morning he rode off on horseback, leaving his family to follow.

One Saturday night, during the Revolution, this surgeon and two officers lodged at his house in Pequea, Pennsylvania, expecting to join their regiment on Sunday.

The parson was very absent minded, and often appeared eccentric. At his usual hour in the morning, he hastily picked up a hat, mounted his nag, and pushed off to church. On the road people ran to the doors and windows, and those assembled at the meeting-house were in the greatest consternation to see their plain Puritan parson dismount, and even ascend to the pulpit with a *chapeau bras*, gold band, and red waving plumes. What could all this mean? As there was no possibility of remedying the mistake, he was allowed to proceed home thus equipped, to the great amusement of his sons, most especially the one who was long President of Princeton College, Dr. Samuel Stanhope Smith.

But the officer to whom this chapeau belonged was in as great a predicament on missing his hat and hearing that it had gone to church. He had no alternative but to wear the parson's plain, low three-cornered cocked hat, quite as outre for full uniform, and he too attracted notice, and made merriment on his way.

In the midst of usefulness, though past the prime of life, Dr. E. Smith was suddenly cut down, and in an unexpected hour he became the tenant of a grave, leaving a bereaved family and many sympathizing friends to mourn.

His eldest son, a physician of promise, was his successor, and seemed to be the staff of his family. His prospects were soon blighted by a disease of the lungs. For two winters he sought relief by a residence in the West Indies. A warm climate proved favorable; it was hoped his life might be prolonged by a southern abode. He was induced to go to Mississippi, where he was confined two years to his bed, in a hopeless state; and being, as he thought, on the verge of the grave, he dictated a farewell letter to his mother, and the family were mourning as for one dead.

The second daughter was most healthy, and as a good manager, with mature judgment took charge of their domestic concerns. Her services were constantly required. The shortest absence was to the family a sacrifice; besides, her usefulness in the church and many religious societies was important. But amid all these duties, within this domicil were hearts sorrowing over the recent letter from a dying brother, so much beloved. Without were dark clouds and a gloomy atmosphere portending a storm.

Here let us pause to recount the thrilling catastrophe of July, 1824. Eliza B. Smith was seated near a back window in the third story, plying her needle. She rose, looked out of the window, and called to her sister in the door below, to whom she made some remarks on the weather and an expected meeting.

In a moment a vivid flash of lightning, with a loud clap of thunder, rent the air and made the earth tremble. A torrent of rain fell, and in the twinkling of an eye the chimneys were torn to atoms, the house shattered and on fire.

Mrs. Smith was seated at the window, in the room below her daughter, and moved her chair just as the bureau was dashed down on the spot. Part of the partition wall falling, the crash prostrated her on the hearth, and feeling suffocated with the sulphurous smoke which filled the room, and seeing fiery sparks thicken around, she crawled to the door, and exclaimed, 'Where is my daughter?'"

She ran up to her daughter, who was seated with her work in hand, her needle in her fingers, and her clothes just ready to burst into a flame, which Mrs. Smith extinguished. Yet she was unconscious that the active spirit had winged its flight, and all her endearing epithets were unavailing " to the dull cold ear of death."

A brother, then on a visit to the family, when he heard the cry of fire, hastened home and rushed through the smoke and showers of sparks. Hundreds who surrounded the house feared to enter, and only one followed him up stairs, Miss A. N. These two bore the lifeless form down stairs, and it was conveyed across the street to Mrs. Elbert's where physicians assembled, but the most prompt means failed to restore life.

The only marks were a single drop of blood from the ear, as if a shot had entered, and two red spots on the breast, near together, resembling a burn just ready to blister. A placid smile beamed over her countenance, which seemed to imply, "Death is not here."

The eldest sister had an iron in her hand, which it was supposed, threw off the electricity and saved her life. She, too, was prostrated, and lay benumbed on the parlor floor, her shoes torn from her feet, and the combs from her hair, which rose from her head, filled with sulphur. Intense pain would seize her limbs for weeks.

The fire was extinguished, though the house was materially damaged. A large closet, close to the chimney, was filled with china; much of this was crumbled into powder. "The clouds poured out water, the skies sent out a sound; thine arrows also went abroad, the voice of thy thunder was in the heavens, the lightnings lightened the world, the earth shook, and thy footsteps are not known."

The absent brother, who passed through much suffering, was mourned as one dead. By a mighty effort he was brought home to die. After lingering in consumption eight years, mostly spent with benevolent strangers, he said, "I will depart to my own land, and to my kindred."

> "Think of his fate, revere the heavenly hand
>   That led him hence, though soon, by steps so slow.
> Long at his couch Death took his patient stand,
>   And menaced oft, and oft withheld the blow.
>
> "Say, are ye sure his mercy shall extend
>   To you so long a span? Alas! ye sigh.
> Make, then, while yet ye may, your God your friend,
>   And learn, with equal ease, to sleep or die."

This bereaved widow's affliction was soothed by the bright prospects of her second son, an exemplary young officer, assistant professor of Mathematics at West Point. On the eve of promotion as principal, the vacation was spent in his family circle. The day of his departure to resume his duties was at hand, when the typhus fever seized him, and the spirit fled from this fleeting world. Three estimable and useful 'inmates of this domicil were prematurely cut down, as flowers of the field. They came home—but to die.

The mother survived these heavy afflictions for years, and as an elder friend of our early days, we pay to her memory our trifling tribute of affection, being an inmate of her family three years. Amid these trying afflictions, we witnessed her daily walk. In joy and prosperity, she was meek and condescending; in sorrow and adversity, calm and resigned. No variableness clouded her brow or darkened an even temperament. An unceasing desire to render her domicil a happy home crowned her life with peace. "Thou wilt keep him in perfect peace whose mind is stayed on thee, because he trusteth in thee."

Capt. Joseph Nicholson, of the U. S. Navy, at the time of these disastrous events, was a neighbor and friend whose noble deeds claim a tribute of respect. He was the shield of his widowed sister, and the orphan's guide, and long before temperance was lauded over the land was an example to men under his command.

He abstained from exhilarating drinks on sea and on shore, and likewise from all amusing games. He was a true believer of the Gospel doctrine, and a regular attendant upon the services of the Episcopal Church. He was not a hearer of the Word only, but a doer of Christian duties, and we trust his benevolent acts were recorded in heaven ere he was so suddenly called to render up his accounts. He could exclaim with sincerity, "I caused the widow's heart to sing for joy, and was a father to the fatherless."

CHAPTER XXI.

Other days—Mr. Crip's Pottery—Sad Incident—J. Keating, Esq.—Peter Provenchere, Esq.—Affecting Incidents—Messrs. Hilles—J. Maule—Boarding School—Baptist Cemetery—Potter's Field—Story of the Water Works.

In the square above, all has changed. Old things have passed away, and new ones rise up before us. The place that was once of considerable notoriety is gone, and strangers inhabit the spot. Yet it is fresh in our memory as a link in a chain of incidents which stretches into the past century, mingling so much with life's vicissitudes, it seems to invite us to substitute our meagre sketch of facts which might fill up a narrative, if well described.

No doubt there are hundreds of females scattered over the land, who could point where the old boarding school stood, and tell of their joyous school days; and a few may remember where their wayward will was disciplined.

But to tell what we have known of this place will turn us back to other days, besides what our fathers have told us, and furthermore an aged female said, when this was a common where cows pastured, and the Stalcup's line cut off the northeast corner; but the town was laid out, and she was offered the whole square from King to French street, and from from Broad to Kent street, for twenty dollars, subject to a small ground rent, to the Swedes' Church. She pondered it in her mind, and counted the silver dollars, laying them aside, and looking over the waste land, declined the purchase.

Two years ago we read an extract copied from the journal of William Penn, stating that on his first voyage to this country he borrowed from a French passenger on board the ship thirty-six pounds, and after Philadelphia was planned, he offered him for the debt the whole square from Market to Arch street, and from Third to Fourth, which the Frenchman declined to take, preferring the cash. Mr. Penn replied, "Thou blockhead, dost thou not know that this place is destined to become a great city?"

Our father said in olden time Matthew Crips owned most part of the square, on which he established a pottery, and in the Revolution his business prospered, for wares of all sorts were scarce and expensive, and his domestic manufacture was in great demand. Even cups and saucers were made, and used by many, though it may be hard to believe by a few of the present generation that their ancestors drank coffee out of earthen cups. Yet it is true, for we have seen specimens preserved as a relic of that eventful day.

Of Mr. Crips we have but little to say, save that he was an old inhabitant, an industrious and useful man, and died wealthy. He knew how to make money, and was well skilled in the art of keeping it.

His oldest son went to sea, and was impressed by the English long before his death. The youngest was cut off by will with a small annuity, and his only daughter. a very deserving woman, was heir to the estate, which she never enjoyed, neither did her heirs. "So that man gathereth riches in vain."

Mr. Crips' residence yet stands with a new front. More than half a century ago, numerous French emigrants arrived here, and increased the population so rapidly that houses were in demand, and rents were raised.

This induced him to give place to a very interesting family, consisting only of Mr. P., his wife and servants. They had made a hairbreadth escape from their native land. Sad reverses, and the unhappy fate of the lady's parents made her the child of sorrow; and though sadness reigned in their lonely abode, for she shrunk from society, yet as they were religiously disposed, gleams of gratitude warmed their hearts to the Disposer of good for a safe guidance to the land of peace and plenty.

Mrs. P. did not seem to possess the national buoyancy of spirit which was so remarkable in her fair countrywomen, whether in weal or woe.

The birth of an infant in this gloomy home seemed as the choicest earthly blessing. As their daughter daily grew more lovely, Mrs. P.'s sadness gradually wore away, and her countenance resumed animation. She was so absorbed in the tender mother's care, that, alas! this little one became a household idol. As its first birthday approached, much pleasure was anticipated, when sudden illness seized its tender frame; but the timely aid of an eminent French physician arrested the disease, and danger was no longer apprehended.

Ah, how sad to tell! the difference of language caused wrong medicine to be sent, and the potion was given by the devoted mother, who anxiously watched over her darling, as she thought she had fallen into a sweet slumber.

But the father's countenance bespoke agonized grief, for he knew that it had gone to a longer and calmer rest, and that the spirit had fled from earth to heaven. There lay the babe, lovely even in death, and when the mother was aroused to the sad reality, she thought of nothing but the inanimate form, and gazed on it in a fixed stupor, and this inestimable lady sunk into a settled melancholy.

> "As the sweet flower that scents the morn,
>   But withers in the rising day,
> Thus lovely was this infant's dawn,
>   Thus swiftly fled its life away."

Somewhere about 1797, Mr. Crips erected the mansion long known as the *Old Boarding School*, which in that day was thought a fine building. It presented a wide front, with a large hall through the centre, and several back rooms were attached by fitting up the old pottery. The premises were extensive; a large side lot, and the whole bounded by French street, that afforded a roomy yard and noble garden.

J. Keating, Esq., rented it for three hundred dollars, and occupied it for years. He married in this town a lovely young lady, the daughter of a very respectable French gentleman, Mons. Deschappelles, who now lies in the old Swedes' Cemetery. He, too, had sought an asylum here when trouble overwhelmed his native land.

An honorable member of this family was too remarkable a personage to pass over—Peter Provenchere, Esq., a highly educated man and accomplished gentleman, whose dignified deportment and courtesy of manners told us that he belonged to another age. Soon after the accession of Louis XVI., he obtained an honorable situation in the household of the king's eldest brother, and under the view of the royal family he was selected as tutor to the Duke de Berri, and when his royal patrons were driven into exile, he continued his instructions.

In 1794 he came to this country, and his first residence was in Wilmington, where he remained until 1808. On the restoration of the Bourbons, Mr. P. was earnestly invited to return to his country, but he preferred tranquility at his advanced age, as the highest enjoyment of life.

The duke did not forget or neglect the friend and guide of his youth, but maintained a correspondence, always addressing him with affection and respect.

After Mr. P. reached his 80th year, he devoted his reading exclusively to religious works. He was a practical Christian in works as well as faith, charitable to his fellow-men, and humble and obedient to his God.

A friend, who knew him daily for thirty years, declares he cannot recollect a single word that he could wish unsaid, or a single act that had better been undone. What vicissitudes had this gentleman seen in his native country! His daughter, Madame M., was also an inmate of the family. She was a very accomplished lady, having been educated with the Princess Royal, afterwards Duchess d'Angouleme. Those persons were relatives of Mrs. Keating, and were highly respected here, and no family were more regretted on their removal to Philadelphia.

Mrs. Keating was handsome, and her figure noble. She was young and in the bloom of health, and her estimable traits of character and courtesy of manners won her the affection and esteem of those who knew her. In that day, the French society in this town was of a high order, and none seemed to enjoy life more, passing their evenings socially at each other's houses.

In August, 1803, Mr. Keating had gone to the west, and at one of their social parties, about eight o'clock, Mrs. Keating was seized with a sudden illnesss and taken home, and another day had scarcely dawned when death entered this happy domicil and bore away one endeared to kindred and friends, and was "a grievous mourning."

The solemnity of that day is still remembered, and Mr. Keating's return to meet his three motherless children. It was a scene of solemn sadness, and his grief was deep and abiding. "It grieveth me much for your sakes, that the hand of the Lord is gone out against me." The sunshine of joy that lighted and cheered those evening circles grew dim on her grave, and set forever.

Year after year, sorrow seemed to invade each kindred household, and remove each brightest ornament. Many of those promising youths are mingling with the dust in the old Swedes' Cemetery.

The little ones were now under paternal care, and early disciplined to obedience, and nurtured in the fear and admonition of the Lord. Being so guarded from worldly temptations, as they grew to riper years, they soared to more glorious joys. Having passed their course of studies with honor, and realized a fond father's hopes, they were promoted to high places in public life. Even erring men estimate worth, as it is evident that he who honors his parent will be most apt to honor his country.

The oldest was engaged in the practice of law in Philadelphia, and six weeks had just elapsed since his marriage, when death bore him to the tomb, and the deepest sorrow overshadowed the household.

The younger son finished his studies in Paris, and was gaining celebrity in the science of mineralogy and chemistry, and but a few years glided by, and he too married and was in London, preparing to embark for his native land, when disease seized his frame, and brought him to an early grave. The moment that his aged father was expecting his arrival, the news was announced that his only son was no more. So little is man's estimate of the joys of life to be relied on. What he cherishes to-day as the choicest blessings may to-morrow open in his heart a fountain of solicitude and sorrow.

In the ardor of youth, and pride of manhood, their tide of life flowed away. As their brief term of years was adorned by walking in wisdom's ways, we trust their spirits were fitted for celestial joys.

The youngest child, a daughter, is a widowed mother, and is superior of the convent at E. Mr. K.'s paternal care embraced an orphan nephew, senior to his sons, and educated by him with the same paternal care. He too fulfilled the duties of a long life in a short one, and died deeply lamented by numerous friends, who sympathized in their family afflictions.

When Mr. Keating removed from this house, Mrs. Capron, from Philadelphia, opened a boarding-school here, but soon resigned. She was succeeded by Joshua Maule and Eli Hilles. Mr. Maule had been for some time a popular teacher, and was esteemed a worthy man, but death summoned him in the prime of life to leave a family of orphans to another's care. His departure was deeply lamented, and the important duty of training youth now devolved on the Messrs. Hilles, whose duties were faithfully performed with great success.

Many females have gone from that seminary with the proof to others of having been thoroughly instructed in the branches of a plain English education, that being the professed principle of the school. A French teacher was employed for those who desired to acquire a knowledge of that language, and occasionally a little of the ornamental in drawing.

In 1816, the Messrs. Hilles erected a fine mansion, surrounded by beautiful grounds, and an extensive view, situated a few squares above, where they continued for years with unusual success. It is now conducted by Dubree Knight, uniting a day school, and it sustains a high character.

The intersection of King and Eighth Streets was long a sand hole, and was so designated. The process of levelling the streets progressed slowly, and it was a dangerous pass in a dark night.

The old Baptist meeting-house is adjoining Mr. Hilles', and opposite the water-works. It is a fine situation now, occasionally used for worship, and has been mostly closed for some years past. There is a large cemetery attached, with numerous graves. The burying-ground for the poor is next, and also quite large, and beautifully situated. The city fathers have lately ordered the remains to be disinterred, and buried in the cemetery, in the north-west part of the city.

Being opposite the water-works, we will sketch its history. As you now will have known of primitive days, you must be informed how the town was supplied with water in our detail of more recent things.

On the highways and in yards were draw-wells, often seventy or eighty feet deep. The limb of a tree was placed upright near them, a pole, balanced, being laid in a notch at the top, and a rope or chain at the end held the bucket, to be borne down till it filled with water, then carefully raised up. Those wells were not covered, and the water was excellent. Wells which had a windlass were more modern, and those enclosed were much safer. Two such were in front of Gov. Dickinson's house, in Kent Street, and thus supplied most of the neighborhood. In those days, half a square was near to get water for family use. Some had a hogshead in the yard to catch rain water for washing. Pumps were the next change; oftimes it was hard labor to pump up water, owing to the well being deep.

A new project to supply down town, where water was not so good, was to bring spring water through wooden pipes from Shipley's brewery, on the declivity of Quaker Hill, from the upper market down. This was choice water, and sufficient for the day. It was done by the spring water company, and such an improvement that it was deemed expedient to supply the higher part of the town, by bringing it more than a mile from Cool-spring, at the country seat of C. A. Rodney, Esq. This was a much more expensive operation.

East side of Market street, above Eighth, an immense cistern was dug, and walled with brick, and lined with an expensive cement. This was to contain a number of hogsheads for extra uses. The latter made the stock unprofitable, and it was sold to the borough. At this time a row of noble trees reached from Brandywine to the Christiana, beautifying the town and making a shady walk, screening old buildings, and giving things a rural appearance.

In spring time, as they put forth verdure and were flourishing, a complaint was preferred by the honorable counsel, representing these trees as troublesome neighbors, invading water-right by working under ground like moles, and perforating logs till the water oozed out. Much contention ensued; parties clung to the side they espoused; for months they grew stronger and waxed warmer, some for "the green tree, and some for the dry."

The rulers assembled, and declared the trees a grievance no longer to be borne. They were invested with supreme power to act, and passed a decree, like the Medes and Persians, that altereth not. It was proclaimed on such a day, within certain bounds, trees of every tribe should be exterminated.

Oh! what lamentation over the trees doomed to destruction, and I am sorry to say that the spirit of rebellion was rife. Even this quiet little town threatened to "nullify." Women were unanimous to spare the trees; but the authority exclaimed, "Cut it down; why cumbereth it the ground?"

Upon much deliberation, it was agreed to petition those uncompromising rulers. Two hundred females and others signed. This was too formidable an array to be easily set aside, and the shade was spared for a season. A few equally desirous to save the trees refused to sign, because they adhered to Gov. Dickinson's maxim, "Let the law be enforced, however bad." Arbitrary laws are ofttimes wholesome to a community; they teach men the importance of selecting competent rulers. "Then I considered it well; I looked upon it and received instruction."

By orders in counsel the next year the axe was laid to the root of every tree within the limits. After all this excitement the logs were found defective, and iron pipes were laid. Besides, there was not sufficient water in case of fire, and the Brandywine water was brought in to supply the whole town, and the water was pumped up by a water wheel at the Brandywine into the reservoir on high ground, from whence it was led by iron pipes for the purposes of the town for public and private purposes.

CHAPTER XXII.

Market Street Bridge—Dr. Monroe—Mrs. D.—An Adventure—Bank—Dr. Pascal—J. Springer—J. Brobson—Hotel—Sailor's Exploit—Smoke House—J. Webster—Post Office—J. Niles—David Bush, Esq.—Major Lewis Bush—Indian Queen.

Before we pass up Market street, we will give a sketch of the rise and progress of the bridge across the Christiana, and the numerous hinderances in getting it constructed. In the olden time, folks never entered heedlessly into new measures. Prudence was a characteristic of the day, so they progressed slowly, and this was thought a prodigious enterprise.

What folly (said some) to talk about throwing a bridge across such a strong current! Why, the spring tides or freshets would sweep away every vestige of any structure that might be built, or the shoals of floating ice rend it to atoms.

Others said, if the mighty work could be completed, no road could ever be made through the marsh, where the banks were continually breaking; for all those meadows did overflow at times, and look like a continuous sheet of water even to the Delaware, and years would glide on ere an ingenious workman could be found to stop these breaches.

Moreover, they said, all the earth carted there would sink or wash away. But a most serious objection was impeding the navigation, and this had a hard struggle throughout the opposition.

Meetings were held and long speeches made. For a time the subject would die away, and then be revived again, when, on a sudden, the rising generation overcame these perils by land and perils by water, and resolved on the undertaking, and it has resulted in great convenience to the traveling community. Yet fully appreciating the progress in useful improvements, we venerate our ancestors, and could wish that their descendants had inherited a portion of their prudence, and also of their honesty and integrity.

Ascending this street many old persons and places will be noted. In this square are the two old residences of the Broom family, which have a renewed appearance. Their pretty daughters were belles of the day.

Dr. Shallcross's dwelling was here, and for years after he left it, it was the domicil of an estimable widow, Mrs. R., whose fair daughters, the Misses R., had a name among the pretty girls of their day.

Dr. George Monroe became the next occupant and owner. He was a surgeon in the Revolution, and married the daughter of Col. Haslet, who fell at the battle of Princeton. She was a lady of worth and beauty, whom death summoned in the prime of life. The doctor survived her for years, and when suddenly called away he was prepared to meet death. Both were members of the Presbyterian church. "O, Lord of Hosts, blessed is the man that trusteth in thee."

The house above, built and occupied by Major Adams, was afterwards owned and occupied by the celebrated architect Benjamin H. Latrobe. He also had a most estimable family and a beautiful daughter.

On the northwest corner of Front Street stood one of the oldest brick dwellings in town, long known as a tavern. Within a few years it has given place to a modern hotel.

When dry-goods stores were few, there was a noted one kept by Mrs. Donaldson, where the best articles could be obtained; and this reminds us of an adventure.

In 1817, as we were traveling from Carlisle to the York Springs, in a private carriage with Mrs. Broom, we alighted at a tavern, while the horses were watered, to make inquiry about the road. A German was giving very incoherent directions, when a stranger kindly came forward and clearly pointed out our way.

We had rode ten miles, and the horses had to rest, and the stranger entered into conversation, and several questions were answered, by which he knew we were from Wilmington.

He observed, twenty years had nearly elapsed since he was once before at this house, to take shelter from a pelting rain, and now for the second time in life was here to be screened from a scorching sun, and it was a singular coincidence that each time he should meet ladies from Wilmington, and should be pleased to inquire for the former, but the name had escaped his memory.

However, he would relate their adventure, and it might be a clue. In 1798, when the fever prevailed in Wilmington, an old lady and her daughter were traveling on to see a married daughter at Shippensburg, and this led to the disclosure that it was no other than Mrs. Donaldson.

The night was stormy, and the rain fell in torrents, and the stage was expected, and much anxiety expressed at the delay, lest the Conewago, two miles below, was so high the stage could not cross, and there was no house on the other side.

In the gloom of midnight, and under pelting rain, they were aroused by the driver with two females, dripping wet, mounted on stage horses partly harnessed, and no saddles.

The stage had been abandoned in the stream. The darkness was so intense that the driver was not aware of the creek being so high, and drove in, and the horses swam almost to the shore, when a wheel loosened and dragged, so they could not proceed.

Mrs. D. was large and heavy, and fears were excited for her safety. The stream continued to swell, and there were no passengers to give aid.

In this dilemma the driver cut his horses loose, and by his most energetic efforts, assisted by Miss D., they succeeded in dragging the old lady from the stage on to the horse's back, he holding her on, and leading the horse slowly, while the daughter mounted the other horse and rode on. In this plight they arrived hungry and weary, but rejoicing at their miraculous escape.

Next day the stage was refitted, and they set off for Shippensburg, with the mail-bag thrown loosely into the bottom of the carriage.

About a mile and a half hence is a very stony place, called Featherbed Lane. One of the horses fell exhausted, and was crippled.

Now the driver commenced to unharness, saying he could no longer be detained, but must hurry on with the mail on horseback, and let the ladies trudge back to the tavern, and wait for an opportunity to proceed.

Miss D. was indignant at the treatment, pounced her mother on the mail-bag, and sitting down by her side, vowed he should not remove it. Their passage was paid to go with the mail, and she would hold on till they arrived at the place of destination.

The driver soon saw that he had a heroine to contend with and must yield, and started to procure other horses, which was no trifling difficulty in that country. However, he succeeded.

And this gentleman with others went to congratulate the young lady for her heroism, and he spoke of it twenty years after as an astonishing feat of firmness and presence of mind. Miss D. was greatly applauded for not submitting to the imposition of a stage driver.

The ancestors of Dr. Nicholas Way resided next to the corner; they were an ancient family. This corner was the last earthly dwelling-place of Col. Thomas Kean.

The Brandywine Bank is of modern structure, on the opposite corner, and Mr. Crampton's old tavern yet keeps its place. Dr. Pascal's drug store, of ancient note, stands, though divided into two. Joseph Bailey, Esq., succeeded in the drug business, but resigned it, and was for a long time President of the Bank of Delaware.

Next was the old residence of our patriotic friend Joseph Shallcross, for many years afterwards occupied by John Sellars, hatter, a very respectable townsman, whose eldest son, his successor, fills his father's place as a trustworthy member of the community.

John Springer's residence and hatter's shop has lately been removed. He was a worthy inhabitant, whose ancestor, Carls Christopher Springer, was a distinguished colonist. John Reynolds' house was another old landmark, but it has been lately demolished. He was for years a respectable, kind citizen, a very large man in the hardware business, but of gentle, soft manners.

In 1806, a low fever prevailed to some extent. It was called nervous. Several young persons fell victims, and none were more lamented than Miss Sally Brobson. She was tenderly beloved by her friends, was beautiful, and in the bloom of youth and loveliness, she fell as the flower of the field to mingle with the dust. Mrs. Brobson was a lady of great literary taste, and also had a fondness for flowers, and made a choice selection. Her garden was on the east side of the square, and though small was tastefully arranged.

James Brobson was at that time in mercantile business, and owned part of several vessels.

Marshall's Hotel, southeast corner of Third street, sign of the ship, was in the Revolution the head-quarters of the officers, and we will relate an incident of the times.

A sea fight on the coast had caused much rejoicing, as the American sloop-of-war Randolph was victorious, and during the excitement a person of some pretensions as an artist painted a representation of the battle on this sign.

When the English fleet lay opposite this town, the sailors passing to and fro were much annoyed by it, and always made some harsh remark as they passed.

One day two sailors, dressed in petticoat trowsers, carrying a bag up the street, arrested the attention of a young girl, who was a great observer of the daily events, and watched their doings. They stopped at the foot of the post, emptied their budget, took out an axe and other tools, ran up the post, and drew down the sign, and split the hateful painting into atoms, and hewed off its support, leaving not a vestige of its former glory.

Seventy years had elapsed since the person who was a witness to this scene, Mrs. Mary Lovering, related it as still fresh in her memory.

In our day, Capt. O'Flinn, a gentleman in the strictest sense of the word, kept this house as an accommodation for travellers, and it was proverbial for order. His sister-in-law, Mrs. Huggins, regulated the household. Her only son was lost at sea.

We are often reminded of the depravity of the present age, and contrast it with the purity of days gone by, and love to dwell on the virtues of an ancestor and the filial obedience of our childhood, till we almost persuade ourselves crime was unknown in the past generation.

But a sudden flash of memory brings out the little old smoke house, the place for the temporary confinement of offenders; it presented its gable end and grated windows, and gloomy door and big lock. Then we remember Jenny Blaney and Kate Magill, and others, passed into oblivion, who had to spend many a dark, lonely night in this dreary prison.

If their crime proved worthy of a trip to New Castle, the culprit was conveyed to the county jail, sometimes favored to ride in a cart, but mostly it was a pedestrian excursion.

Such reminiscences oblige us to acknowledge, depravity existed from the beginning, but they have progressed with the arts and sciences.

John Webster, a most eccentric character, and full of wit, kept a classical school for some time, and afterwards opened a drug and book store. He was also postmaster, and a long list of his drugs and other articles for sale were advertised in poetry, in a most amusing strain, written and composed by Evan Thomas, Sr.

This store was long the post-office, afterwards in the charge of Joseph Bringhurst, a very worthy man. Mrs. Deborah Bringhurst was an intelligent and estimable friend. In mature age, as the child of affliction, we trust she resigned her earthly abode for a heavenly one.

Years have glided on since a sad accident befel one of our old townsmen, J. Niles. Opposite the upper market a sign post had long threatened danger, yet it was allowed to remain. On a windy day, as J. N. stepped out of his door, this post snapped, and the sign fell on his head, instantly crushing him out of life into an endless eternity.

His son, Hezekiah Niles, removed to Baltimore, there published Niles' Register, a very popular paper, and perhaps at one time no paper in the country had a larger circulation.

When he was overtaken by the infirmities of age, he came home to die, and in this place ended his pilgrimage.

The northeast corner of Third street was the residence of David Bush, Esq., whose patriotic sons were so distinguished in the Revolution. Three of them were brave officers on duty; the fourth was a boy, whom we have noted in a later day. A British colonel inquiring the names of officers, hearing that three were sons of one man, exclaimed, "We must exterminate the d— Bushes before we can conquer even little Delaware."

Major Lewis Bush, was called the flower of these youthful heroes. He was handsome, and worthy of remembrance as a hero in his country's cause.

He fell mortally wounded at the battle of Brandywine, having been singled out as a victim. The enemy's balls passed with deadly aim. Being directed by ill-judged kindness, to hasten him from the fatal spot, he was thrown across a horse wounded and in agony, which set the blood to flowing in streams. No soothing hand was nigh to pour in oil and wine, or to stay the bleeding wound, and his valued life gently passed away, and none was more lamented.

Major George Bush was long collector of this port, and a most popular officer. Their only sister, Miss Betsey Bush, was a beautiful woman and a noted belle.

Thomas Spackman's shoe store was just above. He, too, was an old inhabitant; and Joseph Grubb, a most estimable man, married his daughter, who was an excellent woman. Mr. G. was long engaged in the hardware business. Here they both died, ere they were overtaken by age.

Samuel Nichols and wife, a worthy couple, lived to old age. They kept a dry goods store above, and when this was a borough, Mr. Nichols was appointed a burgess. Those people were members of Friends' Society.

During the Revolution, a hotel at the corner of Fourth street was long known as the Indian King, and was kept by Mrs. Allison. In our day it was Brinton's, and one of the most respectable in town. Here the stages all put up, and crowds of Indians were sometimes entertained at the expense of government. We have seen them pass through in crowded stages.

CHAPTER XXIII.

Peter Brynberg—Book Store—Old Bank—Printing Office—Robert Hamilton, Esq.—Adventure of Mons. Bergerac—The Dawes Family—Gen. Stockton—Job Harvey—Town Hall—Michael Wolfe.

THE mansion on the northwest corner of High street was the residence of James Lea, Sen., well known and highly esteemed here in olden days. It was long the Bank of Delaware, the oldest bank in the State. John Hayes, cashier, occupied the dwelling.

An old printing office of Bonsall and Niles was just above. This for some time was conducted by Robert Corum, a reputed literary character.

Many worthy persons lived on the opposite side, who glided so smoothly down the stream of time that we know no incident to relate.

Peter Brynberg, a printer, was a worthy man of Swedish descent. He also kept a book store here, and was one of the publishers of the Episcopal prayer book, altered to suit the constitution of the young republic.

His son-in-law, Robert Porter, was his successor, who was long an elder of the second Presbyterian congregation. Mr. Porter's descendants have continued the book business with respectability and success, and we are happy to add they sustain the integrity of character inherited from their Swedish ancestors.

The residence of Robert Hamilton, Esq., was in the square above. His promptness and decision in his duty as an officer, exacting the like from his subordinates, secured a well ordered police. Under his administration a most extraordinary incident occurred.

A French gentleman, with the best credentials, offered himself as teacher. He also stated he had been a merchant of some note in New Orleans, and there failed honorably. Mr. Hewlings, American consul there at the time of his failure, was now boarding in this town and knew the fact. He, therefore, took lodgings in the same house with Mr. Hewlings, and was much encouraged by a number of respectable pupils, who considered him a well qualified and faithful teacher.

His wife and an only daughter were in Paris, and had promised, whenever he could establish himself in his profession, to provide a home; they would be content even to share his poverty. His prospects were so bright that he expected to send for those absent ones. This buoyed up his spirits with ardent hope, so soon to embrace those whom he held most dear on earth. No one was more joyous, and his happy disposition cheered the whole family, and won the kindest feelings of his fellow-boarders as well as of his pupils.

Amidst all these advantages and enthusiasm, an apparently accomplished French lady arrived and inquired for Mons. Bergerac, and found his residence, and presented herself in Esquire Hamilton's office to demand a summons for Mons. B., whom she accused of forgery to a large amount on the Spanish minister, then residing in Philadelphia.

Consequently Mons. went fearlessly to the office, and faced his accuser, and he recognized her, and said he knew that she had lived in New Orleans.

Her assertions were bold and positive, naming the time and place where the notes were given by his own hands, and the value received. This stranger's story was well told, in the most fascinating manner, and made a great impression; for he could bring forward no circumstances to favor his innocence.

Her firmness induced the squire and most others to believe him guilty, and he was placed under guard strictly, for a short time, to give him a chance to obtain security for his appearance at court. A failure in this would doom him to imprisonment and be fatal to his future prospects, and he seemed to be hedged in, and hardly dared to hope that any one would take upon them such a risk for a stranger.

The Episcopal clergyman, Rev. W. Pryce, was kind-hearted, and took charge of him for the allotted time, entreating him to reflect whether any little incident could be remembered to inspire hope.

He had letters of introduction to Mr. Pryce and P. Bauduy, Esq., and they knew no more of him. Neither of these persons believed him guilty, although the accusation was so strongly made that he was enveloped in a dark mantle of suspicion.

Mr. Bauduy's benevolent heart was touched by the deep affliction of his countryman, in a strange land, and he came forward to offer security to the amazement of the whole community; and the large sum was the theme of conversation, for I think it demanded thousands, and though the act was condemned as so imprudent, yet the purely charitable motive elicited applause.

Mons. Bergerac knew that public opinion was against him, and he most feelingly entreated his pupils not to abandon him, but await his trial. He knew of no human witness to call upon, but faith induced him to hope that the court of heaven would open a way for earthly justice.

His guilt was so strongly impressed upon many that his pupils reluctantly received his instruction. Being aware of this, his feelings were deeply wounded, and it caused a sad depression of spirits. At length the day of trial came. The season was cold and gloomy, and, to save expense and time, he walked to and from Philadelphia in the night.

Mr. Hewlings, who still retained his confidence in him, entrusted to his care a draft for five hundred dollars, to be exchanged in one of the city banks.

There was no trial on that day, and the next it was postponed. Late in the evening he set off to walk home; a threatening storm and cold beset his way. At dark, near Darby, a cart passed. He thought the driver eyed him closely.

As night was closing in, he hastened on, and soon stepped into an inn to warm himself. A little space on this side of Darby he overtook the same cart, and the driver invited him to ride. He thanked him politely, and said "that he could keep warmer walking;" but very soon he was pressed to drive as a favor for a little time, while the man so benumbed with cold would warm himself by walking.

To this request he acceded. With the checks for Mr. Hewlings in his pocket, a valuable gold watch, and new silk umbrella, and a change of clothes in a bundle, he mounted into the cart.

In a few minutes the rascal stopped the horse to get in, and as he stepped out seized him, demanding his valuables. A scuffle ensued, in which his face was deeply cut, and his eye seriously injured. He retained his watch, but the umbrella and clothes were gone, and the villian drove off as fast as possible.

After a long walk in the hail and rain, freezing his face, with nothing to shield it from the sleet and piercing cold, near Chester he took off his neck handkerchief to tie up his face and guard his wound from the weather; and putting his hand into his pocket, he missed the pocket book and checks.

In wild dismay he screamed aloud, feeling that his character was irretrievably lost. How was he to meet his kind friend? The story would appear fabulous.

He ran back almost breathless, praying with his whole heart for Almighty guidance to direct his footsteps. "Behold, I send an angel before thee to keep thee in the way, and bring thee into the place." He knew the spot when he saw the blood that flowed in his struggle; and scrambled in the frozen snow like a maniac, when to his inexpressible joy, he turned up the little package of white paper enclosing the checks, which caused him to rejoice on his way, while his heart overflowed with gratitude for the interposition of a benign Providence, whom he felt had rescued him from impending ignominy.

He seemed insensible to the state of his wounds, and at midnight arrived at Chester, and knocked at Major Anderson's door for admittance.

Their kind attention soothed him in distress. Medical aid was instantly sought and his wounds dressed. A few days quietness was required, and to keep his face from exposure, which time healed, but the mark was borne to his grave.

Previous to the trial being brought into court, unexpected letters from New Orleans proved his departure from that place some weeks before the date of these forged notes, and fully released him from this most unjust accusation, fixing the guilt on those connected with the accuser.

In enumerating his disastrous changing scenes of life, he would exclaim, "But my adventure with *my woman* was the worst of all my troubles." In succeeding years he was an acceptable professor in St. Mary's College, Baltimore.

The mansion just above, now the *Delaware House*, or Brook Turner's hotel, was built by Mr. Abijah Dawes, who was a member of an old and respectable family. A remarkable and well-authenticated incident, that occurred in 1786, may be worth relating.

Edward Dawes, a promising young man, had been a long time lingering with diseased lungs, and now confined to his bed, so debilitated in the last days of his life that he was unable even to raise his hand, and the solemn night of death drew his relatives around him to witness the closing scene.

When they thought the agony was over, and the spirit had taken its flight, and the nurse approached to perform his last duty, he opened his eyes and asked for paper, &c., and to have a table brought to the bedside; then raised up, putting his feet out of the bed without assistance, took the pen, and wrote a letter to his uncle, who had spent years in the West Indies, and had entered into fashionable life in that gay country. He sealed this letter and directed it himself, and handed it to his uncle, Rumford Dawes, at whose house he was, requesting him to present it to his Uncle Cephas, and immediately fell on his bed and breathed no more.

In the morning his uncle C. D. entered the room; this letter was handed him. He walked the floor, evidently agitated, on reading the letter, and exclaimed, "What did the poor foolish youth mean by thus addressing me?" Immediately he ordered a tailor to make him a new suit, and he dressed in so plain a style that no one could recognize him. In a few weeks symptoms of insanity appeared, and after years' confinement in his brother's house, he was removed to the Pennsylvania Hospital, where he spent twelve years. In his later days he was as innocent as an infant.

Great curiosity was excited to know the contents of this letter, and search was fruitless; again and again his papers were turned over, for they were all in R. D.'s possession, and it was concluded he had destroyed it.

Thirty-two years after the event had happened, a son of Rumford Dawes was sent to the same hospital. To employ his mind on that day, he turned out a barrel of old papers, and the first that fixed his attention was the desired letter, handed to me by his daughter, Mrs. E. Massey, with a request to copy it and present it to Mrs. Ann Latimer, who witnessed the fact. Although there is nothing peculiarly striking in it, I have transcribed it for perusal. The following is an exact copy.

24th 1st month, 1786, at night.

MY DEAR UNCLE:—As the agonies of an almost expiring nephew were over me, I queried what was the cause, and it was intelligibly revealed to me. Thou sufferest for thy uncle, C. D. Write to him. It now comes in my view to remind thee that the wisdom of this world is foolishness in the sight of God. It has frequently given me pain to see a person allowed to possess understanding enter my room, in a character and appearance so derogatory to the principles and profession of a true Quaker. My dear uncle, make a change, and repent ere it be too late; trust not to a death-bed repentance.

This is suggested to me for the relief of my own mind, and I sincerely believe for thy eternal welfare. Not feeling any thing more, I wish thy everlasting happiness,

And am thy loving nephew,
EDWARD DAWES.

On the arrival of the French emigrants, this mansion was taken by Mons. Deschappelles, and was long the residence of his son-in-law, Peter Bauduy, Esq.

More than forty years have passed since this house was the dwelling-place of Gen. Stockton, who was well known here. An only daughter, Elizabeth, a very elegant young lady, married John Strawbridge, Esquire, and in the bloom of youth death summoned her to leave an affectionate husband and two infants. "Are not my days few? The eye of him that hath seen me shall see me no more."

The youngest son was killed in an engagement on the lakes in 1813, and the eldest son, Capt. Thomas Stockton, commanded a company in the same war with England, and distinguished himself in battle on the Canada line. He returned home full of honors, and was elected Governor of Delaware. Amidst his popularity he was ordered, in a moment, to resign his honors and mingle with the dust. His death was much lamented by numerous friends.

The northeast corner below was the residence of Job Harvey, of an old family, once engaged in commerce. He died in old age, a wealthy man. His descendants own the property, now a hotel.

Next door to Mr. Harvey lived the highly respectable family, Mr. Geddes, whose handsome daughters were belles of the day. Mrs. G. was an estimable lady, of more than ordinary beauty. They had removed to Philadelphia; and this excellent lady, while on a visit to Miss Vining, was taken ill in the night, and in the morning her spirit had winged its flight for an eternal home.

Above was the residence of an old lady, Mrs. Margaret Marshall, whom everybody seemed to know in her day as "Aunt Marshall," and to appreciate her excellence. Her large garden was kept in the neatest order, filled with fruits and flowers, and the kind reception that welcomed her visitors, on entering her domicil, is still by many held in grateful remembrance.

In 1798, the Town Hall was erected, and thought a very handsome building, beautifully situated. Peter Bauduy, Esq., drew the plan. From the cupola there is a most extensive view. A good bell was presented by Joseph Tatnall, Esq. The yard is bounded by King street, and graced by noble elms. The cells underneath superseded the old smoke house, and a large clock in front, with the clear-toned bell, gives hourly warning of departing time.

Near Market street, on Hanover, was a one-story brick school house, kept by Mr. Jordan, a celebrated teacher. The Baptists fitted it up for a place of worship, from whom it was purchased by the Episcopalians, and for years was used as a lecture room for Trinity Church.

The Bank of Delaware is on the north east corner. In this square was an old hipt-roof frame, long known as the dwelling of Michael Wolfe, biscuit baker. The old people here can remember him carrying a big basket on his head filled with butter biscuit, crackers, Naples biscuit, A. P.'s (so called from the initials of the maker on the cakes, Ann Page, Philadelphia,) and ginger-bread in rolls and squares, passing through the street; and he often walked to Newport and New Castle with this heavy load, and was always cheerful and obliging. He sustained his good character in old age, and ended his weary pilgrimage in this ancient abode.

CHAPTER XXIV.

Abijah Dawes—French Army—Gunning Bedford, Esq.—Dr. Franklin—Dr. McKinley—Governor Dickinson—John Rumsey, Esq.—Old Academy—Its changes—Professor Patterson—Funeral Procession—Old Presbyterian Church and Cemetery.

The mansion on the east side above Eighth street was built by Abijah Dawes. In the Revolution it was the headquarters of the French army. A large sum in French crowns, for their support, was packed in kegs and deposited in the cellar. Be it said to the shame of an American, and one of some standing, too, who found access by night, to break a hole in the wall and secrete a number of kegs in a well in this yard. By an unforseen incident he was detected, to the joy of our allies and the disgrace of the base perpetrator.

The next occupant was Judge Bedford, an officer of the Revolution, to whom General Washington presented his pocket pistols as a token of his approbation of his services. After the general's decease, Lady Washington (so called in those days), as a memento of her regard, presented to him the masonic sash worn by her venerated general. It was of crimson satin. The pistols are in the possession of his daughter. Gunning Bedford, Esq., was also a member of the olden Congress, when this State was nobly represented.

Judge Bedford and his lady were remarkably handsome persons, and of noble stature. Mrs. B. had received an accomplished education, and spoke French fluently, her mother being a native of France. When emigrants from that country crowded this town, Mrs. B. was their friend and patron. Her entertainments excelled in tasteful arrangements and ornamental display—so said foreigners. Her father, James Parker, Esq., of New York, was an early friend and companion of Dr. Franklin, with whom this lady was a favorite and a correspondent during life, and he favored her father's views in giving her a a classical education; and when Mr. Parker edited a paper in New York, his daughter lightened his labor by her pen, both by writing and translating. Some of these papers are now in Miss B.'s possession.

Many remembrances of Dr. Franklin are still in her daughter's hands. The first silver dollar he earned, when a newsboy, he had made into a punch strainer, and he and Mr. Parker exchanged, each having the same, and this is held as a relic. The gold pen and pencil with which he wrote his diplomatic dispatches from England and France, were his memento to her on the close of his useful career; and his own prayer book, which he used at chuch, was affectionately presented with his advice—the same as given to his daughter on leaving her, and in his estimation it was not a trifling gift.

"Go to church constantly, whoever preaches. The act of devotion in the common prayer-book is your principal business there; and if properly attended to will do more towards mending the hearts than sermons generally can do; for they were composed by men of much greater piety and wisdom than our common composers of sermons can pretend to, and therefore I wish you never to miss the prayer day.

"Yet I do not mean you should despise sermons even if you dislike the preacher, for the discourse is often much better than the man, as sweet and clear water comes through very dirty earth."

Abijah Dawes left this property by will to his niece, Mrs. Elizabeth Massey, and it was occupied by Thomas Massey a few years, and sold during the last war with England to Louis McLane, Esq., and was his residence for many years until his appointment as minister to England.

Mrs. McLane has been called in premature age to resign her earthly cares we trust for a heavenly home. A brief tribute to one who passed most of her early years among us may be appropriate. Perhaps her happiest days at school and as a married lady were spent here. No one was a more devoted wife, nor more honored her friends in a foreign land. Her long affliction was borne with calm resignation, and ere the close she confessed her Saviour before men.

The mansion southwest corner of Broad street was built by an emigrant, M. Sarsney, who resided in it for years, and returned to Paris after the restoration of the Bourbons. He was of the household of the Duke de Berri. We regret to pass unnoticed many worthy citizens, of whom no incidents are revived or to be retained in memory.

The square on the east side was the property of Dr. McKinley on ground-rent to the Swedes' Church, and somewhere about 1792 he generously offered to tranfer back his title to the vestry, if they would there erect a church, and occupy the whole lot planting it with trees and shrubbery.

A motion was made to that effect during the rectorship of the Rev. J. Clarkson, and a considerable sum subscribed, with the promise of a fine bell from Capt. Thomas Fort, but so much opposition was made by the country members that it was finally abandoned.

In those days this lot was much higher ground. For thirty years much labor has been spent in digging it down. Formerly it was sown in clover, now and then in wheat or planted in corn, and sometimes used for pasture; and there were a few apple trees that gave it a rural appearance, though the houses were thinly scattered in this neighborhood.

In 1797, Governor Dickinson was in treaty for it to build a mansion in the centre and ornament the surrounding ground, and had increased the sum first offered to nineteen hundred pounds, but Doctor McKinley still demanded a small advance, when a trifling affair caused a misunderstanding, which closed the transaction. This was much regretted by Governor Dickinson, as it would have added little to his expenses and much to gratify his taste. He then improved the old one on the corner of Kent street, renewed the front, and put up extensive back buildings, which made it a costly dwelling; this was his residence from 1798 till his decease.

Governor Dickinson was a prominent actor in the Revolution, and the author of the celebrated *Farmer's Letters.* He filled many high stations, which gave him a conspicuous place in the annals of his country, so that it leaves but little else to be told of him, even by those who knew him best.

But as an honored son of Delaware, we hope our tribute of respect, as a memorial of small things in private life, will not be deemed presumptive from an individual by whom he was long known and valued as a neighbor, nor be uninteresting to those who knew that he remembered the poor of the land.

One family named, which was reduced from luxury to the deepest penury, was for a long season one of his pensioners, and sustained with a beautiful hand.

Others of a respectable class were subjects of his benevolence, and the genial rays of his guardian influence ofttimes refreshed the widow's heart with gladness, and bid the fatherless rejoice, when her orphan boy was educated through his fostering care, for no public schools were here in by-gone days as nurseries for needy children.

It seemed that all the little ones were objects of his interest, and these were so sensitive to his regard that mingled groups of all classes would encircle him in the street, and desirous of his notice salute him thus—"Governor, how do you do, sir?" and they would be so delighted by his kind reply—"Thank you, my little ones; how are all your daddies and mammies?"

Ofttimes he would take them home, and leave them to stand under a window near the door while he threw out pennies or small silver pieces, and apples, nuts, &c., and be much amused to see them scramble for the booty; but the unsuccessful one was always called in for his or her share; and children were so accustomed to get cake, that once, while they were at dinner and several guests at the table, a little urchin slipped in, ran forward and said, "Govenor, will you sell me cakes to-day?" Such things seem trifling to relate, yet they often portray the genuine feelings of the heart. However exalted an individual may be, a portion of his life is made up of small incidents, which often exemplify the real character. The sick and sorrowing were remembered in acts of kindness.

War with England had long been the theme, and this patriot deplored the desolating scourge. Having passed through it once, he most ardently desired his country might never be involved more in such an evil, and it seemed to make upon him a deep and abiding impression. Ere the evil befell us, he was removed, in full possession of his faculties, even with good eyesight, never having worn glasses.

A few months previous to his decease, and while in perfect health, we were deeply impressed by his conversation on the uncertainty of life; when he observed all his worldly concerns were arranged, and his mind in peace on that subject, and he felt that his earthly career was near the close. His ancestors had departed about the seventy-sixth year of their age, and he was waiting a like event, and striving to prepare to enter "the valley of the shadow of death."

One week's indisposition led him to the tomb, lamented as a patriot, statesman, and kind neighbor, and still far better as a Christian. "And he died in a good old age, full of days, riches and honors."

Many worthy neighbors have since then passed into the grave. One of whom, Cyrus Newlin, a benevolent friend, never turned the deserving poor from his door, nor was charity solicited of him in vain, for his purse and hands were open. "Give alms of thy goods, and never turn thy face from any poor man; and then the face of the Lord shall not be turned away from thee."

John Rumsey's residence was in this square, and the family were valued neighbors. Mrs. Anna Rumsey was affable and meek in manner, a sincere friend and practical Christian, a member of Trinity Church, and unceasing in her duties. She attended the Sunday School from its infancy, rarely absent, and never late in attendance. With the kindest feelings, she gave a word in season to the numerous classes as they came in turn.

Mrs. Rumsey was pre-eminent in the religious instruction of youth, and her good works, we trust, were recorded in heaven, where she laid up her treasure. On errands of mercy to visit the sick and needy, our lot was often to witness her retiring modesty and humility. We truly believe very few more strictly fulfil the command of the evangelist, "When thou doest alms, let not thy left hand know what thy right hand doeth."

Mrs. Mary Jones, on this square, was a companion of our school days, and amid the varied scenes of childhood and youth years rolled on with no intermission of friendship. Her amiable disposition and kind feelings knew no change. She died before she was assailed by the infirmities of age, a member of the Presbyterian church. "Blessed is every one who feareth the Lord, that walketh in his ways."

Though the little brick house set back, with a nice paled yard, and pretty shrubbery and trees, has given place to modern houses, and the deserving occupants have gone the way of all the earth, Andrew and Laurette Noels, colored people, are remembered, whose useful and orderly habits, and the good training of their children, might be an example to many of a higher class. Their house was well furnished and kept neat, with a handsome garden in perfect order.

In sickness, they were esteemed the best nurses, ever ready to serve; and none were more acceptable. These respectable colored people came to this place as slaves to French families, and were manumitted by their kind master. None had a more respectable funeral than Andrew Noels, who lived in peace and good will to his neighbors.

Also Abraham and Delia Dores, who were slaves to Dr. Way's brother in the West Indies, were also freed. These two men were long in partnership as noted barbers. Every Saturday night they divided the profits of the week.

Alexander Bauduy, Esq., owned a house above, where his family resided for years. Part of the time, he was an aide to Napoleon Bonaparte. His only son, a promising young man, died in Cuba.

Mrs. Brooks, a worthy widow, lived next to the Academy for years, and had in charge a number of misses from distant places to be educated here. This lady was sister to Major Patten, to whose memory, as the friend of a beloved parent, we will pay a tribute of respect in its proper place.

And what shall we say now of that once honored relic, the Old Academy, on the northern front of the square between Eighth and Ninth and Market and King streets? It is gone! But its usefulness has left a freshness on our memory that ofttimes recalls its former glory—a noble stone edifice, of the neatest mason work, graced by majestic forest trees on the surrounding grounds, commanding an extensive prospect of land and water.

The celebrated Whitefield notices it in his journal, 1774. "In the academy woods, I preached to three thousand people."

The land was Stalcup's, who I think was the donor, to promote knowledge and to bequeath to future generations a most valuable endowment. Public-spirited men erected it, and the fathers of the country were overseers. The trustees were men competent for such an office.

Rev. Lawrence Girelius was chairman of the board while he remained in the country. Bishop White, Hon. Thomas McKean, Dr. Robert Smith, Thomas Gilpin, of Philadelphia, Dr. Nicholas Way, Joseph Shallcross, Esq., Professor Robert Patterson, had it first in charge—he was the father of Dr. Robert M. Patterson, President of the Mint—and this literary institution promised to realize the most sanguine hopes of its founders by the respectability and number of pupils.

As the genial influence of learning was putting forth blossoms and shedding a fragrace o'er the community, the canker-worm of war, ever destructive to good, nipped some of the brightest plants, and withered its prosperity.

Conflicting armies were quartered here at different periods of the Revolutionary struggle, and academical instruction suspended. This noble fabric was converted into a barrack and hospital.

Professor Patterson turned his attention to military operations, and being the only qualified instructor in those tactics, he was the first to exercise the young men of this town. Israel Gilpin was the first captain under his training. Professor Patterson joined the New Jersey line, and was a major in the paymaster's department during the war.

Once more the country was hailed with the joyful sound of peace, harbinger of good to man, and the duties of this institution were resumed with renewed hopes of prosperity. The professors were M. Murdock and M. Maffit. On the departure of the Rev. L. Girelius, it seemed for a time on the wane. Soon after peace was established, an assemblage of scientific men, provided with instruments for observation from the top of this academy, met in town—Doctors Franklin, Rittenhouse, B. Rush, Mr. Madison, and others. Dr. Franklin also made an experiment here on electricity, when a number of the literati were present.

Here, too, one of the first general conventions of the Protestant Episcopal Church met in its earliest days under the new republic, which drew hither many wise men to suit their organization to the laws of the land.

Ere the close of the last century, literary pursuits were abandoned, and this noble building, so beautifully situated for a seat of learning, was changed to a manufactory, every room filled with spinning-jennies and looms.

At length the citizens awoke from their slumbers to an active sense of duty, and appointed new trustees, Drs. J. Latimer, E. A. Smith, Dr. Read, Dr. James Tilton, Sr., Judge Bedford, and R. Hamilton, Esq., by whom competent teachers were elected to fill two departments, one for male, the other for female students. Once more the sunshine of literature brightened up the old academy, if not to gild their hall in glory, at least to honor the vicinity by a respectable high school, where many pupils did credit to their teachers and honored their parents.

In conversation recently with a learned gentleman, Mr. A. was the subject. He was surprised to hear that his education was completed at our old academy. Mr. R. replied that Mr. A.'s scholarship would do honor to any institution. The same might be said of some in the female department, who would reflect honor on any seminary. The public annual examinations were creditable to teachers and to pupils. The boys had recitations, and were examined by day. The evening closed by exhibitions from well-chosen scenes in Shakspeare, which afforded amusement to crowded assemblies of spectators.

To enumerate the varied uses made of these apartments would be a difficult task at this day. To begin with religious instructions promulgated here. Formerly the Roman Catholics had no church in town, and a room on the first floor supplied a temporary chapel on Sunday morning.

In 1814, a Harmonic Society was organized, devoted to sacred music: each member paid fifty cents per quarter, with the privilege of taking lessons once a week or sending a substitute. An upper room was fitted up with platforms and raised benches; four hundred names were enrolled, and several teachers employed. At the monthly concert, instrumental music was introduced by amateurs, and the room was crowded.

During this period Rev. W. Price held Episcopal service here on Sunday afternoons; and purchased an antiquated organ, which was was paid for by a collection taken from the members of Trinity Church. No doubt was expressed of the organist's skill, yet no one could sing when he played, neither could he play if others sang. Sanders, this old German performer, was in perfect keeping with the instrument, and looked as if he belonged to an ancient race. He wore a leathern pouch filled with Scotch snuff, using it by the handful, and making it fly till the room would ring with sneezing in the concert.

This apartment was fitted up in Masonic style, adorned with crimson curtains and emblems of the secret art; thus it was occupied for years.

In 1818, the worthy teacher of languages, Joseph Downing, who will be long remembered by many as a conscientious and faithful instructor, invited the teachers of Trinity Church Sunday School, to occupy the lower rooms; and three hundred children usually attended. A class of German girls was very interesting, to whom the Rev. Levi Bull gave instructions in their own language.

In 1828 we again had afternoon service here, and a large Sunday School until Trinity Chapel was finished. Traveling preachers with or without a creed had access here, and all sorts of debating societies and political meetings.

Many years, on Saturday afternoons, a Dorcas circle met in an upper chamber. More than thirty females, varying in age and religious views, harmoniously mingled to make up garments for the poor. Inclement weather was no hindrance to their endeavors to clothe the naked. The happy reflection of doing good was the stimulus to greater exertion. "Now there was at Joppa a certain disciple called Dorcas; this woman was full of good works and alms deeds; she was sick and died, and all the widows stood by weeping, and shewing the coats and garments which Dorcas made."

Charitable meetings were held here, public dinners, singing and dancing schools, and balls.

In the winter of 1800, once a fortnight there was a well regulated dancing party, called a *whim*. The dress was simple, the refreshments plain cake and lemonade. The company were young persons, who met at candle light, and retired at eleven o'clock. This was directed by a young gentleman now a distinguished statesman.

On the 22d of February of the same year, a funeral procession for the Father of his country was directed by the Cincinnati of the State. Judge Bedford and Major Cass were masters of the ceremony. All the arrangements were concerted in this building.

Though the procession moved from the Town Hall preceded by the military band, a detachment of the regular army led the way followed by nine young girls to represent the Muses, and sixteen young ladies to represent the States, all dressed in white with short sleeves, then fashionable, long kid gloves, little book muslin hats turned up on the side with a black cockade, blue kid slippers, a black sash of broad ribbon over the right shoulder, tied in a bow on the left side. In front was printed in large gold letters the name of a State.

Virginia led the southern, Delaware the northern States. In the outer hand each one held a sprig of laurel; entering the aisle it was laid on the bier, saying, "Sacred to the memory of Washington. We deposit this laurel as an emblem of his never dying fame."

Fortunately it was a very warm day, for no shawls were to be worn to hide the dress. Citizens followed these State representatives down Market street to Second, and up French to the stone meeting house, where an address was delivered.

Now we have told you what strange things happened here fifty years ago.

After all the accommodations this stately building afforded, it was suffered to be sold for a small debt. Previous to the sale one of the counsel suggested to a female that Trinity Church had better purchase the academy than build a lecture-room, for which funds were collected; that twenty-two hundred dollars would buy the venerable relic.

This plan was soon disclosed to one of the vestry, and approved, with a promise that the means should be secured. The Rev. Ralph Williston was to close the bargain with his masonic brethren, as the debt was due to them. A few minutes before the appointed hour, David C. Wilson made the purchase, to our great disappointment and regret, for all things were arranged to alter the building into a church, and erect a large seminary on another part of the lot.

However disconcerted at this failure, and thinking at the time private interest ought to yield to public, we are compelled to own, in justice to Mr. Wilson, that the erection of so many good dwellings on the spot was the starting point of rapid improvements, and as a practical business man he must be ranked among our most useful citizens, who have contributed much to the prosperity of his birthplace.

The N. W. corner of Ninth street was the first residence of Governor Dickinson in town. He lived there several years. On his removal it was occupied by Madame Bauduy, mother of the gentleman named. Hence her remains were carried to the old Swedes' Cemetery.

An estimable widow, Mrs. Reading, with a large family, was the successor to this mansion. Most of her family closed their earthly career in youth—"for the morning was to them even as the shadow of death."

Above this corner in Market street, within a few years a very ancient dwelling has been removed, long known as the Cross Keys, afterwards as the Monumental Inn. It has given place to modern dwellings.

Before us, on the east side of Market street, between Ninth and Tenth streets, is a venerable building. Though small and hipt-roof, it is more than a hundred years old, and is where the Presbyterian fathers in this region first worshiped. It is beautifully situated, and has a large cemetery enclosed with a stone wall, where the dead of two centuries lie.

Many worthies worshiped the God of their fathers in this relic of antiquity. Some we have named are here mouldering into dust. We often pass this spot and reflect on the good deeds of those whom we knew and loved on earth, and doubt not of their being in Heaven. "Therefore are they before the throne of God, and serve him day and night: they shall hunger no more, neither thirst any more; and God shall wipe away all tears from their eyes."

Within a few years a very neat edifice has been erected, called the First Presbyterian Church. The congregation from a very small beginning has rapidly increased to a respectable number, under the charge of their faithful and worthy pastor, Rev. Stephen R. Wynkoop.

Opposite, on the west side, was an excellent vegetable garden, attented to by a good old man, M. Campbell, who supplied its owner's table, Gov. D., and served the market for his own benefit. The cabin adjoining was built by an industrious colored woman, who lived upwards of a hundred years, Lydia Hall. She had two sons in the army of the Revolution; one was carried off by the enemy, and she knew him no more. She was honest and faithful to her employers. Nothing of olden days claims our notice beyond this spot down to the Brandywine. The cornfields, and pasture lots, and orchards, are filled up with fine dwellings.

An old dwelling on the right, fronting the bridge, was long the residence of William Canby, and it bears the mark of the Revolution. A Hessian soldier, striving to get into the house, made a dash at Mrs. Canby with his sword, and cut the window shutter, which was suffered to remain as a relic of that time. In her alarm, she sprang out of the window and escaped to the mill.

CHAPTER XXV.

Front street west of Market—Eleazar McComb, Esq.—Francis Way- Major Patten.

On the south side of Front street, there was a frame used as a workshop. A dock faced Shipley street, where boats landed freight. Just above was a bridge placed over a stream, and in wet weather the walk was nearly impassable. Mr. McComb, being a public-spirited man, had it banked, and a gravel path made to his mansion.

Next house was the residence of Francis Way, whose ancestors were respectable members of Friends' Society. F. Way was remarkably neat in person and in all around him. His grounds and garden were kept in order and abounded in fruits. He married late in life, and was peculiar in his habits.

One dwelling above this was owned by Jonas Canby, who was also a respectable Friend. The house is now a hotel.

On the north side, in later years, a frame was occupied by a heroine of the Revolution, Bell McCloskey, by whom many a soldier's wounds were bound up, and it has been already mentioned of her that she extracted the ball from General Lafayette's knee.

The two good dwellings opposite the Rumford house were erected by Joseph Springer and John Milner, in one of which the latter resided for years. He also built a large house in Market above Front street, now a hotel. He too was a respectable Friend.

Major Patten, an officer of the Revolution, purchased the first house named of Mr. Milner, and resided there in 1798. He belonged to the brave Delaware regiment, and was exposed to the dangers of many a battle. At Camder, in South Carolina, he was made prisoner and taken to Charleston.

Previous to the battle he sent his servant with his baggage to a place of safety, but he never heard of either, and consequently he was marched into the city by his triumphant victors without a change of raiment. The major was a very attractive gentleman in personal appearance and manner. The ladies were compassionate, and many a patriotic one had fled there for protection, whose sympathies were awakened by his destitution, and they supplied him with garments and made a set of shirts. He was treated mildly, and occasionally mingled in society, where he was much admired. No opportunity offered for an exchange, and he remained a prisoner until peace.

As stated by Mrs. Judge Bedford, who was a witness to the return of this worthy officer to his native town, Dover, he appeared without shoes or stockings. An old pair of soles were tied about his feet, his clothes were worn threadbare, and still worse, as small clothes were the fashion, his legs were entirely bare. This portrays the situation of many a poor soldier's return, to whom "the powers that be" are now grudging to grant a pittance, and leave them to pine in poverty.

We have thus paid a brief tribute of respect to the memory of Major Patten's public services, which needed no comment; and as the valued friend of a beloved parent who knew him well, it may be in place here to note that the excellence of his private character was unrivaled.

And the same epithet may apply to his estimable daughter, so recently removed in premature age, from her sorrowing family. Mrs. Ann Wales we knew in early childhood, and in every state of her brief life, and believe we can truly say that the excellence of her domestic character was unrivaled.

A singular coincidence we will note. After a lapse of years, a family from Charleston were boarding in this town. The major and lady had deceased; his two orphans were left in charge of his worthy sister, Mrs. Brookes. One day, in passing with a relative, and attired in mourning, the elder lady inquired whose pretty little children they were? The answer was, Major Patten's.

The name was familiar to Mrs. Logan, and turned her thoughts back to stirring times. She exclaimed, "Can they be the offspring of the handsome officer for whom the ladies of Charleston so diligently plied the needle to make shirts, and I was one of their number?" Verily, this was the person.

CHAPTER XXVI.

Shipley Street—Wm. Jones—Up Second Street—Sheward's Brewery—Tan Yard—Z. Ferris—Cold Bath—In Shipley Street—Dr. Nicholas Way—Post Office—Ziba Ferris, Sen.—The Maid of Erin—A Tale of Other Days.

THE northwest corner of Shipley street was the residence of Wm. Jones, and it is pleasant to tell that his son is the owner, who also bears his father's good name. Here was a fine garden, kept in neat order, and adorned by many a beautiful flower. Even after the street was raised and the garden laid low, attractions were there. The squares almost to Third Street were unimproved still later years.

Up Second street but two objects claim our notice. Sheward's brewery on the north side, of ancient date, prospered in the day when malt liquor was much used. Now it is a decayed relic, though it has long survived the respectable founder.

On the north side, above West street, Zachariah Ferris, an acceptable minister in Friends' Society, owned a tan yard and dwelling house. His son, John Ferris, built a large house opposite the City Hall. He was in the hardware business, from which he retired, and built a house in the next square, where he died in old age much respected. He left a handsome estate, but no children to inherit it.

There was a noted spot in the last century back of Ferris' tan yard, which in my childhood was called Dr. Way's bath. The water was excessively cold. A frame building of goodly size, with benches and pins for clothing, and a large bath, boarded, with steps to descend into the water, which continually flowed in with an outlet at the lower end. This was a great resort for those youths of that day who could save two pennies to pay the woman for her trouble.

A substantial brick dwelling near Third street was long the residence of Griffith Minshall. A very handsome garden was always in good order. A new front has changed its appearance.

Doctor Nicholas Way erected a large commodious mansion at the southwest corner for his residence. He was an eminent physician, and a gentleman of the old school. His popularity was unbounded. He commenced practice in 1775, and associated with the officers of his own nation and with the foreigners, also with other distinguished men of his day, which gave him notoriety abroad, and drew to him many students, especially from South Carolina. As a practitioner, he was highly prized for his skill and affable manner.

In 1793, when the yellow fever first appeared in Philadelphia, crowds of citizens sought an asylum here. So great was the dread of that epidemic, many were refused admittance. Doctor Way thought change of air would counteract its contagious effect; and used his influence by interceding for their reception. Immediately every door was open and houses filled.

In the prime of life he was thrown from a horse, and had his leg broken. The inconvenience of riding induced him then to resign his extensive country practice. His patients were unwilling to yield, and this was so perplexing he knew not how to limit his visits.

He therefore came to the conclusion to change his residence. In the autumn of '96, he went to Philadelphia, but yet so undecided as to remaining there that his house was kept open till the following spring. He was appointed by Gen. Washington President of the Mint. In his domestic character Dr. Way was a gentleman of worth. He never married. In the fall of 1797, he fell a victim to the yellow fever in Philadelphia, and no one was more deeply lamented.

His house was purchased by Mons. Hammond, a French gentleman, who occupied it for years, and sold it to Jacob Broom, Esq., who resided there for some time. It is the present residence of our Senator, the Hon. John Wales, who, with his worthy family, the descendants of Mrs. Ann Wales, already noticed as the daughter of Major Patten, have been long our particular and intimate friends.

At the northwest corner was the Post Office, for near twenty years. Nicholas G. Williamson, Esq., was postmaster during that time, and he was also elected mayor of the city. At his decease, he left a widow and many daughters to mourn the departure of a husband and father.

The old hipt-roofed dwelling above was long the abode of Jane Farson, a Friend, who lived and died here. A relic of other days occupies its ancient spot in this garden. A white rose bush has bloomed annually for a hundred years, and still flourishes in vigorous beauty from youth to old age.

The southwest corner at Fourth street was owned by the Richardson family. Those two were fine houses in that day; with a large garden kept in neat order, which seemed the usual appendage, and this one was of the first class. At the close of the Revolution, Joel Zane, a respectable Friend, kept a hardware store on this corner. Mrs. Hester Zane was a most worthy, benevolent woman. One of her good deeds was to make soup daily for the poor French soldiers when quartered in town during the Revolutionary war.

"Come ye blessed of my father." "I was a stranger, and ye took me in."

On the northeast corner of Third street, the ivy that clings to the wall and creeps into the crevices of yon old mansion is an emblem of the past, and reminds one of the family of by-gone days. Ziba Ferris long resided here. It is now occupied by his son, who bears his name. An elder brother, whom we have noted, was a martyr to humanity in 1802.

The personal appearance and winning manner of Mrs. Edith Ferris were lovely, even in old age; and her acts of mercy were followed up, wherever charity claimed her attention, in giving alms, or in visiting the widow in affliction, or soothing the child of sorrow. One of her good deeds we here relate.

On the approach of autumn, the day was cool and damp. One came to Mrs. Ferris, and said a stranger in affliction was her neighbor. Ever prompt on errands of mercy, she hastened to the abode. On entering, the interior presented an impressive scene. The absence of many comforts was apparent, and an interesting young woman, lingering on the borders of the grave, conscious of her slow and sure decay.

It was evident she had seen better days, and had mingled in refined society. Unfitted to struggle with adversity, or yield to its stern demands, disease was progressing, and sadness and sorrow beset her passage to the tomb. Intense anxiety was depicted in her countenance; a lovely little one fondly clung to her arms, and seemed to bow down her feeble frame with maternal grief. The family consisted of three foreigners, just arrived, with limited means, in hopes to improve their fortune in America.

The young man, as a husband and father, was much perplexed.

He deemed it important immediately to pursue some business for his livelihood, and his wife's delicate health forbade his absence to seek or engage in lucrative employment. The sympathies of one so kindly disposed as Mrs. Ferris were aroused, and it was a touching event.

On another visit, she advised the young man to accept an offer that would secure the means to sustain his family, assuring him that she would attend to his wife's comforts, and take charge of the little girl in his absence.

Such unexpected benevolence in a stranger overpowered them with gratitude, and seemed the dawn of a brighter day in their cheerless abode. With the most assiduous attention, the duty was fulfilled by this good Samaritan. No omission chilled the warm affection enkindled in the heart of one far from relatives and native land. It burned more brightly, and was most ardent, when the shadow of death was over her, whispering to the senses, "Behold thy days approach, that thou must die."

She again requested this kind friend to take the little one and train her in virtuous ways. To her fostering care she could resign her earthly treasure, and leave the fleeting world without a sigh. In a moment, her spirit fled from earthly scenes.

The father was desirous to have the care of his child, and kept her for a short time. He was a gentleman, unacquainted with labor, and entered upon farming, but was unsuccessful. Then he requested Mrs. Ferris to take charge of his little girl. This lady replied that her plain habits and domestic employments would not accord with his views, but to these he freely assented, and she received the child as her own.

His wife's relatives were indignant at the resolve to come to this country, and vowed to know her no more. Yet a rich maiden aunt did adopt their only son ere they sailed, and spared no expense on his education at home, nor in France, whither he went for three years to complete his studies.

We now leave the little girl in kind hands, to pass on to her teens, and pause ere we draw near the pith of our story. When she had become inwardly and outwardly as decided a Friend as ever ascended yon hill, to her this mansion was a little world. Its inmates were the objects of her affection. Here all her pleasures and cares were centred. Beyond the precincts she had little concern, for she was a stranger to the endearing ties of kindred, and was gliding so smoothly down the stream of time, thus far, that the first moving of the waters ruffled the even tenor of her way on entering her eighteenth year.

This rich aunt—her mother was of a noble family, Miss Stevens, of Stevens' Green, in Dublin—had heard of her niece, and solicited an introduction to Captain Geddes, of Wilmington, then in that city. To him she communicated her intention to receive this relative into the bosom of her family, and make ample provision for her future support, and empowered the Captain to furnish funds, and bring her across the ocean under his protection.

On his arrival home, the Captain had an interview with Mrs. Ferris, who communicated the intelligence to the young lady, Deborah Jones. The unlooked for kindness surprised her, but did not enkindle in her bosom any ambitious views. Being happy in her home, she was therewith content. Yet, on listening to the story, it agitated her calm spirit. She knew not how to express gratitude to her kind aunt, accompanied by the refusal of such an offer, which she felt no desire to accept.

Not so with Mrs. Ferris, ever anxious to promote the welfare of the little stranger, whom she had taken in tender age, and led on, by careful steps, to years of discretion, and now so worthy, and striving to make ample returns for all her solicitude in childhood by affection and usefulness. Besides, her services in the family were important, and their attachment was reciprocal, and the parting would be painful. With deep feeling, her benefactress urged her to accept the advantageous proposal. Being trained by the rule of obedience, to yield to the counsel of one in whom she had the most implicit confidence, she acquiesced, and prepared for the voyage.

In arranging her outfit, Mr. Ferris thought it expedient to make her dresses a little more in fashion, to better suit her aunt's taste, and not to deviate from Friends. But D. was conscientiously opposed to any innovation in the old path. So her garb was of the plainest order. The separation was a trying scene—to bid a final farewell to beloved friends and a youthful home.

About 1789, the heroine of our story was escorted to New Castle by Governor Dickinson; his daughter, Mrs. Ferris, and herself in Gov. D.'s carriage; Mr. Ferris and children in another; Mr. Wright and daughter, relatives of Gov. D., in their coach. Capt. Geddes sent his long boat to take them all on board, where they bid adieu, and sailed with a fair breeze to the Emerald Isle.

Their prosperous voyage, arrival, and reception at Stevens' Green, were stated to the writer by Capt. Geddes. Favorable winds wafted them speedily o'er the ocean. D. was a stranger to sea sickness, and, though so sad at leaving her friends, not a murmur escaped, nor was a frown seen on her brow, neither did she spend time to bemoan her departure. She was endowed with a mind of a high order.

The cabin arrangements were under her care, and order and neatness presided. Excellent desserts were provided for dinner every day. Not a button hung loose on a coat, nor was one wanting from the cabin to the caboose; neither did a stocking want a stitch. Every sailor was an object of her care, and his comfort regarded.

These little favors and attentions kept the ship's crew in perfect good humor from land to land. Besides fitting up garments and nice cookery, she was often employed in reading useful books to the sailors.

At length the eventful day was ushered in by a delightful morning, and the ship safe at her mooring in Dublin harbor.

An express was sent to inform the aunt of her arrival, and in their best dress they waited an answer. A coach and four splendid horses drove up. A man in superb livery handed the captain a note, as they stepped into this fine carriage. D.'s heart went pit-a-pat, and, with her head bowed down, they drove through Dublin. The captain bid her cheer up to meet the lady patroness.

They alighted at the door of an elegant mansion, and entered the reception room, where they were greeted with a cordial welcome by the noble aunt, and met by the brother, who had just arrived from Paris, with all the airs and graces of a French fop. The aunt was an elegant, dignified Irish lady, richly dressed; the niece in the simlest garb of an American Quakeress of the plainest order. No three persons from either quarter of the globe could come in contact to form a more striking contrast.

The scene was so novel every one seemed to lose the power of speech, and sat gazing at each other astounded, in solemn silence; while the captain had to exert his powers to restrain his risible faculties. If the countenance was an index of the mind, and could be read, each one queried, Do kindred ties unite us?—and does the same blood flow in our veins?—or can any sympathy exist between us?

The aunt was evidently disappointed both in nephew and niece. When the shock had subsided, and conversation resumed, the voyage was the topic; and occasionally the niece was addressed, who faintly answered "Yes!" or, "No!" The aunt was so anxious to draw her out that she observed the sight of land must be cheering after passing weeks on sea! "Yes!" again. To bring out a sentence, she asked her, "What day did you make land?" "Last First day!" The aunt amazed, softly repeated, "Last First day?" Turning to the captain, she said, "Pray sir, tell me what day is that?" This was about the amount of the introductory visit.

On taking leave, the captain observed his young companion shed tears. The hostess noticed it, and most politely invited him to partake of the hospitalities of her mansion, whenever it suited his convenience.

To cheer the stranger in her new home, he often spent an hour there, and was always made welcome by the aunt. As he became more familiar, he ventured to give a few hints of the manners and doings in this town, "where," he said, "females usually attended to domestic duties, and her niece being brought up in a plain Friend's family, whose daughters were conscientiously instructed in household affairs, he had no doubt that she would be much happier to be employed, and better reconciled to the change."

The aunt thought the hint good, at once proposed to her to feel herself at home, and take an interest in the family.

This was most agreeable to one used to every-day duties. The captain said, "Not much pains had been taken there in little matters, such as washing windows; the glass was usually pretty well dimmed, and the absence of neatness was annoying to one so accustomed to order." Therefore, she immediately commenced ablutions. By inducing a servant to rise at morning dawn, they cleaned the paints, washed windows and floor of the breakfast-room, and set all things in order before the lady entered.

This extreme neatness delighted her. The windows were so clear she thought the glass new, and the transition was sudden, like magic —all was done in a few hours. But when she found that her niece had taken a very active part, her dignity was touched, and she hastily exclaimed, "Do you suppose I brought you to Dublin for such menial services? Are there not servants in my house to do all you command them?"

D. modestly replied, "Active employment best suited her turn of mind." In fact, she could not live so listless. If her aunt could condescend to allow her to take a part in domestic duties, it would add much to contentment in her new sphere of life. But she was willing to submit to her decision. This calm submission to her aunt's pleasure was conclusive. The aristocratic lady yielded to the Yankee notions of her republican niece, and confidence and good feeling were reciprocated.

An elegant wardrobe was ordered for the niece, which caused some altercation. The primitive one was wedded to her simple garb, and scrupulously rejected to adorn her person by dress. Though so dissimilar in opinions and taste, years glided on in great harmony, each being blest with good temper and kind feelings.

This lady's business concerns were extensive, and a young man was often employed, in whom she placed full confidence, as he was faithful to his trust. He too was a member of Friend's Society, and on business visits sought an opportunity to converse with D., whose religious views accorded with his own. These interviews were pleasing to one who seemed to be cut off from associates, holding her own principles, and they became mutually interested in each other.

But he feared to make further advance, lest it would displease the lady patroness. At length he ventured to introduce the subject. The aunt respectfully listened to the proposal, but her manner was repulsive, and it was evident did not accord with her designs, who had anticipated a more honorable alliance for her niece.

However, upon reflecting that she was a plain, unpretending girl, with no great personal attractions, she felt that such pretensions were delusive, and to this young man she could make no reasonable objection. His moral character she highly appreciated, and there was a congeniality in their persons which promised a happy union; and she reasoned away her more aspiring hopes, and sanctioned this marriage.

They adopted the name of Stevens, and it was solemnized in troublous times, in the day of Emmet and Rowan, and others of the "United Men," so that Dublin was the theatre of discord, and it was most prudent to withdraw to a less populous place. Wexford became their residence. Here the aunt purchased a house, and fitted out her niece with every comfort, and their prospects daily brightened.

On a visit of her husband to Dublin, a person whom he knew begged the favor of him to deliver a letter to a friend. He was not aware it was addressed to a "United Man."

The police were vigilant in examining all who entered the city, and said this letter contained treasonable expressions enough to condemn him. He pleaded ignorance of the contents, which availed nothing. He was dragged to prison, and treated with all the rigor of a traitor, and denied the privilege of conversing with visitors.

In the mean time his wife anxiously looked for his return. As weeks elapsed, and no intelligence arrived, her distress was intense. It was concluded he had been murdered on the way It was, alas! the too common fate of travelers passing conflicting parties. Her aunt decided it best to break up her establishment, and return to to the home she had left.

During this extreme distress at home he was closely confined in the most rigorous manner, and pining away under disease. His keeper seemed to pity his case, and a way opened for him to whisper in his ear where the aunt lived, and to intreat him to make known his pitiable condition. The man was trustworthy, and conveyed the tidings, but in so hurried a manner that it seemed improbable. The servant said a rough-looking man told him Mr.——was in prison, and the number of his ward, and quickly he was gone.

Though it might not be the truth, the kind aunt did not delay to visit the prison. Being a loyalist, she gained access, and was shocked to find him such an object of compassion. By perseverance, she obtained leave for him to visit her once a week for a few hours, on her own responsibility to see him safe back. On one of these visits his escape was planned. The aunt gave him a silver basket, under the pretence of getting some confectionery for her a few doors below; and he was borne away by men in disguise to a ship ready to sail for America. His wife had prepared to depart with him. They arrived safe in Philadelphia, where he soon died with a disease contracted in prison. On the news of his death, the aunt wished her to return. But she said nothing could induce her to recross the ocean.

Years winged away, and D. engaged once more in married life. Though no such disasters befell her, there was cause for unhappiness, and after a lingering disease, she died, and left two daughters, one of whom was brought up by the friend of Mrs. Ferris. They were very respectable, worthy women. The youngest, contrary to the advice of friends, made an adventurous voyage to a land of strangers, and is at present in China.

CHAPTER XXVII.

School—Henry Pepper—Wm. Cobbett—St. Andrew's Church—Billy McDougall—Dr. Gibbons—College—M. Bradford—Woman in a Well—John Bull—Boarding School—Caleb Seal—St. Peter's Church—Sisters of Charity—Friends' Meeting House—Cemetery—School.

In olden days, the north corner was M. Andrew's printing office. His son edited a paper; then James Wilson, his son-in-law. It was for years the only Democratic paper in the State.

Nathaniel Richards, who long occupied this house, died recently in the 93d year of his age. These persons were respectable members of the Society of Friends.

Edward Hughes lived near. He had a worthy family, and was long a clerk in the Bank of Delaware. He and his wife died in old age. They and most families who resided in Shipley street were of the Friends' Society.

An old fabric on the east side, yet standing, where most of the respectable children of suitable age were in part educated, will be long remembered. The teacher, Henry Pepper, was a graduate of Dublin College, a teacher of languages, and a proficient in French, which was deemed so essential when the town was teeming with emigrants. Besides, it was so genteel to say you were learning French, if only a few monosyllables were acquired—to say "Parlez vous francais?" and this was about the amount that many did learn. Yet there were a few hard students who had much knowledge of the language, obtained from books.

A number of French gentleman came to take lessons in English. For a few hours each day they occupied a room. Many amusing incidents occurred between the scholars in exercising their skill to speak a strange language.

Mrs. Pepper was young, sprightly, and very handsome, in those days, and she was dearly beloved by all his scholars. In the spring of 1797, Mr. P. removed to Philadelphia, where his prospects brightened. But in the autumn he fell a victim to the yellow fever, leaving a widow and four small children to depend on her own exertions. "As God tempers the wind to the shorn lamb," under his providential care he raised up for the destitute widow a most benevolent friend in E. J. Dupont, Esq.

In our school days, a stranger of some notoriety resided on Quaker Hill, in the house afterwards owned by Col. McLane. This was William Cobbett, an Englishman, who became afterward so celebrated as a writer, both in America and in England. He was a teacher of French here for some time, and an eminent scholar. He published a grammar of the French language, which was highly approved. His own history was as follows:—

Once a common soldier in the British army in the East Indies, at a pay of sixpence per day, he managed to procure elementary books, and studied nearly the whole night. His thirst for learning was so ardent that he never lost a moment, and he thus advanced himself to pre-eminence in the language. He came to America about the year 1794, and resided at Wilmington. He often assisted Mr. Pepper in teaching, as he had several large classes. Some of those gentlemen were distinguished scholars, from whom he gained much knowledge of the sciences, and they were his friends in a pecuniary way.

He gave the credit of being initiated in political debates to this town. Said, "he had lived in the hotbed of Democracy." On Quaker Hill, amid the *Stars*, whose political horizon was so brilliant, he scarcely dare defend royalty.

Hence he removed to Philadelphia in 1796, opened a book store, and became notorious in public life. About to publish a paper, he enlisted Mr. Pepper's services by a great offer to write for it. He resigned a flourishing school to engage with Cobbett. Being struck by the name of his gazette, he inquired why he called it *The Porcupine*. He answered, because he meant to shoot his quills wherever he could catch game.

Mr. P. soon discovered a want of principle in it, and withdrew, for those who had been his best friends in his poverty were the first attacked. Wm. Cobbett's political career is well known—it ended in his being a member of the British House of Commons.

The northwest corner of Sixth street was the residence of Miss S. Hanson, an estimable lady, and celebrated for the excellent government of misses. Many from distant places were placed and educated under her care. In this house an adventure of the Revolution has already been related, in which Miss Hanson was a participant.

St. Andrew's Church, (Episcopal,) southwest corner of Eighth street, was erected in 1829, by a minority of the congregation of

Trinity, Old Swedes' Church. In a few years it inherited a large legacy by will from the estate of Mrs. Mary James.

In the midst of prosperity, a calamitous conflagration consumed the interior, destroyed the bell, and rendered the walls irreparable. But the energetic measures of the members surmounted this disaster, and reared a larger and more complete edifice. Recently the exterior has been much improved. The church is in good condition, and has ever sustained a flourishing Sunday School. It is at present under the pastoral charge of our excellent Bishop, Alfred Lee.

Delaware Avenue.—On the northeast corner of Orange street is a foundry, established some years ago by James Rice, with machine shops in operation. This family are old inhabitants, and are deserving people.

In years gone by, the southeast corner of Tatnall street was of some notoriety. A large pond, from time immemorial, was in possession of the bull-frog tribe, and it seemed their lawful inheritance. Mischievous boys now and then would disturb their repose as they popped their heads out of the muddy water.

But when "Les Messieurs" became residents here, even the villagers learned to cook them into a savory dish, and a price was offered for their legs, which induced young anglers to invade the premises with hook and line, and capture many noble fellows. Yet they were prosperous, and had a numerous progeny; and, when spring put forth its blossoms, they tuned their pipes—and such a merry clan greeted the whole vicinity in evening concerts!

On the verge of this pond was the noted Bull-Frog Tavern, not forgotten by the children of that day. A lonely old man cut timber from Mr. Shallcross's woods, and put up a shantee. Though harmless, he was a terror to the young folks, because he was intemperate and unsightly. He was like the man of "the house that Jack built," "all tattered and torn," and, like "the maiden, all forlorn." But, unlike the priest, he was never "shaven or shorn." Some waggish boys painted or caricatured an enormous frog on a board, and nailed it on the side of his shantee, lettered under—"The Bull-Frog Tavern, kept by Billy McDougall, but no entertainment within or without for man or beast."

The large mansion on the south side of this avenue was erected more than thirty years ago by the late Dr. Wm. Gibbons, and is the residence of his family. The doctor was a prominent citizen, eminent in his profession. He was likewise distinguished for his literary attainments, and deemed an instructive and agreeable companion. Though in the decline of life, his faculties were in full vigor; and, ere he was overtaken by the infirmities of age, death entered his chamber, and the spirit fled to happier regions. The doctor left a large family, and many sympathizing friends to mourn his loss.

Those extensive buildings adjoining are a Roman Catholic College, of considerable notoriety, under the direction of Priest Reilley, who sustains the character of a worthy man, and of a competent instructor. A number of pupils and students from a distance are placed under his guidance.

The premises on the east of the college, with the ancient hipped-roof tenements, was owned and occupied, in olden times, by John Hedges, Sr., whose family were of Swedish descent, and his descendants are still here to witness the changes from early days.

The very handsome new stone mansion on the north side was erected by Moses Bradford, Esq., but a few years ago, and the spot was suddenly transformed from a rugged cornfield to cultivated grounds, with a large house, an ornamented lawn with trees and shrubbery, and a flourishing garden. It seemed as if all was done by magic.

To Mrs. Phebe Bradford's fostering care much was due. Her taste in arranging trees and shrubbery, fondness for flowers, and perseverance to accomplish her designs, seldom failed to succeed. But, alas! like "the grass that groweth up and flourisheth in the morning, in the evening is cut down and withereth," so in the midst of her labors "her sun went down at noon," leaving her family and friends to lament the mysterious providence. Many with whom she was associated in religious and benevolent societies will long feel her loss.

Trinity Church may truly lament a most efficient member. We look up to the choir, for "lo! thou wert unto them as a very lovely song, of one that hath a very pleasant voice, and can play well on an instrument." We look around and see few to fill her place, and fewer who have the courage to encounter the lion in the path of duty.

> " 'Tis sweet to remember: I would not forego
> The charm which the past o'er the present can throw,
> When in calm reminiscence we gather the flowers
> Strown around us by friendship in happier hours,
> I would not forget, though my thoughts should be dark,
> O'er the ocean of life, I look back from my bark,
> And see the lost Eden, where once I was blest,
> A type and a promise of heavenly rest."

On the south side, between Shipley and Orange streets, yet stands an old stone fabric built by a worthy Swede, Andrew Vanneman, whose family lived there for years. In this yard is a very deep well, out of which a woman was miraculously rescued more than thirty years ago. On a stormy night, the wind blew almost a hurricane, when a man came in who had business with her husband, and he had not returned from his work.

She invited this man to wait till he came, and partake of their supper. She then left him to prepare it, and, in drawing a bucket of water, the windlass gave way and threw her into the well. The rattling of wind prevented her screams from being heard; but her long absence induced the man to look for her. He found that she was in the well, and it was not in his power to extricate her. In terror he ran to the Cross Keys Tavern for help. Men came with ropes, and tore the sheets from the bed, by which they drew her up, almost lifeless and excessively bruised, having been in near three-quarters of an hour. In a few weeks she recovered, and acknowledged a special Providence in her wonderful deliverance.

Orange street.—Orange street, though of ancient date, affords but little to tell. On the southwest corner of Eighth street is a foundry of some note, established by Betts & Stotsenburg, men well known and esteemed for their enterprise, fair dealing, and integrity of character.

Having legends to narrate in other streets, we regret to pass this old trodden way in silence; yet we must confess it is without much incident. But a building on the west side may excite surprise, and we will tell you an achievement of a descendant of John Bull.

The time of which we speak was somewhere about the last contest with Great Britain, when an Englishman and his family arrived here. He was of so goodly a size, one might suppose he had fed well on the underdone roast beef of old England. A ruddy and demure aspect comported with his steady habit. He used the plain language, and in a simple garb attended Friends' religious meetings. By industry and attention he won the good opinion of his neighbors, and it was noised abroad he had funds, and intended to establish a malt concern on an extensive scale. "Verily," said they, "he is a man of business powers, and will astonish the natives."

Well, this lot was purchased, and the odd fabric erected for a malt house, one end of which was fitted up for his abode. In the meantime, he sought employment, was a good penman; drew up instruments of writing very satisfactorily, and boasted of his tact in collecting moneys, and even was ready for an agency.

In this too he was energetic, and had wonderful success. But the winding up of his affairs it is hard to credit.

The contest alluded to was ended. The Yankees were successful and triumphant. He too had seen in this little town, night after night, brilliant illuminations for victories by sea and victories by land, and you will scarcely believe, in the face of all this, an apparently inoffensive man unarmed would dare attempt to outwit those whom his powerful and brave nation, with sword in hand, had just failed to conquer. Yes, with his own hand did he filch Yankee pockets to fill his own, and make a quick trip to enter Canada victorious, and left some to bemoan their credulity in preferring an unknown to a competent and worthy neighbor. Verily, Joseph Reed's audacity did "astonish the natives."

'In olden times, William Shipley erected a fine mansion N. W. corner of Fourth street, which will pass for a good dwelling at this day. On the S. W. corner was one of the first brick houses—but it was then built in the Village of Willingstown, and before the name was changed to its present one in honor of the Earl of Wilmington—the same nobleman in England to whom Thompson the poet of the *Seasons* has dedicated his Address to Winter.

Tatnall street.—On the southeast corner of Delaware avenue and this street was the bull-frog pond—on the west side was a boarding-school for boys, established by John Bullock, a Friend. Both Mr. and Mrs. Bullock were worthy people, eminently qualified for the arduous task of instructing youth. Their duty was so faithfully performed as to secure success, and fill the seminary with boarders from distant places. But few day scholars were admitted. In the prime of life Mrs. B. died, and in her station could not be filled by another. No one was more lamented by her family and friends. Mr. B. continued his charge for a few years; then he resigned it to another, and was suddenly summoned to depart, we trust to a happier region. This event was deeply lamented. He was a friend to the needy, and a useful citizen. Mr. S. Alsop has the charge of this establishment.

Opposite is the Orthodox Friends' Meeting-house, a very neat place of worship, amidst noble trees.

Shipley's brewery, at the foot of Quaker-Hill, in days gone by was a place of note. From this never-failing spring, that once supplied the town, a stream issued through a pipe under the street, where a fountain supplied many with pure cold water. Raising this stream many feet has changed the face of things, as may be seen by the houses on the south side, now almost buried.

West street.—The stone house on the west side of this street was built under the direction of Joseph Shallcross, and sold to Mordecai Woodward, who erected the large rope-walk. On the street west of this, he followed his occupation for years. After his death, John Dauphin, a French emigrant, became owner of the whole property, and employed agents to conduct the operations of rope-making. Mr. Dauphin was concerned in the shipping business, and during the embargo was involved in difficulties. After a short attack of disease, he was suddenly removed. As an affectionate husband and father, he left a bereaved family to mourn. Although known to be a wealthy man, much of his estate escaped from his heirs into other hands.

The N. W. corner of Sixth street was the residence of Frederick Schrader, gunsmith. Here was a public garden, kept in excellent order many years. Mr. S. was a constant attendent at Trinity church, and lies mouldering in the dust of that ancient cemetery. At his death, the lot was sold, improved, and enlarged, and now a Roman Catholic seminary of some celebrity, erected upon it, is conducted by the Sisters of Charity.

The northeast corner was the residence of Caleb Seal, who died in the ninety-third year of his age. His son, William Seal, inhabited this ancient spot till death, in advanced age, summoned him to his final abode, to leave a widow and children bereaved of a kind husband and father. As a citizen, his departure was found to be a great loss. He had been long the President of the Bank of Wilmington and Brandywine; he was repeatedly elected into the Delaware Legislature, and often chosen executor, or appointed administrator to settle estates, and usually gave satisfaction to the heirs. He was a worthy Friend, and left a large estate.

St. Peter's Roman Catholic Church is on the southeast corner of of Sixth street. It was built more than thirty years ago, and has been twice enlarged, and is now of considerable size. The congregation has increased rapidly, mostly by emigration. The cemetery within that time has been nearly filled.

William Gailey's residence, where he lived for many years, was adjoining this cemetery. He and his wife were members of Trinity church. She was of Swedish descent. By care and industry, he had acquired a competency, and leaving no children, he bequeathed to Trinity church one thousand dollars.

On the northwest corner of Fifth street is an ancient dwelling. In olden time, it was the residence of J. Bennett, who was the first burgess when this village was promoted to a borough. He was the father of Major Bennett, who became Governor of the State. His son, Capt. Joseph Bennett, sailed from this port, and was a very worthy man. He had several daughters.

On the opposite square is the Friends' burial ground—an ancient spot, in which interments are continued. The first Friends' meeting-house was built in this square, but, though commodious, had become too small for the society, and was taken down to give place to a very large one, erected on the site in 1816; it is beautifully situated, and shaded by many noble trees.

Opposite is a Friends' school house of long standing; it was built before the Revolution, and it has been kept up with much respectability. Boys and girls are taught here in separate apartments. It is under the superintendence of Friends, and much attention is paid to order.

That venerable dwelling on the southwest corner was erected by Wm. Shipley, and his heirs have always inhabited it to the present time.

Some years ago, there was a flourishing boarding school for boys in this square, under the superintendence of John Smith, who built a large house. He removed from the town, and this school was given up. Next to the corner was the residence of Gen. Washington during his sojourn in Wilmington, while the army lay here. Joseph C. Gilpin is the present occupant and owner. The house has been much improved, but the parlor floors, on which the General so often trod, have been preserved.

Captain John Lea sailed from this port in other days, and when he retired from life on the ocean, he was appointed chief magistrate, and served a long term. His old residence just below has given place to a modern mansion.

Next door below was once the residence of William Cobbett, already mentioned as having been notorious among politicians in later years.

And here are two ancient dwellings so dressed up in modern style that even their inhabitant, the shrewd lawyer Johnson, were she on earth, would be puzzled to find her old abode. As it is not the custom of women to practice law, a sketch of one may not be amiss, who flourished early in this century, and who was a personage of great notoriety in all the country towns around, Westchester, Old Chester, New Castle, and the lower counties, as the most independent woman of the age.

We must own her personal appearance was not very attractive. So masculine a mind was incapable of studying the small and delicate arrangements of dress; an olden-timed petticoat and short gown suited her fancy. With a man's hat and staff she regularly attended courts, and read or imbibed law, which her capacious mind drank in like rivers of water. The technical terms were studied, and she was familiar with all the quirks and quibbles of attorneys. With her it was a perfect mania to be involved in lawsuits. As a land holder she was often gratified, and would enter the office of any noted lawyer to tell her story, but never to offer a fee.

When the courts were in session at New Castle, she made her pedestrian excursions over there; and with her staff and her papers in hand entered the court house with the confidence of a chief justice, and pleaded her own cause, in the places named, and even this, too, in the day of E. Tilghman, A. J. Dallas, and others of Pennsylvania, and of John Vining, J. A. Bayard, and N. Vandyke, and others of Delaware. Mrs. Mary Johnson is still remembered in this town for her ability as well as for her originality of character. She died in old age.

All large towns have some places more noted than others. On the East we named such in passing, and must not omit those on the West. Love Lane on the western part, and its hills and valleys, were traversed in other days, and Mount Racket, which now deserves a better name. And the tan flats must not be overlooked, for here a portion of our colored population is accommodated with dwellings. On a level, walled up by high streets, the entrance descends by flights of steps, and it is rather a novelty to strangers.

In this section there are several tan yards and leather dressing establishments on quite a large scale. There are a number of foundries and factories, where locomotives and cars on the most approved plan are built, and coachmakers' establishments of older standing. Our ship builders seem to have inherited the spirit of their fathers, to stand unrivaled, especially in the steamboat line, and we leave their works to commend them. A slitting mill, cotton manufactories, and rope walks, sail makers, and stone cutters, and in fact every trade creditable to the operator is pursued in this town. And few places of the same size can boast of as orderly a population.

CHAPTER XXVIII.

A Legend of the Revolution—D. D. B.—Gen. Robertdeau—Miss V.'s visit—Marriage—Seclusion—D. D. B. enters His Majesty's Service—Mysterious news—A Perilous Journey.

When glimpses of the past lead our wandering thoughts back, to renew scenes of youth long winged away, the mind is crowded with pleasant themes. Although fleeting years have severed the strongest earthly ties, and tears of sorrow flowed over many a dissolved link which bound us to those we loved, as we reflect on days gone by, and upon those who are mouldering in the grave, we could fill pages, in recounting their story, and exhibit many a romantic picture in real life.

But there is one now who rises fresh upon the mind, interwoven with many incidents which awaken a deep interest; and as a narration of the thrilling events of life, at all periods, has enlisted the sympathies, or excited the passions, if skillfully portrayed, this may, in its simple garb of truth, as a faithful delineation of incidents in the history of the Revolution, have its claim to our attention.

Dr. Daniel Bancroft was the descendant of English parents. He was born in Massachusetts, but went to England in his early years; and was thus called an Englishman. He was endowed with superior intellect, highly cultivated. He chose the medical profession, and in a small town near London studied with a physician who was an eminent chemist. As this science was particularly attractive to him, he devoted his time to it. Aided by every facility, his arduous labor was rewarded by his pre-eminence in the study.

In compounding drugs, when sugar of lead was used, he was apt to taste it, and was not aware of its pernicious influence on the nervous system until he was brought to a critical situation, which affected him in declining years.

His only brother was a distinguished physician in the royal household, of whom the historian, and the British surgeon noticed hereafter in this story, were sons. The yellow dye from the black oak bark—now known in commerce as the quercitron bark—was the discovery of these two gentlemen, who were honored by a patent from King

George the Third, granting for seven years the exclusive right of importation of it into England.

They were calculating on an immense revenue during that period. It was the beginning of troublous times when the hero of our story embarked for this country to select a place suitable for his exports. The brother in London, who was to be the recipient, so warmly espoused the American cause, on the side of the Earl of Chatham, that it portended ruin to their schemes.

When hostilities commenced, he deemed it most prudent to retire to France, where he educated his children, and the surgeon and Mr. Montgomery were classmates.

Dr. Bancroft leaned to royalty, though he resolved to remain neutral, and not express his views. However, neutral ground was scarce, and he found no spot whereon to rest his foot, but with a few families of similar views in Philadelphia he cautiously formed an acquaintance. Among these was a wealthy widow, and in her house he mingled with the *elite*. Her only son, the heir to a large estate, was idolized, and indulged in extravagance. He was an ardent, thoughtless youth, openly espousing the rebel cause, which was a great annoyance to his most loyal mother.

Dr. Bancroft foresaw his own critical situation, and felt the propriety of retiring to some sequestered spot, where he might remain unknown. He apologized to this hospitable lady for his abrupt withdrawal from her delightful circle.

She manifested great regret at this conclusion, for an interesting niece was daily expected from New York to visit her. She had relied much on his gallantry to promote her pleasure, and had intended to surprise him by the introduction. A brilliant reception was to crown her arrival, and surely he could wait a few days to be present. The request was too impressive to be resisted, and he complied.

This niece was Miss Vallois, the daughter of her only brother, who lost his wife young, and under most afflicting circumstances. This lady had been on a visit to a sister, and on returning home, a storm arose, and upset the packet on the Delaware. Instantly the cabin was filled with water, and the gangway blockaded with floating furniture, so that the prompt assistance to rescue the passengers proved of little avail. The only hope of release was through a hole to be cut in the quarter-deck. But while this was progressing, the lamp of life had ceased to burn with all but two. One passenger and this infant only were spared.

The mother was brought home a lifeless corpse, and the father became a wanderer. A sister, married to Dr. Bard, an eminent physician in New York, adopted the child and educated her with care. At this time, she had just entered her eighteenth year, and, with an elegant figure and fascinating manner, she was esteemed a beauty, and endowed with great conversational powers. She was the pride of her uncle, who had long been solicited by this aunt, and reluctantly yielded his consent, to make this visit.

Dr. Bard, of New York, was a devoted patriot, and when the enemy's fleet was expected, he removed with his family to a country seat near Livingston Manor. As it was an eventful era, it may be well to intersperse our story with anecdotes of the times.

Brigadier-Gen. Robertdau took charge of this young lady to Philadelphia—then a journey of two days. During the first dinner, at a hotel, some one had heard of his antipathy to cats, and was disposed to play a trick, by letting a cat into the room just as they were seated at the table. He turned pale, dropped his knife and fork, faintly exclaiming, "A cat!" and fell back in his chair stiff as a corpse.

All present were alarmed, and after he revived, he assured them it was a weakness over which he had no control, and he would rather face the cannon's mouth, or point of the bayonet, than encounter a single cat. Hence he was dubbed "The Pussey General."

The young lady, introduced into society, fell under the influence of a magician's spell. The aunt prided herself on her appearance, and was so caressing, her friends so devotedly attentive, that everything around her was gilded with pleasure, and diffused a bright aspect over all she saw. Hitherto she had been treated as a child; confined to her studies, or usefully employed. Now she was the object of attraction.

The doctor's judicious plan was not so easily imagined as he had thought. Society had more captivating charms, while his intellectual powers and courteous manners were not overlooked by the lady. Nothing was omitted by the aunt to make a favorable impression on either, and she rejoiced at his attention, although fully aware that her niece's guardians would spurn a connection with a Tory. Talents, consequence, nor wealth would avail.

Miss Vallois's honorable principles and warm affection towards her benefactors made her aware that her path of duty pointed homeward, and she resolved to pursue it and forsake her pleasures, by bidding adieu to her admiring companions. The intercourse between the two cities was suspended, and proved a hindrance to performing her intention. The doctor adhered to the royal side amid popular discontents. In the gathering storm, the time came when her decision was to be made, and she adopted his views.

Under the auspices of this aunt, a private marriage was hastily concluded upon, not to be consummated within her mansion, which would effect an insuperable barrier between the friendship of two sisters whose political views were so opposite. This one thought her niece was forming an alliance so splendid as to justify or excuse any intrigue on her part.

At the little town of Burlington, in New Jersey, the marriage ceremony was performed, and they retired to a farm house. Here the doctor's sentiments were known, and he was closely watched—but an occasion soon offered which led him to prison; and he most indignantly denounced such harsh treatment merely for opinions, not having committed any condemnatory act. When released, he openly espoused the royal cause, and entered on board the Roebuck ship of war as surgeon, to be exchanged for a situation in the army.

In a few weeks, his interesting wife was left in solitude. The family were plain Friends, kind in their way, but no society for her—not being at all intellectual; and books in those days were a locked treasure, when all valuables were concealed, and people were on the wing.

The faithful guardian of her infancy had resolved to know her no more. To both the separation was heart-rending. This communication was made to her in retirement, where she reflected much. Good common sense and a cheerful disposition led her to secure the friendship of the inmates, though so different in their views, tastes, and habits. They were laborious farmers, rising with the dawn and retiring at twilight, and so occupied with domestic concerns as to leave little time for relaxation.

Yet, in this rustic circle, a young female, nurtured in intellectual refinement, devoted to social pleasure, and possessing a discriminating mind, with genius to search for hidden treasure, discovered traits of character that would have ennobled many in high stations.

In her character there was a union of dignity and companionship. It was desirable for her to have associates, and she sought the regard of the household by manifesting gratitude for their attentions, and by conformity to their habits wherein she could yield. Her respectful manner engendered a reciprocal attachment dissolved only in death.

Hitherto ample funds had been supplied, with affectionate remembrances. Now months had glided by without news from the doctor. Her last guinea was treasured up, and she was in arrears for a quarter's board. A veil of gloom was thrown over the future, and dread seized her mind lest a life so dear had fallen a victim to a southern climate. Her efforts to maintain cheerfulness were on the wane, her kind hosts observed unusual sadness, and were striving to keep from her the unfavorable rumors afloat, when she was informed of the arrival in the vicinity of a gentleman direct from the encampment where the doctor's regiment lay.

Mrs. Bancroft made a visit to him, without an introduction, and inquired how the regiment was situated, and then for Dr. B. He, being a stranger to her anxiety, related what he knew. He said he had spent an hour with Dr. B. and his bride the morning of his departure, and had attended his wedding three evenings before.

After listening to the stranger's story, she was overpowered and silenced for a time; then she exclaimed, "*Impossible, sir,* for he is my husband!" Her informant was deeply confused; however, on comparing incidents, he was convinced of his identity, and felt so indignant at being a participator in any way in such a base procedure, and the companion of a villain too, that would abandon so interesting a young creature, with an infant—in the warmth of ardor, he vehemently denounced his baseness, which aroused her to check his rashness, by repeating with composure, "Sir! it is impossible, for he is my husband; and I will not believe him guilty of dishonor."

Late in the evening, she returned to her solitude, and retired. After a sleepless night, her cheeks were bedewed with tears, and her eyes betrayed a sorrowing heart, and she resolved to inform this benevolent family of all that had passed in her interview with the stranger, and of her destitution, hopes and fears, and to conceal nothing, confiding in them as friends capable of sympathizing in her sorrow.

Mingling with the group at the breakfast-table, she communicated her sorrows, and few would have believed such an impression could have been made on persons so bound to worldly cares. Their warmest sympathies were enlisted. How sweetly does the spirit of a kind affection steal over the heart! for they did "weep with those who wept." The duties of the day were laid aside, and they devoted their time to soothe her agitated feelings, and alleviate her sorrows, by offering her an asylum for life under their roof.

Mrs. A., with whom she resided, clasped her arm around her, and embracing her, said, should poverty befall her in those perilous times, she should share her last half loaf. As such an incident could only be felt—we leave it.

The mysterious story of the marriage winged its way through the country, adding fuel to the Tory cause, and condemning both parties upon the most uncharitable suppositions. With a few, she was an object of pity; but as it was generally thought no good thing could come out of Nazareth, more censured her, and said it was a visitation for marrying a Tory.

Amidst all this commotion, letters brought remittances and the cheering news that the Dr. enjoyed health and cheerfulness, and proved that absence had not chilled his affection.

The British were in full glare of prosperity. In the south, the Dr. had good quarters, and the best accommodations were provided for her reception. In a few days, a vessel was to sail from New York with stores, and a few passengers. Capt. Lee of the army had engaged to take her in charge, and she was entreated to embrace the opportunity, as no other would soon offer, and to expect only the protection of Capt. L., as he was an unpolished man, but faithful to his trust.

Then the marriage story was solved. The Dr. B. named had been a surgeon in the same regiment; the spelling of their name differing only in two letters, and pronounced very similar, induced the Dr. to fear the circumstance might reach Mrs. B., and be circulated to his discredit, and wound her feelings. He therefore gave an explanation. No hesitation obscured her mind—at once she resolved to go; but a paragraph in this happy epistle mingled her joy with sadness.

The Dr. advised her to bid farewell to country, kindred, and friends, for the cloud of war was darkening, no cheering gleams of peace were gilding the horizon, and ere the joyful sound should be hailed, his patent right might expire, and the verdure of the plant be nipped ere it advanced to a golden harvest. His brother had pursued a course which blighted a hope of its renewal.

When he could resign his commission with honor, the vicinity of London would be the place where he designed to engage in his profession.

To leave the guardians of her helpless years, without manifesting the least gratitude, or sorrow for eluding their authority, filled her heart with anguish. In the midnight gloom of a sleepless night, she made a solemn vow to hazard a pilgrimage to their retreat, implore their forgiveness, and in the bonds of union with those beloved, invoke a blessing for Divine guidance over her impending fate. As sleep had fled, the hours were spent in maturing her plans with calmness; not a moment was to be lost. A suitable woman had been engaged to attend her infant, in the event of her going South; and her residence was in Elizabethtown, where Capt. L. was to meet Mrs. B. in fifteen days, equipped for the voyage, at a moment's notice.

She was fully aware that many dangers must be encountered in her journey up the North River, and partly on foot, and alone. She provided suitable apparel, and her kind hostess supplied a dark homespun dress, fitted to her person. On the following day, her host conveyed her child and baggage to E., and in the care of the trusty woman she left her treasure, suited herself with a bonnet and coarse shoes. Her guineas were quilted in a girdle, and fastened around her waist; with her bundle, she set out on her adventurous way.

Uncertain how to proceed, a large reward enabled her to stipulate with a man for a passage to New York. From thence, through the influence of a British officer, she was conducted to a town some miles distant, where she was informed that, at a village, seven miles hence, a packet touched twice a week, and that the morrow was their regular day. It was the afternoon; no money could procure a conveyance, not even an escort. The way was rugged. Soldiers passing to and fro, military stations of conflicting parties, were a dread to the wayfaring man, often subjecting him to danger. But these perils must be met, for her time was limited. In sober times, such an enterprise would be deemed arduous; now there were many risks, peculiar to the distracted state of the country; besides she might be detained as a spy. All these perils seemed to require a masculine mind.

CHAPTER XXIX.

The Hermit--Recruiting Party- Evening Mists--Village--Tavern--Gen. Green--Secures Her Passage--Recognition--Dr. B.--Retreat--Susy--The Meeting--Reconciliation--Dr. S--The Parting--A Ride--Baggage Wagon--New York--Crosses to New Jersey.

It was the season of spring, and the afternoon of this pedestrian excursion was damp and cool. Evils which might beset her crowded her mind until it was like a bewildering dream. She wandered from the road, and a solemn awe seemed to whisper peace, where all animated nature was still; even the leaves had ceased to quiver. The foot-path was devious, and the cart road forked; not a human being, or a habitation, to mitigate her loneliness and sadness. Even the creaking of her coarse shoes was startling; and being aroused by the sound of a drum, with hasty steps she reached the woods, where an opening presented the cheering sight of a cabin. It was the abode of a hermit, who admitted her with kindness, which was balm to her wounded feelings. While she rested, conversing with him, the recruiting party passed by.

Here information was gained, which, had it been communicated at the time, would have been important to the rebel cause; but her loyalty silenced the disclosure; besides, it might lead her from the path of duty she had resolved to pursue.

The recluse stated that these soldiers were marching to the village, where a detachment of Gen. Green's regiment was quartered, and the packet would leave there the next morning, for the last trip that week, and no conveyance or escort could be obtained so late in the day. She told him that necessity compelled her to go on, and he advised her to follow the drum, as she had strayed, though not far.

This road was more intricate, and, nearly exhausted with fatigue, she kept the cheerless path at a respectful distance from the drum, and this apparent mishap insured her a safe guidance, when other efforts must have failed.

The dusky shadows of evening were thickening around her, and the distant drum and shrill bugle from the barracks warned her of the approaching hour for the sundown reveille. The stately hills and rocks rose upon her view, and the blue vaporing mists were gathered about its summits, and hanging like curtains in the air. Soon the twilight died away, and the glimmer of a few lights marked the place of her destination, when an officer glanced suddenly by her; yet she thought she recognized his features.

Entering an ordinary tavern, she seated herself in the bar-room by the fire, hungry, chilled with cold, and weary, and so dejected that she hesitated to order a meal or a night's lodging, even with a full purse to pay her fare. She sighed for a glimpse of a familiar face, or even the sound of a voice to address her. In this disconsolate state, she wept. A quick footstep arrested her attention, and the well-known face of Gen. Green was presented. To introduce herself would insure aid and counsel, so much needed; yet she shrunk from this, and even tried to conceal her face.

He paced the floor, evidently an attentive observer, and advancing, addressed her politely, inquiring the cause of so young a female being alone amid such peril. An evasive and confused reply was given, when he demanded an explicit answer. To tell her motive was a hard struggle, it simply concerned herself, to induce the captain of the packet to set her on shore at Dr. Bard's landing.

The general listened to her brief reply with intense solicitude, and exclaimed, "Can it be possible! Am I deceived, or is it the voice of M. Vallois?" A conflict of feeling agitated her, and almost choked with sobs, she said, "Yes, Gen. Green, you do know the voice! It is that of a penitent wanderer, on a pilgrimage to her foster home, an exile, rushing into the arms of her early friends to beg forgiveness, and implore a parting blessing, ere she bids them a final farewell."

The recognition, though grave and silent, was deeply exciting. The general was cautious, and dared not converse freely, lest it should be known that he had an interview with the wife of a Tory. He begged her to betray no knowledge of him, but to receive any little attention as charity towards a helpless woman.

The walk of seven miles in fear and trembling was wearisome. The day had been passed without refreshment, and now she was exhausted. The general relieved her embarrassment by ordering supper and securing her lodging, and, still more important, he ordered the captain to land her where she desired. This could not have been effected without his influence, and her scheme would have failed. This event she deemed an interposition of Providence in her behalf, and her anxiety and care were soon banished by a refreshing sleep. "Upon this I awaked, and behold, and my sleep was sweet unto me."

Early in the morning she went on board the packet. The captain was kind, and told her she was indebted to General Green's influence for being set on shore at B.'s landing. She ascended the frowning hills with her bundle; the path lay beside the skirts of a forest, where the wind sighed mournfully through the broken boughs of many an ancient oak. The winged tribes had ceased to sing, and were retiring from their airy flights, flitting among the branches to nestle into rest.

The sun, descending the western hills, threw its lengthened shadow over the noble trees, as an emblem of departing time, and the golden tint fringed the borders of the verdant fields, inspiring her with sublime emotions. She sat down on a mossy seat, feeling her need of support and guidance in the difficulty of entering the abode of her offended relatives, doubtful of meeting a reception, after all she had passed through.

Thus agitated and veiled in gloom, a tall figure came forth out of the forest glade: his snowy locks were hanging over his shoulders, and a bundle of sticks in his arms. The recognition of his features startled her; he arose upon her sight like a spirit of other days; a nervous shiver shook her whole frame, and she shrieked and fainted. His attention was arrested, and when she revived, she exclaimed, "Oh! my father!"

His wanderings had separated them since childhood; remembrances of the past flitted across her mind to sadden their meeting. They conversed until the evening shades gathered over them. Her parent could give her no advice, for the family were so exasperated at her marriage with a Tory, that even to name her was prohibited, and the youngest son only ventured to allude to her. She was his favorite cousin, and, being ardent in his feelings, he vowed that, when he was a man, he would traverse oceans, and scale mountains to meet his beloved cousin P.

Being left to pursue her lonely way to the mansion, she met an old servant, who was milking a stray cow near the kitchen door; the servant had always been treated by the family more as a relative than a slave. Of her she inquired for a night's lodging. Her familiar voice astonished the woman; she sprang on her feet, knew she was not mistaken, and burst into a flood of tears. She repeated what her father had told her, and advised her to rush into the parlor and surprise her uncle and aunt, for Master B. was there, and he was a host in her favor.

She acquiesced, following the woman to the parlor door, who

waved her hand to her mistress, and said, "A benighted traveler begged lodging." Mrs. B. answered, "Susy, you know we have no spare room." "Mistress, she looks like a lady, and so young." "Let some one go with her to the farm-house." "Oh, mistress, just come and speak to her yourself." "Why do you persevere so, Susy?" "Oh dear mistress, do come and see; she is so tired, besides so pretty." Mrs. B. replied, "Susy, you always manage to gain your point."

The niece now came forward, saying, "Madame, will you have the goodness to give me a shelter under your roof? Overcome with fatigue, I am too feeble to proceed further." Her voice and manner were impressive.

The aunt started, and sighed heavily. The whole company were attracted, as they were silent at the moment, for her young cousin had just been reproved, in their presence, for alluding to his Tory cousin. In his excited state, he had grasped a heavy chair, and recognizing her voice, in a frenzy of joy dashed the chair so forcibly, it broke against the wall. They saw it in time to escape the stroke, or it would have leveled the three.

However, their screams alarmed the household, who all ran. The chair touched Susy's elbow and she fainted, and amid the consternation this hero exclaimed, *"It is my own cousin Polly!"* (her name having been Mary Magdalen Vallois,) and he affectionately embraced her. He alone was regardless of the passing incident, and the whole was a most pathetic yet ludicrous scene! Their awakened sympathies subdued their displeasure. The transition was so sudden, from the severity of the rebuke addressed to the youth, to the most affectionate greeting of the wanderer. Here the offender's presence "lulled the angry passions into peace."

It was as overpowering as unexpected to her to be blended once more with this interesting family, in the bonds of affection, and feel that the flame of love still burned brightly around the domestic hearth. Her most sanguine hopes did not reach beyond a cold reception—to be permitted to acknowledge her error, and to bid a final farewell in good will. "Behold, how good and how pleasant it is for brethren to dwell together in unity; it is like the precious ointment upon the head, and as the dew that descended upon the mountains of Zion, for there the Lord commanded the blessing!"

When the flurry had passed over, her dress was scrutinized, and queries arose, why in such a garb, and alone? how was it possible for a female to travel from New York, and pass the different military stations? Circumstances seemed to confirm their opinion, that her condition was forlorn, cross events and sorrow had induced her so rashly to encounter the hazardous journey, and hope only had buoyed her up, that as a repentant exile she could recover her foster-father's protecting care.

The only information they ever had was the story of the Dr.'s marriage in Georgia. Even in primitive days, ere telegraphic wires were stretched, to convey news from the Atlantic shores to the mountains, evil reports were borne on the wings of the wind, but they knew her high spirit must have passed through the furnace of affliction ere it was melted into such humility. Her destitution was evident, for she was meanly clad, and without a change of raiment. This conclusion rekindled their most ardent love, and in pity, they vied with each other in kindness, resolving to let the unpleasant past be buried in oblivion, and to give her a cheerful welcome to the home of her youth, though events had separated and made their path in life so opposite.

After the excitement produced by the extraordinary scene had subsided, every one was anxious to know how a lonely female could travel the road in such wild and stirring times. Her physical strength was exhausted, but her mental energies were exhilarated by the deep interest manifested towards her. She began to recount her adventures, omitting that part which referred to the absent ones, and this required considerable skill to manage, for she had designed, when about to depart, to state in few words the object of her visit. "I kept silence, even from good words, and this was pain and grief to me."

Many incidents peculiar to this trying season, when related by the adventurers, were truly affecting, and as she progressed, they drew nearer and melted into tears. Those touching scenes, if remembered at this day, would be grown dim and old—or not understood. But she was famous at narrative—there was a freshness and life in all her descriptions, and no one was ever disappointed or wearied by them.

Many little occurrences are still fresh in memory, which, if narrated with her powers, would add beauty and effect—such as the scenes mingling with the dreary walk in the wood, as the shadows of evening advanced, with the cottage bursting upon her sight—the hermit's reception—and the old man's tale of the war, never before disclosed. And the solemn thoughts in following the drum to the village—the recognition of a friend in General Green—and the sudden appearance of her father, whom she had not seen since her childhood; all these were related with so much feeling that a thrilling interest was kept up until the dawning light of a new morn aroused the group.

The following day was the only one she could devote to her loved friends, and the thoughts of a separation from her family was a painful trial, but was submitted to with firmness. Towards noon the next day, she ventured to disclose the design of her visit, and refer to her future destiny. This was harrowing up their feelings, so that every word sounded on the listening ear like time's parting knell. Strong objections were eloquently argued against her return to New York, and experience convinced her it was a dangerous path—but that maternal duty bid her " brave the lion in the way."

Her kind uncle pledged himself to have the child brought on, a less hazardous enterprise, and seeming to meet every obstacle. He depicted in glowing colors the toils and crosses attendant on life in a camp; but neither entreaties nor remonstrances availed. She resolved to encounter the perils and hardships incident to military duties, and share her husband's fate, and neither her courage nor powers of endurance ever failed.

They were amazed at the readiness with which she was hastening to cross the ocean to meet her husband, and the diseases of a southern climate. While they condemned the rashness of so young a female, they applauded the faithfulness of the wife.

About one o'clock, company was announced: Dr. S., of Philadelphia, his daughter, and son-in-law, Mr. L., of New York. Their arrival introduced a different subject. On the threatened invasion of this city by the British, Mr. L. had retired to the manor; so repugnant was it to his lady's inclination, that she resolved to abandon her husband and home rather than forego the gayeties of a city life, and insisted on her father taking her to Philadelphia.

Dr. S.'s intimacy with Dr. B.'s family induced him to request their influence with his daughter, and prevail on her to return with her husband. In compliance with his wishes, they most affectionately entreated her to give up the rash resolve to meet her husband no more in an earthly home, and pointed to the heroism of their niece.

This high-toned lady could not tolerate such condescension, nor respect such passive women. She was inexorable, and all their arguments failed. This extraordinary incident whiled away a few hours, and by contrast enhanced Mrs. B.'s character.

Early in the morning, Mrs. B. set off on her journey, accompanied by her uncle, about forty miles on horseback, over a very rugged road, and neither of them accustomed to the mode of travel. The parting with her family was sad, and the way was gloomy. She resolved to make an effort to cheer him, by recounting a series of amusing anecdotes peculiar to the times. As evening was drawing to a close, they were much fatigued. The last three miles she fainted twice, and was held upon her saddle by a man till they reached the place of rest, where a refreshing sleep fitted her for new trials. Her affectionate uncle dare not venture beyond these bounds, and she bade him adieu with a sad heart.

Loneliness encircled her path, and tears flowed to her relief. Tedious miles were passed over, and fruitless inquiries were made for a conveyance, till convinced her only safe way was on a baggage wagon, mingling with soldiers' wives. Meeting with one of whom, she solicited a seat; the women objected, bawling aloud to the driver that they were "now too scrowdged." He as roughly replied, they must make room, for his orders were "to take up all the sogers' women."

Those in the next wagon with much civility admitted her, though they were crowded to excess with those of the very lowest order. They strove to be so civil, she felt herself under a lucky planet by having escaped from the other.

The afternoon was spent in the most boisterous manner; at nightfall they encamped in the woods, midst a darkness like "the Egyptian, which could be felt." It was drizzling and chilly, and no cover for their defenceless heads. A slight cold had affected her previously, and the exposure caused a swollen face; and it was very painful. In the morning, one of the women assured her it was the mumps, and advised her to bandage it with a handkerchief, as sometimes it was dangerous, and they all seemed disposed to soothe her by kindness and to cease from their noisy mirth. During the ride she had expressed no displeasure at their boisterous conduct, nor of her own inconvenience. They knew she was not one of their class, and were pleased at her not interfering with their amusements.

In this humble garb, on the top of a baggage wagon, midst a group of the lowest order of women, she entered the city of New York, where she had been educated and associated with the most refined society. Her thoughts reverted to the past, and made her deeply sensitive to the present event. They were all dismissed at the barracks, and went in search of their husbands, while she sought a conveyance to New Jersey.

In a forlorn condition, she wandered around to find a boatman to ferry her over. It was so difficult a task to cross, that none were willing to encounter the risk. At length she met a man of whom she had a faint recollection. He consented for a large reward, if she would meet him on the wharf about midnight.

In the house of a poor woman, she sought shelter till the appointed time. The night was unfavorable, and with two men in a boat, in terror and almost despair, she was ferried over and landed in the salt marshes, paying her last two guineas, and left to grope the dangerous way, sinking in the mire; she was fearful of rising no more till the last trumpet sounded.

CHAPTER XXX.

Safely Landed—Meeting her Infant—Captain L. hastens her on—Contempt of the Officers—Unsightly Dress—Apologies—Prosperous Voyage—Joyful Meeting—Charleston—Noble Lords—Royalty Triumphs—Anecdotes—Rebels Revive—Gen. Green—Sails to Nova Scotia—Their Arrival—Gloomy Scenes —Usefulness—Visit to the Barracks.

THE dawn of day favored her escape. A Jersey wagon drove by, and in it she secured a passage to Elizabethtown. Her child was well, but unhappy in her absence. The family were amazed to see her in such a plight, a swollen face, and covered with mud-draggled clothes. Fatigued and really indisposed, she required refreshment and rest; while the former was preparing, water was brought, and she changed her shoes and stockings, intending to rest a few hours before arranging her dress.

The nurse had an errand a mile distant, and Mrs. B. urged her to hasten back, as she expected Captain Lee.

The nurse had just left, when the bustling officer appeared, hurrying her into the vehicle, sick and weary, not allowing her a moment to change her unsightly dress; nor could entreaties move him to wait for the nurse.

However, he did make an arrangement with the clever host to hurry her on. Though his manner was rough, the object was kind, to place Mrs. B. and her child safely on board ship before dark. Her mind was so absorbed by harassing scenes and fatigue, suffering with the pain of her face, she was regardless of her appearance, as if unconscious of the impressions it would make on strangers.

The ship was at anchor ready to sail by morning light. It was nearly dark as they went on board, and Captain L. pushed her into the cabin, and went for the nurse. Having no introduction, and in so mean a garb, she was gazed at with the utmost disdain.

The haughty officers and their wives made many observations, which awakened a sense of her mean appearance.

As they were plotting to get rid of her, a young officer, with a full complement of assurance, said, "Where are you going?" "To Georgia, sir." "May I ask your object?" "To meet my husband." "Is he connected with the army?" "Yes!" "So you are, I suppose, a soldier's wife?" "No!" "To which regiment is he attached? and what rank?" She answered "the —— regiment, and his rank a surgeon," with a muffled face, and painful to speak. He did not understand, and replied in a contemptuous manner, "So madam, you are not a soldier's wife, but a 'sargent's lady?'"

At this remark, drawing the bandage off, she spoke aloud, with a scornful look, and said, "Neither am I a sargent's lady, but you are a British officer, and ought to be a gentleman. As you see me an unprotected female, your influence should induce those present to treat me civilly." They were all amazed and silent for a moment. One said, "Madam is a keen one." "She is rather smart," said another; "pretty good looking, too." Then they noticed the child, and attempted to caress her; but the child shrunk from their embrace, seeming to feel her mother's displeasure.

When the passengers entered, berths were selected and there was none for her. As the captain of the ship was applied to, he appeared to know nothing about her. However, in compassion he did his best to have a bed fixed on the cabin floor. There was no alternative at this late hour; and even this accommodation to one so wearied and indisposed invited a refreshing sleep.

Warmth and rest relieved the pain, and removed the swelling from her face. She was suddenly aroused from a sound nap by the tossing of the ship, for it blew a heavy gale, and some were thrown out of the berth, and all were wretchedly sick. To her discomfort the floor was defaced, and if her plight in the evening was mean, the morning light presented her a disgusting figure.

At gray dawn all who could, arose. They were weighing anchor and getting ready to sail, as Captain L. arrived with the nurse, calling aloud, "Hallo, captain! what have you done with my woman?" Again they eyed her sharply. She seemed doomed to perplex them and to keep up an excitement. There was yet no clue to her history.

When the ship was under way and regulations established, a state room had been secured for her, where she made her toilet, and came out in the new character of a surgeon's lady. The whole company were astonished, as if a new star had appeared to eclipse the cluster. Her face had resumed its shape, and the gallant captain introduced her at the eleventh hour.

Several officers were on board, friends of Dr. D. B., attached to the same regiment, and they overwhelmed her with apologies, and she readily forgave them all. Her good common sense attributed the slight that passed to her unsightly dress, which induced them to feel she was an intruder. Being highly gifted in conversation, she proved a charming companion at sea. Her recent adventures were an entertaining topic, and a prosperous voyage landed them safely at Savannah.

Adventurous wanderings, sorrowing days, and sleepless nights had embittered the years of absence, and meeting the doctor in good health to her was unexpected joy, affectionately reciprocated. Great success awaited this detachment of the army. Soon they entered Charleston triumphant victors. In the zenith of their glory, they reveled in luxurious living, masters of the queen city of the South.

A spacious mansion was assigned to Dr. D. Bancroft, and his bounteous table never failed in guests. The skilful services and intellectual acquirements of the Dr. were highly appreciated. Besides, he was an instructive and cheerful companion. Mrs. B.'s personal charms, intelligence, and fascinating manner lured to their domicile refined society, and the most distinguished of the army, admired and esteemed by the noble Lords Cornwallis and Rawdon, gave her celebrity; and perhaps the happiest days of her married life were passed in Charleston—if splendid living, added to many gratifications could make her happy.

But all this pleasure was ofttimes mingled with painful feeling. However deeply enlisted under the banner of royalty, with great faith in kingly power, as fittest to rule a nation, her heart was still warmed by the love of her country, and yearned over many a rebel's tale of woe, as their hard fate tingled in her ear. Melted into tears of sympathy, she would burst forth in declamations against the heartlessness of the powers that be.

This was deemed offensive, touched the honor of the nobles of the land, and drew from the Dr. an apology for his lady's warmth of expression, declaring all her dearest relations had espoused the rebel cause.

This was an epoch in which independence was veiled in gloom; defeat succeeded defeat; battle and pestilence swept off its hundreds, on the right and on the left. The rebel army was dwindling away, and too enfeebled to compete with a powerful foe. Harassing marches, with deficiencies in military stores, resulted in disasters, and depressed the spirits of brave men who were without sufficient food or raiment to sustain them under the exposure of a southern climate.

His majesty's forces were fully aware of their condition; and they being well paid, clothed, and fed, were exulting in the prospect of a speedy conquest. Tories were perpetrating the grossest excesses, plantations were devastated, and peaceful families driven from their homes, pennyless wanderers, "to seek a shelter in an humble shed;" many were compelled to sue for protection, and be shielded under the royal banner in Charleston.

Of this class were a few patriotic ladies. Though bowed down by adversities and their humiliating position, their fixedness of purpose and patriotism ofttimes astonished the noble lords, in whose presence even they dared to make a pithy reply to ill-timed taunts, or contemptuous allusions to the imbecile rebel army; with undaunted courage they never flinched to avow their faith in their ultimate success, though apparently they were beaten and laid low in the dust.

Anecdotes and heroism of women in the South, in those Revolutionary days, are too numerous to be noticed. One now might be more than a tale twice told. Yet we will venture to detail one or two of them, which may have slipped into oblivion, or be new to you. Col. Tarleton had been wounded in the hand by a rebel officer of high rank. It left an ugly scar on his hand, and being vain, he took care to hide it.

One day, in conversation with a lady, he referred to the sad condition of the rebel soldiers, and said, "What have you to inspire hope? Only contrast the armies. One commanded by gentlemen, trained in military tactics, and consisting of well-disciplined troops. The other, raw recruits from the plough or workshop, under the command of officers but little better qualified for service. I grant that a few of your officers are gentlemen, and many brave men have acted well their part, but mostly, they are composed of the former class, and I am pretty credibly informed that Gen. —— cannot distinctly write his name." "Ah!" said the lady, "I never heard that; but be it so; it is very evident he can make his mark," looking archly at the scar. "You know, sir, that will do in law." He bowed in silence, and withdrew.

Two officers, after a morning's ride, called to pay their respects to a lady, and the common topic of the army was discussed. They spoke of having rode through her estate; she inquired how they were pleased with the country, and situation of her residence. Said one, "So well, that I have selected a place near you for my adopted home, and hope we shall be friendly neighbors."

The lady expressed surprise, but he went on to say, "It must be owned, the rebels are subdued, and peace will be soon proclaimed; confiscated estates we shall claim as our own rightful possession."

She replied, "Sir, as conquerors you will never—no, never, possess one foot of land in these States. But it is probable, before the contest is decided, many of you may require 'six feet by three;' and should any of your friends select such a portion of my estate, most willingly I will convey the title."

Reverses soon altered the position of the conflicting armies. Great sacrifices were made to aid the cause of liberty. The rebel soldiers became more healthy, noble examples of patriotism were recorded, and to crown the brightening hopes, Gen. Green was appointed commander at the South, and the defenceless patriots raised their drooping heads. The enemy saw on all sides they were possessed only of a tottering power, which must soon fall, and they became irritable and revengeful.

At this crisis an event occurred to present a victim for retaliation. The execution of Major Andre had borne heavily on their indignant feelings, and their prosperity waning refreshed the memory on this painful subject. The solemn fate of Col. Hayne is too well known to repeat.

> "A story should, to please, at least seem true,
> Be suited well, and told, concise and new."

Suffice it to say he was the object of vengeance; nine of his family were dangerously ill with the small-pox, of whom Mrs. H. and four children died. The deepest sympathy was excited. All the ladies in the city signed the petition for his pardon. The coffin of Mrs. H. was brought before Lord Rawdon to arouse a better feeling. All this was unavailing. Col. H. was hung. It was said this act was ever after regretted by his lordship.

Years glided on, and his son, Col. Hayne, had a temporary residence in London; and being invited to dine with the Duke of Sussex, as he entered the hall, the first object which arrested his attention was a full-length portrait of Lord R. It harrowed up his feelings, and his thoughts wandered back to other days.

Here we pause to say memory fails, or dreamy recollections of touching incidents that would fill the chasm are too faintly impressed to narrate, and we make a sudden transition to the North.

Lord Cornwallis had surrendered, and peace drew near. The bark scheme had failed; nothing seemed to present for the future, and Dr. D. B. resolved to continue in His Majesty's service. His regiment was ordered to Nova Scotia. Ere the social joys and balmy clime of the South were bid adieu to, the second infant daughter was presented at the baptismal font, sealed Carolina, a memento of her birth-place and her parents' happy days.

Towards the close of autumn, they sailed to the wild stern shores of their destination. The forces landed on a chilling morning. Nature was assuming its wintry garb. Every green thing was nipped; the streams had ceased to flow, and were thickening and frosted over with glassy ice. No longer the beasts were seen to roam, nor fowls to flicker, nor were winged families soaring in the air; none tuned their notes amid leafless branches. No echo of their cheering voices resounded through the immense forest. No sound save the howling wind, in terrific grandeur, among naked trees which seemed the boundary of the northern world, where all beyond was the frowning sky.

The rugged way was strewed with broken boughs, even to the very wicket gate of the lowly cottage designed for their abode; exhausted by sea sickness, and weariness in clambering over and under fallen trees, sliding down and leaping from one to another, with the fragments entangling their clothes, so as to impede their progress.

Under such circumstances, to find a shelter was cheering. Here a frugal meal was easily prepared, which good appetites made savory, and being refreshed, invited rest. On retiring, Mrs. B. acknowledged her gratitude for the special 'providence that had guided them over the dangerous seas and safely thrown them ashore to enjoy repose.

"Blest be the hand divine, which gently laid
My heart at rest beneath this humble shed."

Ample bedding had been provided and arranged for their comfort, and fuel abundant to warm an apartment, where the fresh air blew in at every crevice. They enjoyed a sweet peaceful sleep till the morrow's dawn.

The hurry and bustle of turning over and examining a quantity of baggage, that each one might have their own, occupied the day.

When they arose the next morning, the premises bore a gloomy aspect, surrounded by a dreary wilderness, and the absence of comforts, so unlike everything that they had ever seen. They felt as if a sudden convulsion of the elements had cast them upon a new planet, where neither beast nor winged tribes could exist, and that man alone, of all animal creation, was fitted by nature to atmospheric changes, alike indifferent to every clime, whether to scale icy mountains of frozen regions, or to pass through icebergs, traverse the trackless ocean, or, under the scorching sun of the tropics, wander over the burning sands of the desert.

A dusky morning portended a gathering storm, and induced melancholy reflections and thoughts of home. All was hurry and bustle to secure doors and windows, when thick clouds of blackness overshadowed the land, and blew a hurricane, threatening devastation. In a moment, every tenement seemed doomed to destruction, and in the pelting rain and hail whither could they flee? An awful solemnity pervaded the hamlet, till the Almighty Ruler of the raging tempest bid it cease.

Mrs. B.'s nervous system was convulsed; a shivering seized her, and an unusual sadness. She now saw her airy castles crumbling into dust. In wiping the tears from her cheeks, a suppressed sigh would escape, and the doctor looked sad and was silent. Although she felt so anxious to know how long this station was to be endured, yet she dare not ask, for any fixed time would appear an age, and she knew there was no alternative.

Some days were employed in assorting baggage, and arranging this rude but roomy dwelling, and the aspect of the interior brightened, and her countenance was more cheerful, and her spirits calm.

On glancing over the doctor's well furnished library, and large accessions of new works received from Europe just as they embarked from Charleston—and seeing the abundant roots that had been gathered in the South, hoarded up, besides an untold number of gallipots, her heart sickened at the sight, for she felt that the days of her pilgrimage in this barren land were not yet numbered.

Here was spare room for chemical operations; fuel to keep up fire for stews; and in short every facility to pursue the science which all his life had been his hobby. Moreover, the great advantage of seclusion favored his designs, and he entered into the study with all the enthusiastic ardor of youth, regardless of the cares or comforts of the world. Locality to him was merely a name.

Mrs. B. had been trained in society, and was fitted to adorn it. Early habits had implanted in her a love of the world, and she felt it had charms and snares; she concluded evil must mingle with the good, and was willing to endure her portion of the one, and enjoy the other; consequently, her thoughts recoiled from the idea of living as a recluse.

In this sequestered spot, lonely hours would renew reminiscences of early days and absent ones, and scenes of youth often crowded her imagination and gave a sombre tint to her evening meditations. Her arrival at the solitary farm house in New Jersey would rise up before her, and her lacerated feelings when she bade the doctor adieu, as fanatics hurled him to prison for opinion's sake, and the dread of meeting him no more. Amid these gloomy forebodings and loneliness, an evil hour had come.

In the bloom of youth, she was cast off by her dearest relatives, inexperienced in the world; and years glided on in this retreat, where sorrow crossed her path, and oft bore heavily on her head. No books were there to amuse a tedious hour, nor companions but the rustic inmates, so uncongenial to her. Yet even there she had enjoyed happy days, and a portion of content was mingled in her cup.

The absence of books, so deeply regretted, had produced its happy effect, inducing her to read and study carefully individual character with as much assiduity as if she was searching for hidden treasure. Yet in this underrated family were found gems beyond price. In coarse clay tenements, lay hidden hearts which, if polished, might adorn the palace. In their midst, as the child of adversity and sorrow, feelings were aroused that would have ennobled any state, and called forth her gratitude, to cement a friendship only to be dissolved in death.

On a dark rainy night, in the woods, on a baggage wagon, crowded by the very dregs of society, whose boisterous vulgarity melted her into nothing, even there a spark of human kindness enkindled in their bosoms, warmth to shield her from the damp, when they saw she was suffering pain produced by exposure, and they ceased their noisy mirth.

In all her perilous ways, she owned a providential care, guiding her safely through; and to her Almighty Benefactor her heart ofttimes glowed with gratitude, and she resolved no more to murmur or repine, but strive to be useful in her station, and be therewith content.

Fully convinced of her indebtedness to that class, she resolved to render to such some essential good, and the soldiers' wives at the barracks claimed her attention. On the morrow she designed to visit those, and enter into new duties. Retiring with unusual solemnity, the night passed in sweet repose, and the renewed morning opened with a clear and bracing air.

Or if, during the day, the sun was seen struggling in misty clouds, its momentary escape cheered this desolate region. "Truly the light is sweet, and a pleasant thing it is to behold the sun." Mrs. B.'s destiny no longer depressed her, yet she was sensitive to the absence of natural beauties to charm the eye and animate the heart. This was a memorable day, and opened one of the most magnificent spectacles Mrs. B. ever beheld.

Many a lofty tree had been shorn of its leafless boughs by the recent storm, which scattered them to the winds, and left the more tender branches to hang wildly waving to the gentler breeze, fancifully adorned by the nightly frost, and gilded by the beams of the glorious sun as it arose in grandeur; and the whole firmament appeared a brilliantly illuminated archway, glittering over the boundless forest, seeming to bend 'neath the falling stars, or jets of diamonds spouted down to carpet the earth, sparkling beneath the feet portraying the majesty of Omnipotence, at whose bidding the desert will blossom as the rose.

This sublime display of the heavenly orb surpassed all description, and Mrs. B., ever an admirer of celestial views, was enraptured, and glided over the icy way to the garrison with an imagination as elastic as her footsteps. She felt a guardian angel was guiding her to the spot to pay her debt of gratitude so long due.

> "Friendship, mysterious cement of the soul,
> Sweetener of life, and solder of society,
> I owe thee much. Thou hast deserved from me
> Far, far beyond what I can never pay."

On approaching the enclosure, they saw the women running to and fro, peeping through the embrasures. Curiosity was on tiptoe. Soon voices were heard. One said, "Surely the surgeon's lady is not coming here!" Said another coarse voice, "Where else can she go in such a barren place?"

A large hall was the entrance where these women had assembled, and were in much confusion. When Mrs. B. advanced, and her soldier guide with a basket on his arm, a few bold ones looked inquisitively, ready to demand the object of her visit. Others shyly hung their heads, and not a few were slipping out of her way.

At once she disclosed the design of her visit, and expressed so much interest in their welfare, that her mild and dignified manner commanded respectful attention. Few words passed at this interview, yet each one was noticed, and a few seemed overpowered by the beauteous morning, and their exclamations impressed Mrs. B. favorably to repeat her visit. Their own dislike to the station was evident.

Time winged its way so imperceptibly, that, on her return dinner was waiting. The doctor's spirits were exhilarated by the magnificent display of the morning, and the children were joyous—the elder one was of an age to observe, and endowed with an inquiring mind, cultivated by her parents—had much to tell of the great sight, and was sure it was the "burning bush" that Moses saw, for it burned so long and did not consume the trees. Then she inquired how far it was to "Mount Horeb."

It was more than a month since the family group had assembled for conversation or amusement, and such an enlivening scene was a jubilee in Nova Scotia, where clouds and darkness had reigned triumphant, and they seemed once more to be under a new planet.

Amid this cheerfulness Mrs. B. found it no easy task to recount her morning's excursion, aware it would not accord with the doctor's idea of propriety. But it was a duty she must perform, and happily this was the moment. The doctor was astounded, deeming it a rash adventure. In alluding to the martial spirit which pervaded the camp, and how those amazons often killed time in skirmishes, ending in sore bruises and black eyes, his remarks were humorous and amusing, warning madame to beware of frequent interviews, lest she should mingle in such sports and mar the pleasure of her visits by requiring his surgical skill. Then observed, had she overstepped the bounds of etiquette it might not have surprised him, as he knew her fondness for company. But he was never more amazed than when he heard Mrs. B. had entered the ranks, to associate with soldier's women.

Madame was pretty shrewd in her replies. His odd fancies and Yankee notions in his study were playfully exhibited. However, he yielded to her entreaties to visit the barracks, by compromise—but no one was to disturb his bivouac, nor touch his fixtures, where he was to reign a monarch o'er heaps and pile upon pile of musty roots. The gathering dust might add weight to the relics. Neither was a brush to molest the clan of hairy-legged spiders, or to disturb their ingenious labors in spinning fanciful webs, till majesty extended the golden sceptre.

The evening was whiled away so agreeably that the knell of time warned them of the tenth hour. Rain, hail, and sleet rendered the following day most unpleasant—Mrs. B. was fully occupied with domestic duties.

In the South, an intimacy had been cultivated with a few of the officers' ladies who were in this station, and those claimed morning calls. The inclement season had prevented any friendly intercourse, and this visit was most acceptable, yet they expressed much surprise at her braving the intense cold; while they, clad in woollens and furs, were hovering around a large fire, so sensitive to the bleak winds, that every crevice was stopped. Some of those ladies were educated in affluence and acquired luxurious habits, and the sudden transition from a warm climate,

"'Twas a hard change, an evil time had come,
We had no hope—and no relief could gain."

To all such, it was indeed a desolate land, and their theme of conversation were bitter regrets, especially as there was no limited time for their sojourn—weeping and mourning over their gloomy abode.

In vain Mrs. B. strove to cheer them, and left in sadness to make her way home over the rugged pathway, meditating on the diversified characters presented in this small district, conscious of her own foibles of repining and murmuring, as the mantle of gloom enwrapt her domicil. She resolved to fit her heart and home for the reception of the feeblest ray of light or hope that might creep in to warm and cheer the inmates, fully convinced that real or imaginary woes were increased by pondering over the dark side.

The third visit contemplated was, to a class much more pitiable; refugees, who clung to royalty in the Revolution, and fled hither, leaving country, friends, and wealth, with slender means of subsistence. Their estates were confiscated, and here they were poor and dependent, martyrs to the cause of royalty on a barren soil—on all those, privations and disappointed hopes bore heavily. Some had fled through fear, having no desire to espouse either side. Others were prompted by mercenary motives. Each class were now indulging in sad despair. A goodly number of Friends mingled in this motley group, to fill up the variety of character.

The morning was clear for this excursion, and Mrs. B. set out with her faithful soldier guide, to visit those neglected exiles, by whom she was graciously received. For the improvement of their condition, there was no apparent prospect. Discontent and murmuring were unanimous in the private cabin and in the military station. It seemed unavailing to strive to soothe their drooping spirits or pour oil in a wounded heart. This class, more than others, aroused the sympathies of Mrs. B.

On her way home, with theirs she measured her own position, and found it by far the most eligible. In looking to the future in her own, there was much to inspire hope, and her mind was fully bent on being useful in this station, in which Providence had placed her.

And as Gideon was the name of her soldier guide, by the blessing of God she was untiring in her efforts, "whether the fleece be dry, or watered by the dews of heaven." In all her wanderings she had been protected by an invisible hand, and mercifully sustained.

CHAPTER XXXI.

A fortnight passed—Resolution—Mrs. B. studies medicine—Coarse fare—Discontent—Stores arrive—Energy—Popularity—Amusing incidents—Improvements—News from London—Sails for Boston—Explores the States—Wilmington selected—Black oak bark exported—Death of Dr. B.—Mrs. B.'s residence in Virginia—Devoted to Slaves.

A DREARY fortnight had gone since they first trod these rugged shores. In the south, many hours were spent in compounding and weighing drugs to aid the Dr., and she had paid strict attention to the art, and made some progress, besides acquiring a smattering of Latin. This evening she was impressed that the study of medicine was clearly pointed out as a duty in which she could most effectually serve that class of beings. Dr. D. B. was consulted and acquiesced. He thought it was an admirable idea to occupy so active a mind, even were not a human being benefitted.

Leisure, books, and an eminent professor facilitated the study, arduously pursued for two years or more, during the time of their sojourn in Nova Scotia, where much practical knowledge was gained on attending women at the garrison; and testimony was borne to her skill and judgment, and also to acts of charity and mercy; and in streams of happiness a sweet reward flowed into her own bosom, which turned this wilderness into a pleasant land cultivated by benevolent acts which had a salutary effect upon others.

Luxuries were unknown here, and their daily fare was coarse. Being used to such, the privation of many things was submitted to without a murmur. But the want of good bread was sorely felt, as they had to feed on coarse, tough biscuit or unleavened cakes. Out of this trivial matter grew much discontent. Like the Israelites of old, who longed for the fleshpots of Egypt, and loathed the manna in the wilderness, and murmured against Moses; so these people longed for the fat of that land, once their sweet home, and loathed the unleavened bread, and murmured against their rules.

Their destitution was proclaimed to the ear of royalty with effect. Stores arrived at this crisis. They were remembered by absent and unknown friends. Many packages were welcomed. Mrs. B.'s presents contained a most desirable offering, portable yeast, with the receipt to prepare it; and the donor was no less a personage than the Queen of England. This was cheering, and without delay, a quantity was set to rise.

Women were called from the barracks—to them was given a portion of leaven and flour to bake early in the morning. When all was ready, Mrs. B. with Gideon and other soldiers, their baskets loaded with bread, went to the officers' families to distribute a portion, while the women liberally served the ranks. Cheerful faces and grateful hearts cordially greeted them. On the morrow the refugee families received their portion from Mrs. B.

Three days were spent in distributing bread, and those were days of feasting, joy, and gladness, and this simple incident foreboded much good, and brightened every object. To Mrs. B., it was a memorable event, and those three days were deemed among the happiest of her life. In many a sad moment afterwards her heart was soothed and cheered by the reflection of that trifling incident.

Spring was opening, and the Dr. spent much time in searching for roots. Mrs. B. often was his companion in the woods, from the rising to the setting sun. The first green thing discovered was wood sorrel, under a log covered with leaves. The acid was so delightful to taste, Mrs. B. gathered a quantity, stewed and seasoned it as green apples, and made pies, so rare that these were relished as a delicious morsel, and the news flew through the colony with increasing demands on her for small pieces to taste, and Mrs. B. was celebrated as a pastry cook; for her pies were unrivaled in excellence; her recipes were copied out over and over, for them.

The Dr. was exceedingly amused at his wife's culinary fame, which he had never discovered, and she confessed that the pies were an experiment which made such a hubbub in this little world and incited ludicrous scenes.

Ladies hitherto shrinking from the chilling winds, or even a balmy breeze, would hie to the forest in scores, be exposed to the dews and torn by briers, scratching over dead leaves and scattered branches for wood sorrel, with all the energy of the men at the gold diggings in California.

Excitement was a preventive to colds, and exercise created appetite and invited refreshing sleep, and a better temperament was the consequent effect. The country was assuming a more enlivening aspect, though vegetation was slow in putting forth buds. The favorable change excited emulation in each one to improve their home. Trees and shrubbery were planted, gardens plotted and vegetables cultivated; all were aroused from their slumbers.

In this improving state of the colony, strange news arrived, very mysterious, yet true. Letters were written by Dr. Edward Bancroft, of London, who had retired to France during the contest with America; stating that he was now reinstated in royal favor and his patent right renewed for seven years. Dr. D. B.'s speedy removal to the United States was urged, where he must travel over the land and select the most eligible location for the exportation of the *Black Oak Bark*, for the yellow dye. The Dr. resigned his commission and prepared once more to cross the ocean.

Mrs. B. was overjoyed, anticipating the pleasure of embracing her dearest relatives on her native soil. Yet in her checkered life—whether a city mansion or a lowly cabin in the wilderness was her abode—even a tent in a camp—or tossed on the ocean—there was some attraction to regret on taking a final leave, and individuals to bid farewell to—even among the lowest order, that would excite a tender feeling and a falling tear.

Here was no visible attraction, but the last look on her destitute cottage was sad, and taking leave of those for whose welfare all her powers had been exerted, and with success, too, in their moral improvement. The parting was solemn. They were sorrowing because they should see her face no more.

The accidental residence of Mrs. Bancroft among the rude settlers of Nova Scotia, in the cold and uncultivated regions of the north, and her services to them, both in the improvement of their minds, and of their domestic life, may most probably recall to my young friends the account they have so frequently read of the banishment of Telemachus among the shepherds of Egypt.

In numbering her days in Nova Scotia, more happiness than sorrow was mingled in her lot. Many trials had beset her way. Yet, she was fully convinced, more happiness than misery was allotted to man. Each one had their portion of good and evil. If the good was cherished, the evil would wither and pass away as the evening shadow.

At Saint Johns, they embarked for Boston, and had a pleasant voyage; there the Dr. had relatives, and Mrs. B.'s reception was so kind, the Dr. was induced to leave his family, while he explored the Eastern States. As it occupied more of his time than was expected, Mrs. B. often accompanied him—and in the North, she was his constant companion. Her visit in the city of New York, to her uncle's family, was transient; their having been so recently opposed to the Dr., an introduction was not thought advisable; no unkind feeling was evinced, and a pleasing reconciliation was anticipated.

Philadelphia was their residence, while the State of Pennsylvania was carefully traveled over. During the war, the whole South was passed through, but Delaware being so narrow a strip, was easily overstept, into Maryland.

By invitation of Daniel Heath, Esq., they were nearly two months guests at his hospitable mansion. In his tour, the Dr. was accompanied by a gentleman from each section of this State. In the meantime, Mr. and Miss Vining made a visit to Mr. Heath's family; as Dr. D. B.'s pursuits were a theme of conversation, Mr. V. became interested, and advised the Dr., before he decided on a permanent situation, to visit Delaware.

He acquiesced—and he accompanied Mr. Vining to Wilmington. These two gentlemen soon rode over the State, and his months of laborious research, and wanderings, were here crowned with success. Thus we disclose the connecting link in our chain of narrative.

Dr. D. B.'s exploring expedition, in detail, may not suit the fancy of all, yet a few will no doubt estimate the motive, to show by authentic facts, that valuable and useful articles of trade, are the produce of *Delaware*.

Black Oak Bark, now the Quercitron Bark of the export trade, was first sent out from Wilmington to England by one of the discoverers of this yellow dye, and after a fair investigation of the thirteen States, Delaware had the precedence.

Here we will state a singular coincidence. Two of the greatest chemists of the time selected Wilmington for an abiding place, one from England in the last century, the other from France. John James Ullman, Esq., early in the present century.

In 1786 or 1787, Dr. D. B. occupied the house on Quaker Hill, now in possession of Benj. Ferris, and engaged largely in the exportaion of the bark. His mind was too much absorbed in scientific works to bend to business, for which he had no tact.

He was easily imposed on; plausible and flattering promises often drew from him large sums of money in advance for bark, which proved a failure—not having had a proper inspection, his shipments were made and condemned in England. Such remissness had to be accounted for on this side of the Atlantic, and proved a heavy loss. On the other side great profits flowed in streams to benefit the importation there.

Mrs. B.'s personal appearance and character have been exemplified; living in extremes of climate and exposure; yet, on her arrival here few could believe her beauty had faded, or that the vicissitudes in life had withered her attractions; she was admired and caressed. Preceding parts of her narrative state her wanderings, and the diversified characters with whom she seemed doomed to mingle, unprotected in society, and in solitude; yet, she averred none treated her rudely, nor was she ever subject to insult. The trifling incident on board the ship was a solitary case of incivility.

During a residence of twelve years or more in this town, trials and crosses were endured, that if related by a fanciful pen, would vie with many a tale of romance. Though the incidents are fresh in memory we will leave them to pass into oblivion, and hasten to the conclusion of our narrative, now far beyond the lines we had prescribed.

Two daughters have been alluded to. One more was born in Wilmington. The eldest was a handsome brunette, and an elegant figure. Four lines, quoted by a gentleman, on his introduction to her, accord so well with the opinion of many, they may suffice.

> "Her form is perfect elegance,
> Her face the image of a heavenly mind,
> Her manners true---the effect of genuine sense,
> Like nature and like art refined."

In 1796, she married young, and went to Virginia, accompanied by her sister, who was very fair and handsome: though smaller, she had a fine form, and was too sensitive to the changing scenes of life. The elder was dignified, self-possessed, and seemed fitted to encounter adverse events—and many were mingled in her cup.

The elder son of Dr. E. B., of London, had traveled through the United States, and was on a visit to his uncle, and one of the bridal party. At the close of the year, he was to sail for England. John Vaughan, Esq., of Philadelphia, was his father's agent, and gave a dinner party before he embarked. His uncle was a guest, and sat down to table apparently in perfect health. Ere its viands were carved, he fell in an apoplectic fit, and when he was raised from the floor his pulse had ceased to beat, and the lamp of life to burn.

The winter of the doctor's decease, Mrs. B. boarded in Philadelphia. Her youngest daughter had entered her seventh year, and was a sprightly and sensible child. A few of her witty remarks are fresh in memory.

The lady of the house had no children, and was too exacting of others. On taking leave and affectionately admonishing this one, she said, "Mary, you are a sensible, and a very pretty little girl, but you have not won my affection, nor do I believe you will win the love of others, as you have so independent a spirit, and seem to care so little for the world or anything in it." On listening attentively to Mrs. D. C.'s advice, she replied, "Very true, madam. I have read in the book mamma says was written for our instruction and guide in life, that we are not to care for this world, nor the things thereof."

On the anniversary of her ninth year, she observed, "I never saw the sun arise in such splendor as this morning. It awoke me, and shone so bright and cheering on my birthday, that I felt it to be a reproof for my disobedience, and resolved never wifully to offend any one. Then I can shine too, and cheer all around me, by being dutiful and good. And, my dear mamma, I will strive to be prepared to be your companion and friend, as my sisters were."

Being an inmate of our family for months, her good intentions were adhered to. At times she had been disagreeably wild and rude. From this day she became an exceedingly interesting and amiable little girl.

In the Autumn of 1797, during the prevalence of yellow fever in Philadelphia, the younger son of Dr. E. B., of London, who was Surgeon-General to his Britannic Majesty's forces in the West Indies, was making a tour through the United States, and visited his aunt in Wilmington, and in compliance with his father's request, invited Mrs. B. and her daughters to accompany him to London, and make it their permanent abode. Her married daughter was too strong a tie to sever, and this advantageous offer was declined. However, she did accompany him to Boston, and visited their relatives.

Having long contemplated a visit to her daughter, she set off in the Autumn of 1798 to Virginia, uncertain of her future destiny. Her youngest daughter, near ten years of age, was her companion.

The following Summer, Miss B., a beautiful girl of eighteen, her second daughter, on a bridal party, was riding, and they alighted at a gentleman's mansion, where refreshments were offered. Twelve persons partook freely of preserved plums with impunity. Miss B. grew sick and was taken home.

A physician was called in, and the next day it was announced to her mother she was poisoned. Inquiry was made what she had eaten. The plums were examined, and having been preserved in a copper kettle affected her stomach, previously diseased. Her sufferings were agonizing for three weeks, when she expired. She was in the bloom of youth and loveliness, and was her mother's friend and companion. Of all her trials none bore so heavy or bowed her so low, for no tears came to her relief. Her beloved Harriet Carolina was no more.

> "Cold drops the tear which blazons common woe—
>   What callous rock retains its crystal rill?
> Ne'er will the softened mould its liquid show:
>   Deep sink the waters that are smooth and still.
>
> "Oh! when sublimely agonized I stood,
>   And memory gave her beauteous frame a sigh,
> While feeling triumphed in my heart's warm blood,
>   Grief drank the offering ere it reached the eye."

When a few more years had gone, her youngest daughter married; from early life she had walked in religion's ways, and was an exemplary and consistent Christian, with whom her mother spent her latter years in peace and happiness; though a permanent home in the South was not in accordance with her wishes. But it was her fate.

Mrs. B. being inimical to slavery, she was conscious of prejudice. Yet she was just—and averred, that in a long sojourn in their midst, neither cruelty nor ill-treatment beset her way, more than was exhibited towards others in a like station in free States, where much more labor was exacted, and in general where the blacks were less cared for by the employer.

As Virginia was her future abode, this class of the human family claimed her unwearied attentions, and there was ample scope to labor for their welfare and moral improvement. In 1808, in a visit to her friends here, many interesting incidents were recounted of her efforts to do them good, and though not often successful, she continued to persevere.

Her son-in-law, M. Turpin, owned a tract of land with four hundred slaves, distant four miles from his residence; many of those were too old to labor, and numbers too young. Such swarms to be fed and clothed, consumed the annual crop, the failure of which incurred a heavy debt. Yet master said "old family servants could not be disposed of, while there was land to sustain them."

Mrs. B.'s medical knowledge was important, and her services in constant requisition, unless domestic duties had higher claims or inclement weather proved a hindrance. Every morning she rode around this farm, visited each quarter, and gave a word in season, not passing the laborer in the field.

She playfully said, in striving to impart instruction to the most ignorant of the race, she was daily learning something new. Even from the field she returned wiser; there she learned how to plant cotton—to raise tobacco, and to grow corn. At the quarters, she learned to spin, to weave, and to make hoe cake. Yea, more, to eat a piece with a slip of bacon after her morning ride, ere returning to a late dinner. From the slaves she acquired all this useful information.

In summer it was her delight to walk into the cornfield on Monday morning, and meet the cheerful black faces with clean white cotton garments, mingling among the green stalks two feet high or more, and to be so pleasantly greeted by the slaves, calling to each other "*our lady has come.* Oh, missee look so well." In the woods on horseback, or rambling on foot in their midst, she was a stranger to fear.

A very fatal fever prevailed among the slaves in this region, one season, and many fell victims on neighboring plantations—only three of her patients died with the epidemic.

Though her task was arduous, it was her peculiar characteristic to fit herself for any station in which it pleased God to call her.

Mrs. B. might truly be called a pilgrim of the world—having resided in the thirteen old States, besides Nova Scotia in its primitive days—and having passed through so many vicissitudes in life. It may be regretted that the preceding facts have not been more skillfully described. But it should not be forgotten that those incidents of other days are gleanings of memory that come "like a shock of corn in season."

In her adventurous wanderings many sorrows crossed her path—adverse events bowed her low—anticipated ills, that make up a portion of life's woes, never were mingled in her cup—but a cheerful temperament gilded all her hopes, and lured her to the bright side of the future, to extract some sweets from every bitter portion.

A sane mind, trained in religious ways, was an endowment that filled her heart with gratitude for every blessing—strewed her pathway with content, and taught her to believe that the Almighty Disposer of events dispenses happiness more equally than man is willing to acknowledge,

CONCLUSION.

Having thus far completed my intended narrative on "The Reminiscences of Wilmington," I commit it to my friends, to whom it has been addressed.

I own I am much gratified in having been able to preserve those incidents, some of which are traditionary, but many of them are—to adapt a poetical description—

"All that I saw, and part of which I was,
A forest land become a peopled place—"

during my long residence in my native city—and I transmit them to you, as those of practical experience in the course of our history,

When these occurrences are adverted to, we may almost conclude they have been singularly numerous and interesting, and perhaps such a conclusion is not without reason.

The village of Wilmington had always been a favorite and an agreeable residence, from its locality and its aspect; and being at a kind of middle limit of our northern and southern country, with a foreign intercourse of no inconsiderable extent, it obtained a population of interest more diversified than the usual average of our settlements.

Being also surrounded by a fine district of country, and originally settled by a people of plain manners, and great integrity of character, it has afforded every accommodation without the larger expense, pretension, and embarrassment of some of the greater cities, in consequence of which a higher degree of sociability and confidence has attended a general intercourse among those persons who were entitled to enjoy it.

It is a very striking fact in the settlement of various parts of this country, that an impression of the character of many of the colonists continues to influence, with great advantage, the conduct and manners of their descendants.

Foreigners from abroad have observed Wilmington to be the welcome home of the emigrant, the exile, and the stranger, and from these, as well as from its own citizens, many rising characters have appeared on an extensive arena in the annals of our general history.

The neighborhood has also been the seat of successful industry to persons who have chosen to engage in several of the domestic manufactures and improvements, honorably to themselves and usefully to the community.

Yet the incidents which are thus brought up to our time, are by no means so terminated as to cease in interest—and if in former life the author has led the way to the instruction of others who may kindly preserve her in remembrance, she hopes she may now induce them to continue the same kind of local history, for it will increase in importance with the general increase of our country.

As it regards herself—she considers she is justified in her labors—for there is before her the emphatic language of Scripture—

"In the morning sow thy seed, and in the evening withhold not thine hand, for thou knowest not which of these may prosper."

ELIZABETH MONTGOMERY.

WILMINGTON, DELAWARE, *May 28th*, 1851.

THE END.

www.ingramcontent.com/pod-product-compliance
Lightning Source LLC
Chambersburg PA
CBHW031902220426
43663CB00006B/732